Vision Critical Studies

General Editor: Anne Smith

George Eliot: Centenary Essays and an Unpublished Fragment

GEORGE ELIOT: CENTENARY ESSAYS AND AN UNPUBLISHED FRAGMENT

edited by
Anne Smith

VISION

Vision Press Limited
11-14 Stanhope Mews West
London SW7 5RD

ISBN 0 85478 314 8

Printed in Great Britain by
Redwood Burn Limited,
Trowbridge & Esher

Typeset by
Chromoset Ltd.,
Shepperton, Middlesex

MCMLXXX

Contents

Introduction

Cecil Parrott's review of the latest volume of George Eliot's letters in the *Spectator* of summer '79 sparked off the kind of exchange that she and George Henry Lewes would have enjoyed. The *casus belli* was Sir Cecil's remark that her books had languished unread for a long time until I. A. Richards' lectures in Cambridge in the twenties had restored her reputation as a serious novelist. Of course there was the predictable "no it was F. R. Leavis" row, but more interestingly, there were letters from people who, wholly and blissfully ignorant of Eliot's disappearance from the list of approved authors, had gone on reading and enjoying her work all through the period. That they had done so is not surprising; that they took up their pens to write with such passion about it is.

The *Spectator* correspondence provides a chastening reminder to the academic critic that his efforts at interpretation and analysis are after all no more than a kind of optics: turn the lens this way and you see some of the finer detail; that way, and you see the overall pattern. Every way you look at George Eliot's work you find something to satisfy the intellect and delight the aesthetic sense, whether it be the superbly good-humoured Dutch-painting detail of country life at the Hall Farm, or the broad illustration of the *Middlemarch mappa mundi*. And everywhere in it you are conscious of her benign creative presence, that rare combination of tolerance and commitment.

It is with some humility then, and the certain knowledge that her work will outlive ours, that these essays are offered as a celebration of her centenary year.

A.S.

Edinburgh, July 1980

1

A New George Eliot Manuscript

by WILLIAM BAKER

In the Hugh Walpole collection at the King's School Canterbury, beautifully bound in blue morocco with tinted gold embossed edges, with five blank leaves at the back and three at the front are eleven lined leaves measuring 25.2 x 20 cms on which (with the exception of a few lines) are ten pages of writing in George Eliot's purple ink hand.[1]

Some of the contents of the manuscript have similarity with material in "George Eliot's Notebook for an Unwritten Novel" now at the Princeton University Library. The opening leaves of this notebook inhabit a world of espionage and intrigue during the Napoleonic Wars. The contents of the notebook then move to George Eliot's more familiar provincial scene. An eighteenth-century family pedigree is presented with "Old Rupert b.1720" and dying in 1783 as the oldest member, two sons, born in 1752 and 1759, the "Eldest grandson, b.1780" and the "second grandson b.1782" both eligible to fight in the Napoleonic Wars. In addition there is a "Rich. Forrest b.1751". We have also a Bishop, a Grammar school, and a legal dispute over who owns "school-revenue".

The Midland setting, "Old Rupert" and "Rich. Forrest" appear in the King's School manuscript. George Eliot started work on what is now the Princeton manuscript "either between early 1877 and mid-1878 or between mid-1879 and her death on December 22, 1880".[2] References in the King's School manuscript to "Buonoparte", "Cobbett", the England of Queen Anne and Ireland, all point to the 1877 period, and to

9

George Eliot's researches at that time.[3] Other evidence suggests a later date. The telephone reference on the first leaf may relate to 21 March 1878 when George Eliot and George Henry Lewes "went to the Telephone office to have the Telephone explained and demonstrated".[4] The presence on leaf nine of what appears to be John Walter Cross' holograph suggests for the transcription of this passage a date sometime after Lewes's November 1878 death.[5] The clean physical appearance of the text, relatively free of deletions, erasures and without squeezing,[6] suggest a late draft. There are signs that George Eliot was experiencing difficulty with names especially those of Rupert Pollexfen's child and his Irish relatives. The presence of George Eliot's textual subdivisions—"I" and "II"—suggests that she was copying from something planned and already drafted.

The plot outline of two families long settled in the Midlands, the attention to detail of setting and domestic history, the story of misspent youth, a foolish marriage, and a long-lost son standing to inherit much, combined with the espionage, Napoleonic War and Irish themes present in other sources, has rich fictional resonance. Judgements as to whether the King's School George Eliot holograph manuscript contains her prose at its best must remain subjective. In the present writer's opinion, what we have at the King's School Canterbury is some superb hitherto unpublished George Eliot descriptive writing and the fragment of another work from George Eliot's pen—one uncompleted or yet to see the light of day.

[1]

This story will take you if you please into Central England and into what have been often called the Good old times. It is a telescope you may look through a telephone you may put your ear to:[7] but there is no compulsion. If you only care about the present fashions in dress & talk in politics and religion pass on without offence as you would pass the man with the telescope in the Place de la Concorde,[8] not mounting to look through his lenses and then abusing him because he does not show you something less distant and more to your taste than the aspects of the heavenly bodies. Allow those who like it to interest themselves in the sad or joyous fortunes of people who saw the beginning of the Times newspaper, trembled or felt defiant at the name of Buonoparte, defended bull baiting, were excited by the writing of Cobbett[9] and submitted to some invisible power which ordained that their back waist buttons should be nine inches higher than those of their Fathers. These people did not manage the land well; they knew little about subsoils and top dressings, allowed trees and hedgerows to take title of their acres & in all ways helped the weather to make bad harvests. But their farming was picturesque & it suited the preservation of game. A large population of hares partridges & pheasants had short but let us hope merry lives between the times when they were made war on by the superior race who intervened between them & the unscrupulous foxes that would have killed & eaten them without ulterior views. And as many foxes were allowed to remain & enjoy their known pleasure in being hunted

[2][10]

were handsomely provided with covers. It was a bosky beautiful landscape that was to be seen almost everywhere in our rich Central plain, when a little rise of ground gave the horseman a possibility of seeing over a stretch of tree-studded hedgerows enclosing here & there the long roofs of a homestead & merging in[11] woods which gave a wide-spread hint of the[12] landowner's mansion[13] hidden with its park & pools & resounding rookery far away from the vulgar gaze.

One such mansion, whose parapet & curling smoke were[14] to be seen by the traveller in riding down the slope from Upper Lawtrey, was called Longwater & so far as the parishioners generally cared to know had always been the property of the Pollexfens, though it was understood that the family had waxed in importance & that some time or other their Estate had been enlarged. For there was another house in the parish, called Gatlands, which was believed always to have belonged to the Forrests until the Pollexfens bought it & the former owners sank into tenants, at the same time entering into a further relation with their landlord which had lasted ever since. In fact, as far back as the reign of William the Third a General Pollexfen who had served under that monarch had rounded his possessions by buying various smaller properties in Upper Lawtrey & among them the farm of Gatlands belonging to a Walter Forrest who[15] remained on the farm & accepted the office of bailiff for the whole of the Pollexfen Estate[16] which now extended over Upper &

11

Nether Lawtrey. Since Walter Forrest sold his own land & was chosen bailiff on another's, we might infer either that he was one of those able persons who manage everybody's property better than their own or else that he was only the inheritor of a gradual decay such as was

[3]

apt to befal the families of small Squires who had little margin for imprudence, & that he had the good sense to part with his embarrassed proprietorship at once instead of continuing to pare it away. Ingenious inferences; but they may happen to be false, for gallant generals have not always chosen their agents wisely, nor are there only two ways in which a man might be brought to sell his land; & a hundred years after the fact there was no evidence of Walter Forrest's motives, any more than of the family history before his time. In most cases even now, the commonalty of England knew little of their Great Grandfathers.

But in the house at Gatlands there was a carved oaken press filled with miscellaneous family relics, tattered silk garments, odd spurs & shoe buckles, hoops & maimed toys, some of them having a dignity & antiquity which made Richard Forrest, the actual tenant, refer them vaguely to his forefathers among the Cavaliers[17] who had injured the family prosperity by their unrequited exertions in the royal cause. He liked to think that his family fought for the King against the Roundheads. As to their having been Jacobites & drunk the health of the King over the water, his wishes were less decided, for these shades of sentiment seemed less reconcileable with his own loyal satisfaction in King George;[18] besides, the threat of Catholicism disturbed everthing. The General Pollexfen who enlarged the estate & began the connection with the Forrests had behaved as became a Protestant in transferring his loyalty to William the Third, & though under Queen Anne the Pollexfens had ranged themselves with the Tories, they had probably held it reasonable in a point of practical[19] politics like the Succession to the Crown,[20] to be a little on both sides till only one side was left. But, whatever side they had taken, since the families of Longwater & Gatlands had been brought into connection the Forrests had been wont to think that the

[4]

Pollexfens were right in their opinions & not with propriety to be

12

blamed for their actions: an attitude of mind which if their forefathers were cavaliers must have been hereditary in the stock for a good part of two centuries, the only material change being that the name of Stuart was overwritten by that of Pollexfen.

Gatlands was a quaint place. The house stood on a slight rise from the highest level of Upper Lawtrey & unlike the wide-wooded Longwater could be well seen from the road. It was[21] built of greenish sandstone, had a walled court in front & two goodly stacks of chimneys relieving its long roof, & it bore above the entrance the date 1613. The latticed windows were low, the court had no other ornament than grass & gravel with an inadjusted sundial in the middle of it, & the place looked rather sombre except when the westwood sun made its latticed panes glow like rubies. The farm-yard & stackyard lay at a little distance from the house, & so did the garden, which stood in a green close like a bushy islet fenced with clipped yew & holly. A passer-by, looking at the venerable but substantial building might have been disappointed to learn that it was only inhabited, not also owned, by a descendant of the yeoman or small squire who probably came into possession of the land long before this house was built. Richard Forrest, however, was not an ordinary tenant farmer. He was a man of weight in his district & in some quarters was held more of a power—in other words was more grumbled at by people who did ill for themselves—than the master of Longwater himself. Forrest was contented enough with this proportion in things, being less indignant at unjust blame which only touched him personally than he would have been at presumptuous complaints against Squire Pollexfen.

The name Pollexfen of Longwater has not now a stirring sound for the English nation, & even in the times this history is concerned with would not have

[5]

commanded immediate & deferential notice throughout the length & breadth of the land. Its conjuring power was at the strongest in the parishes of Upper & Nether Lawtrey & the neighbouring market town of Wynnover; already in the borough of Ripstoke, hardly ten miles off, the power had become doubtful with any but a small, better-informed minority, & at the cathedral town of Sudlow just within driving distance, whither churchwardens went in their gigs to hear the Bishop's charge, the name Pollexfen had no more command over men's service than if it had been a foreign copper. But to the mind of Richard Forrest it was hard to imagine how even in London when he spoke of Mr. Pollexfen his hearers should remain cold & require explanation. He had twice visited the metropolis on business & had felt some disgust at the indifference with which certain tradesman there had received his mention of the personage for whom he was fulfilling commissions.

It must not be supposed from this touch of simplicity that his ignorance was of a deeper sort than any now extant, for in these days too our feelings make us liable to such mistakes of the imagination about other men's celebrity—perhaps in some cases about our own. And even as knowledge goes now, Richard Forrest had a useful share. His letters were written in good English & his neighbours said of him emphatically that he knew the 'natur' o' things'; adding, at a later period, that it would have been better for him if he had not known anything beyond this. For some were of opinion that he might have escaped the chief calamity of his life if his schooling had ended with the well-known academy of Jonathan Grosbeak at Wynnover, who taught figures & measuration & penmanship exerted on the Lord's Prayer left nothing to be desired in the same line; whereas Forrest had been for two years[22] under the Reverend Mr. Roach, master of Ripstoke

[6]

Grammar School, from whom he was supposed to have brought a tincture of uncertain book-learning having little to do with the nature of things, & suited only to the clergy who could see through it or to the Counsel at Assizes whose business it was to confuse people.[23]

II

As to the past history of the Pollexfens we need not now inquire beyond the youth of[24] Rupert Pollexfen, the father of our Squire who was christened Dudley.

This Rupert was not the eldest son, but the third, & an arrant scape-grace, who declined the army & navy as well as the church & led an eccentric vagrant life, consorting with horse dealers, jockeys, cock-fighters & boxers; not merely making use of such people & treating them with the contempt they deserved, in the way customary with young gentlemen of his epoch, but identifying himself with them & seeking no better company. With all this, a merry & a well-built fellow, inclined to give though unaccustomed to pay, & on the whole one of those who are frequently declared to have a good heart, apparently because you might not have inferred it from their bad conduct. Among those who thought less favourably of his heart, being most annoyed by his conduct, were his own family, who held it a mercy that he was the third son safely out of requirement as nearest male, & ceased to care whether he were in the Isle of Man or in Ireland, in His Gracious Majesty's Hanoverian dominions or in the more distant

[7]

British possession of Nova Scotia, provided they heard little of him. But contrary to all reckoning the two elder brothers died, the one without offspring, the other unmarried; the entail suddenly wanted the vagrant Rupert, & before he was thirty[25] he became Pollexfen of Longwater, owning the best part of Upper & Nether Lawtrey with two livings in his gift, & having a power of doing as he liked with his own which would have enabled him to lay the longest of the long pools dry & kill all the fish in it, quite as if he had been a convulsion of nature. That was the sort of powerful unreason which the opinion of the neighbourhood expected of him. But here doubtless his good heart came into play, for he did not happen to like killing all the fish at once, & what he liked to do with his own differed little from what was done by many of his contemporaries in Loamshire: Sometimes when a younger son who has led a wild life & got[26] tired of moneyless dissipation, succeeds to a handsome inheritance, he becomes close-fisted, strait-laced, the contrary of his former self. But it was not so with the returned prodigal of Longwater. Property had not the effect of making him prudent, & with regard to his pleasures his reform consisted chiefly in his being able to afford them.

But what concerns us mainly about this unillustrious Rupert, who began to sow his wild oats by running away from School in the days of George the Second, is that during a vagrant visit to Ireland at the age of two & twenty, he fell in love with the grey eyes & long dark lashes of a modest Irish Girl, the daughter of a small innkeeper in whose house he[27] lodged, & persuaded her to marry him. He wandered away from her soon after, but not with the intention of forsaking her; rather, as he said to put a sum of money in his pocket & return to set up a

15

[8]

small inn on their own account. For he had already come to the pass of renouncing his station, not even caring to boast that he had renounced it, so that for aught his wife knew, the venerable house of Pollexfen might have had no higher head than the cattle-drover or corn-factor for whom she had been accustomed respectfully to draw beer. He did in fact write to her & let her know his whereabout, but before he could return with the desired sum of money he received the news that Kathleen had died in childhood leaving a fine boy which, if the father had nothing to say against it, was to be christened Rupert Crommelin[28] Pollexfen; Crommelin[29] being the name of its Grandfather Matthew Crommelin[30] publican, at the Sign of the White Bull in the outskirts of Cork.

Why from that time the Crommelins[31] heard no more of Rupert Pollexfen, never came out clearly into evidence, & perhaps was never known with perfect clearness to Rupert himself. A self-indulgent young fellow of four & twenty, informed that he is the father of a child whom he has never seen & whose mother is dead, may be willing enough to persuade himself that the grandparents will like nothing better than to have the entire charge of the baby. What a man objects to doing himself easily appears to him in the light of a pleasant task for others, & it is astonishing how much good nature is shown in this imaginative way. That Rupert's conscience had in the first instance been quite unstirred towards his own & Kathleen's offspring is hardly credible, because seven years afterwards on coming into the estate he lost little time in setting on foot an inquiry after Matthew Crommelin, who it appeared had for some years quitted the White Bull without caring to advertise his new[32] address, having burnt his

[9]

fingers with politics. The search was not successful, but meanwhile Rupert Pollexfen, under the touch of tender compunction & also perhaps with the design of rendering the due tribute to the mother of the legitimate heir whom he was then hoping to recover, placed a handsome marble tablet in Nether Lawtrey church with an inscription in memory of Kathleen, daughter of Matthew Crommelin & wife of Rupert Pollexfen, who died in childbed Dec. 22. 1743.[33]

16

But the heir was not found, & some years later—such is the instability of human wishes, at least in the case of our country gentleman under the earlier monarchy of the House of Hanover—the father was no longer very sorry for the failure; for he was wooing his second wife, a blooming dame of good family who would not have liked him as well if he had had an heir. Nay, he let it be understood that Kathleen's child had died with the Mother, & thinking that the mere suggestion of his former marriage might be bitterly unpleasant to his bride, he was brash enough to raise the oaken panelling of his pew in order to cover the tablet, saying to himself that the tablet was there all the same, & he had not 'five Inch' from his own deed. For he flattered himself that he had a strong will. And it seems indeed that he was a powerful animal; but his early irregularities & renunciation of rank did not turn out to have been signs of a powerful mind or of any revolutionary democratic leanings beyond the spirit of the time. So that his strong will had now without difficulty turned in the usual direction of a wealthy Squire's addicted to most of the Sports known as manly & British—epithets which then included Crab-fighting and bull-baiting.

[10]

Some of these Sports he carried on expensively, keeping a pack of hounds, glorying in his stables & preserving his game so as to satisfy the ambition of having the best covers in that part of the country. Whence the suspicion of insanity which the neighbours had attached to his early courses gave way to the judgement that Pollexfen of Longwater lived like a gentleman; & if he carried things with a high hand in point of game & rabbits & damages to his tenants, he did what he had the money for. And this was true, only the money soon ceased to be ready.

The Forrest of Gatlands who managed the Longwater estate at that time had also sporting tastes, & the only sign Rupert gave of retaining his early eccentricity was that he made this Forrest much of a boon companion. The Squire & his managing man, who was quite as much of a gentleman as his principal, were on very easy terms,[34] & when there was little or no other company at Longwater, rode together, went shooting together, drank together, & this with greater frequency as the Squire advanced in life & became more indifferent to approval in the drawing room.

NOTES

1 I should like to thank Professor R. A. Foakes for drawing my attention to the Walpole collection, the King's School Canterbury for allowing me to publish material in their possession, and David Goodes of the School for his kindness. The contents of this George Eliot manuscript are published with the kind permission of Jonathan G. Ouvry who holds the copyright. Sir Hugh Walpole bought his G. Eliot Ms. from Maggs Bros. who purchased it "at Sotheby's in 1935, when a large collection of [G. Eliot] manuscripts was sold. They were the property of Miss Elsie Druce, niece of the late J. W. Cross" (Uriah Ernest Maggs to Sir Hugh Walpole, 29 October 1937—typed letter now with the G. Eliot holograph at the King's School Canterbury).

2 Jerome Beaty, "George Eliot's Notebook for an Unwritten Novel", *The Princeton University Library Chronicle*, 18 (1957), 182, 175-78, see leaves 1-4,6 of the Morris L. Parrish Collection G. Eliot Notebook.

3 See my "George Eliot's Projected Napoleonic War Novel: An Unrooted Reading List,", *Nineteenth-Century Fiction*, 29 (1975), 453-60. There are "autograph manuscript notes, possibly for a projected novel, on the back of one card of a card calendar for Jan. 1876" (described by the Index Card) now at the Beinecke Library, Yale University. I should like to thank Professor Miriam Allott for drawing my attention to these notes. A transcription may be found in B. C. Williams, *George Eliot* (New York, 1936):

> "Agent who forswears himself— / Intriguing agent. / Old lady under the tyranny of her servant companion. / Mrs. Lane. / Hornung / Mrs. Locke. / Baronne de Ludwigsdorf and Cousin Rosa. / Simple man of crudition. / Widow supporting himself by keeping a school: imperfectly instructed: domineered over by her head teacher. / Itinerant players. / M. Maunoir and Mde. Courier. / Scilly Isles. / Plongeon. / Mischief-making son-in-law. / Dr. B. surgeon's assistant at K. / G. Morris and his books. / Proud of a Common Function (W.Works). / M. Lefevre. Bishop Mont. and Welsh Vicar. / Passion for poverty. Marriage on a death-bed (Scheele). / Daughter educated for a governess (simple parents). / Only daughter spoiled. / Young woman left with her friend's baby. / Showy clergyman: Translr of Pascal. / Ideal working vicar. Hen-pecked scholar. / Organist and singing girl. Forger: clergyman. / Clerical busybody. Aristocratic bachelor clergyman. / Whitsuntide visit to grandfather's / Leicestershire Farm." (/represents the end of G. Eliot's line length whilst noting: I have run the items together). Williams comments that these "are notes for a new novel . . . What would she have contructed from these data?" (pp.290-91).

I should like to thank Professor G. S. Haight for drawing my attention to Blanche Colton Williams' discussion and transcription.

4 See *The George Eliot Letters*, VII, 16. Of course G.H. Lewes through his many scientific contacts would have known of the latest developments

with telephones. Cf. fn. 7 below.

5 George Eliot did not allow John Walter Cross into her company and confidence until late April 1879. Following Lewes's death she shut herself away from the world. See G. S. Haight, *George Eliot: A Biography* (Oxford, 1968), pp. 525-26. Cf. my "J. W. Cross to H. Spencer, 23 December 1880: an unpublished letter concerning G. Eliot's death", *ELN*, 13 (1975), 39-40.

6 For a detailed description of the physical state of a George Eliot novel manuscript see J. Beaty, *Middlemarch from Notebook to Novel: A Study of George Eliot's Creative Method* (Urbana, 1960), pp. 35-6, 56-104. Beaty notes that G. Eliot used "very dark brown almost black ink, changing some time in 1872 to a violet ink" (p.133). The manuscript now at King's College is written on 26 lined ruled paper lacking margins. Since, as Beaty points out "George Eliot frequently had more than one stock of paper on hand at any one time . . . and used them almost haphazardly", (p. 15) such evidence seems not to be useful for dating purposes in the present instance. Similarly with watermarking: leaves 1,2,3,4 and 5 have 10 vertical chain lines and the watermark "JAL". The fourth leaf also has a full emblem crest beehive-shaped with a horn on the top of a central ampersand and a three-corned pinnacle watermark. The other leaves show various fragments of this emblem. Leaf 6 has 10 vertical chain lines, as have leaves 7 and 8, which also have a crown water-mark and no "JAL" initials. Leaf 9, containing G. Eliot's and what seems to be Cross's hand, has two kinds of paper: the top section measuring 7·7 × 20cms with 3 vertical chain lines; the bottom, measuring 15·5 × 19·5cms has the watermarking "TREVOR" and underneath this "SUPERFINE". In my transcription of the King's School G. Eliot holograph, [ ] represents material supplied by the editor.

7 "Commercialization" of the telephone "began early in 1877", see *Encyclopaedia Britannica-Macropaedia* (Chicago, 1975), 18, p. 84. For G. Eliot's fascination with the new machine see *The George Eliot Letters*, ed. G. S. Haight, 7 vols. (New Haven, 1954-55), VII, 16, 28. Cf. fn. 4 above.

8 Possibly an allusion to material in Emile Saigey's *Les Sciences au XVIIIe siècle, la Physique de Voltaire* (Paris, 1873). Notes from this work are to be found in G. Eliot's late holograph notebooks which the present writer is now editing. G. Eliot's and G. H. Lewes's copy of Saigey is now at Dr. Williams's Library, London.

9 "Selection from Cobbett's Register" are noted by G. Eliot as having been read "from June to Oct." 1877 - see *Nineteenth Century Fiction*, 29 (1975), 454, citing Carl H. Pforzheimer George Eliot Holograph Ms. 707, folios 83-4 back.

10 George Eliot has paginated at the top leaves 2-10. On the verso side of the first-leaf, in her hand is a "I". The first leaf shows signs of having been folded into half, and the top half then into three sections. The purple inked "I" is in the middle of these sections.

11 Following "in" G. Eliot wrote "ample" which she has erased.

12 "the" is added above the ruled line, cf. fn. 6.

13 G. Eliot wrote "residence" which she then erased.

14 "whose parapet & curling smoke were" added above the line. G. Eliot wrote "chimneys" which she erased, placing "parapet" above.

15 Following "who" G. Eliot wrote an erased word, which is now difficult to decipher - possibly "brother"?

16 The words following are an addition. G. Eliot originally wrote "in that neighbourhood." which she erased. "Pollexfen" was a common-name amongst the Anglo-Irish ascendancy.

17 The "C" has two lines underneath it—emphasizing that G. Eliot wished it to be capitalized—evidence that this ms. is in a late draft form—for such a sign G. Eliot used to instruct printers in her manuscripts, cf. fn. 6.

18 Following "King George;" there is an erased ampersand, "besides, the threat of" is an addition above the line.

19 G. Eliot wrote "political" which she erased and replaced by "politics".

20 A short erased word follows "Crown," but I have been unable to decipher it.

21 Originally "It had".

22 Originally "eighteen months". "Grossbeak" is the name of a large bird of prey.

23 Following is a new paragraph and two and a fraction of a third line of erased material mentioning Richard Forrest and the Pollexfens.

24 Following "inquire" there are approximately nine erased words which have been replaced above the line by "beyond the youth of".

25 Originally "three and thirty".

26 Originally "become".

27 An addition placed above the line.

28 This is above an erased name.

29 In the margin and following two erased names.

30 Again above an erased name.

31 *Ibid.*

32 Above the line.

33 Following are 7 ruled lines of purple ink writing finishing with "Dec. 22. 1743" is a fresh sheet of paper glued on to the other. It has 17 ruled lines, 15 of them are written on in what seems to be John Walter Cross's black ink hand. See fn. 6 above.

34 Originally "easy terms together".

2

Critical Approaches to George Eliot

by TERENCE WRIGHT

It may seem a strange way to begin a new collection of essays on George Eliot but it is nevertheless true to say that there has already been too much written about her. Her novels have lent themselves to a large amount of moralistic commentary that is sententious and critically naive. Any addition to the canon must make clear from the outset that it is not going to increase the number of bulky volumes which make George Eliot appear as boring as her enemies would claim she is. Not that her ethical standpoint is an unsuitable object for study. All her ideas, thoroughly articulated in her essays, letters and notebooks as well as her novels, demand constant reinterpretation and evaluation. It is difficult to write about her without discussing the religious and philosophical framework of her novels. But critics should be more self-conscious. For the sake of clarity as much as honesty they should be more explicit about their aims and methods. "The overall danger in the modern critical scene", as a recent review complained, "is the combination of spurious objectivity with hectic pluralism".[1] Too many critics pretend that they know everything and believe nothing.

Inevitably, certain critical ideologies are given labels: Leavisite, Marxist, Structuralist and so on. Such broad differences of approach are easily distinguishable. It is often clear from the language a critic uses whether he is articulating an emotional response to the novels, whether he is attempting to place them within the historical context which gave them birth, or whether he has some model of literary forms into which he is trying to make them fit. But not all critics are transparent in their use of language or dogmatic in their point of view. Nor am I saying that they should be. What I am saying is that they should admit quite openly what their critical approach entails in terms of beliefs about literature and about life. They should abandon the pretence that they are being somehow "objective" in a sense which does not call for discussion.

This introductory essay considers various examples of the way in which critics of George Eliot have found it impossible to say something significant about her work without revealing their own standpoint. She has been attacked and defended primarily for her beliefs. Even where criticism has been based ostensibly on artistic grounds, the aesthetic criteria employed have indicated a different attitude to life. The history of George Eliot criticism mirrors the changing religious, philosophical and aesthetic assumptions of the past hundred years. What has made that criticism good or bad, however, is not so much whether writers have agreed with George Eliot's position as whether they have understood it, whether they have realised its intellectual and imaginative subtleties. The best critics, whether sympathetic or antagonistic, help readers to understand her better.

This is not a bibliography. The aim of this essay is to consider the relative merits of different critical approaches and to bring out any implicit assumptions they contain. After considering some of the attempts to bring out the intellectual content of her work I pass on to various analyses of her "art". In addition to these two obvious approaches I examine other possibilities, in particular the psychological, the political, the historical and the feminist. I suggest that the alternative to a "hectic pluralism" in which uncommitted and uninteresting critics try to cover too much ground is not relativism but a healthy individualism in which a number of different outlooks contribute to a vigorous debate about her novels, their significance and their achievement. For an object is better known and a belief better based when it is seen from all possible angles.

Some of the most fruitful contemporary criticism of George Eliot was ideologically hostile. An unsigned article as early as 1863 by the liberal Catholic Richard Simpson brought into the open the theological strategy of her novels as well as the major philosophical influences on her thought. He traced the "organic unity" of the careers of George Eliot and George Lewes, the "double mouthpiece of a single brain", and the importance of their joint study of Comte, Goethe, Strauss and Feuerbach. He made no attempt to conceal his distrust of their condescending sympathy towards Christianity and her disingenuous defence of providence in *Silas Marner*,

> making Marner's conversion depend altogether on human sympathies and love, while he, simple fellow, fails to see the action of the general law of humanity, and attributes everything to the "dealings" which regulate the accidents . . . hiding a subtle argument for error under a specious defence of the truth.[2]

Whether or not we agree with Simpson that George Eliot's ploy fails because "the disguise is more wholesome than the well-concealed purpose", our understanding of the novel is undeniably sharpened by his attack on its theology.

Another liberal Catholic to point out the strength of George Eliot's reliance on contemporary humanist thinkers was Lord Acton. Asked by John Cross to revise his *Life of George Eliot* in 1885, Acton may have overstated the extent to which "she was in the clasp of the dead hand" of Auguste Comte. But he appreciated both the intellectual solidity she gained from her close study of Positivism and the additional life it derived from the creative process:

> If the doctrine, separate from the art, had no vitality, the art without the doctrine had no significance.

Acton showed how inseparable were George Eliot's beliefs and her art. He also placed her firmly within her historical context, paraphrasing Carlyle's description of the "generation distracted between the intense need of believing and the difficulty of belief" to which she belonged inescapably.[3]

A continued interest in the intellectual roots of George Eliot's work is essential. The ground may seem to have been well covered, from Cooke's *Critical Study of her Life, Writings and Philosophy* in 1883, through innummerable international treatments of the subject between the two great wars,[4] to more recent American work. But most of these products of thorough scholarship are so broadly based as to lack incisiveness.

Bernard Paris, for example, presents an impressive portrait of George Eliot's "intellectual milieu" but fails to distinguish adequately between the different strands of thought he describes.[5] Ulrich Knoepflmacher reveals some of the similarities between the work of George Eliot, Matthew Arnold, Walter Pater and Samuel Butler, yet he fails to bring out the precision of her position, the result of close study of specific philosophers other than Feuerbach.[6] Felicia Bonaparte betrays complete ignorance of the different philosophical traditions which lie behind her seemingly random combinations of Hume, Mill, Spencer, Darwin "and others".[7] The vagueness of these studies encourages the misguided attacks on the undogmatic emptiness of "George Eliot's Rhetoric of Enthusiasm" such as Ian Ker's.[8] Unlike his nineteenth-century counterparts, Ker's criticism is invalid because of its failure to understand her position fully.

There is still ample room for more precise studies of the intellectual sources of George Eliot's novels, in particular her relationship with the Hennells and Brays, her translation of Strauss and Feuerbach, her close study of Comte, and her co-operation first with Spencer and then with Lewes. K.K. Collins' account of her revision of the last two volumes of *The Problems of Life and Mind*,[9] for example, illustrates the kind of definite contribution research can make to an understanding of her novels. To read her own clear outline of the gradual development of "The Moral Sense", limited as it is by the physiological knowledge and assumptions of her time, is immensely more valuable than anyone else's general paraphrasing of stock Victorian attitudes.

Many of George Eliot's notebooks remain unpublished. These can of course help critics to reconstruct her reading and her general areas of concern while planning her novels. But they are so scattered and so little known that they have until now been too little searched for the background material which can give greater exactness to the consideration of her ideas. In addition to those noticed by Haight and Baker,[10] there is another notebook for *Romola* in the Bodleian Library[11] and a philosophical notebook at Nuneaton[12] which have yet to be used to proper advantage. These notebooks and the catalogue of the Leweses' books now in Dr. Williams's Library[13] should be the starting point for further research into George Eliot's reading.

The attempt to do justice to the precision and subtlety of George Eliot's intellect is only one approach to her work and it was in reaction to the Victorian inability to appreciate anything but the philosophical and religious content of her novels that Henry James emphasised "The Art of Fiction". He constantly argued that the philosophical assumptions of her time weighed against the natural simplicity of her genius, which lay "buried" in *Romola*, "less . . . a work of art than . . . a work of morals". But while he complained of her seriousness he was also aware that this was her strength, the reason why she was "alone" among English novelists, approached only by Fielding. Even he was only "didactic — the author of *Middlemarch* is really philosophic".[14]

The post-Victorian attack on George Eliot for her moral seriousness, exemplified by Leslie Stephen and Virginia Woolf among her admirers, was little more than a statement of preference for "lighter" novels. Stephen attributed the decline in George Eliot's popularity to "the misdirection of her powers in the later period" rather than the change in taste at the end of the century.[15] His daughter ostensibly rejected "the late Victorian version of a deluded woman who held phantom sway over subjects even more deluded than herself". But she also went on to complain of "the absence of charm" in her novels. The problem with George Eliot's heroines, she elaborated, is that "they cannot live without religion".[16] But this is the very essence of George Eliot's writing. The fact that the struggle for faith failed to interest a later more sophisticated generation tells us more about them than it does about her. Lord David Cecil's urbane distaste for George Eliot is largely disqualified as criticism for the same reason.[17]

Any critical approach to George Eliot, if it apprehends her work at all accurately, returns to the central concern with religion in the broadest sense, the attempt to give meaning to life. The most incisive analyses of imagery in her work relate to this theme. Mark Schorer's examination of the metaphorical consistency of *Middlemarch* reveals five particular themes which reflect the underlying concern with the Religion of Humanity: unification, antithesis, progress, "creative purpose towards

25

absolute order" and "'muted' apocalypse".[18] David Carroll traced the way in which images of disenchantment illustrate the "archetypal pattern upon which all her novels are constructed", the movement of the main characters through the three Comtean stages of illusory faith, disenchantment and regeneration. The moment of disillusionment itself is symbolised by disconnected objects, purposeless fragments or ruins, which faith sees in meaningful relation.[19] Brian Swann studied the symbolic significance of the mirrors and windows in *Daniel Deronda*, reflecting George Eliot's concern with varieties of egoism and altruism.[20] All these articles illustrate how the study of her techniques can contribute to a fuller understanding of her ideas.

Concentration on the conscious elements of George Eliot's art runs the obvious danger of committing the intentionalist fallacy. From her letters and notebooks we can see that she did often follow some predetermined pattern for each novel. In the two notebooks for her unwritten novel to be set in the Napoleonic wars, one at Princeton, the other at Canterbury, published for the first time in these essays, she can be seen gradually working out the characters and their inter-relationship. A card calendar for 1876, now at Yale, also contains jotted notes for potential characters in this novel, including a widow, a teacher and an "ideal working Vicar".[21] This seems to bear out what she told Frederic Harrison about basing the real on the ideal, as do her discussions with Lewes about "her scheme for *Daniel Deronda*".[22]

Most of George Eliot's notebooks are only repositories of information which she felt might be useful for her novels. But the "Quarry for *Middlemarch*", as opposed to the "*Middlemarch* Miscellany",[23] shows her working out both characters and situations before finally dividing the book into scenes and chapters. Jerome Beaty's very thorough study of the development of *"Middlemarch" from Notebook to Novel* concludes that, in spite of this, the "greatest 'planning' stage was the writing itself". He qualifies George Eliot's romantic account of her composition of the Rosamund-Dorothea meeting in Chapter 81 without alteration, erasure or planning, from inspiration by a "not herself". Blackwood's explanation of what she meant by saying that her novels suddenly passed "into the irrevocable" was nearer to the truth:

> she thinks and thinks over what she is going to write. It "simmers" in her mind as she says and when she puts it upon paper it seems to pass in into a reality not to be altered.[24]

In spite of her thorough philosophical preparation and her painstaking collection of historical details, however, there was clearly a very "unplanned" element in her writing. Perhaps her friend and translator, Alexandre D'Albert-Durade, best describes

> sa puissance de conception et de création, qu'une fois son plan déterminé la faisaient assister aux scènes qu'elle écrivait si les acteurs parlaient et agissaient devant elle.[25]

Her preparation and planning both triggered her imagination and gave it a solid base on which to build.

Even if it were not critically naive and ponderous to work from George Eliot's stated aims and objectives to the final product without any consideration of unintended effects, it would not reflect the large element of spontaneity in her writing. The strength of the best treatments of her "art" is that they are not bound by any concept of intention and are prepared to evaluate as well as describe the formal aspects of her work. Barbara Hardy realised that George Eliot needed to be defended against the charge of constructing plots to illustrate a rigidly preconceived moral:

> There is no President of the Immortals sporting with Esther or Bulstrode, but a novelist working within a convention of a certain allowance of contrivance, arranging events so that they will force her characters to demonstrate their moral direction.[26]

That direction is often determined organically, from within the nature of the character as she came more fully to understand it, rather than mechanically, imposed from outside in order to fit the moral scheme. After examining the varieties of authorial voice evident in the novels and the way in which themes and images are interwoven, Hardy concluded that Eliot's strength lay in her successful integration of the real and ideal. Instead of exemplifying "Lewes's hated detailism", the particular events of each novel are placed within a wider context of character and action and so given significance.[27] This is the difference between what Lukács called description and narrative, contrasting Tolstoy's narrative of events which are integral to the moral themes of the novel with Zola's accumulation of picturesque but insignificant detail.[28]

The critical controversy about realism in George Eliot was first raised in France in the 1880s when Zola was forced to defend his concept of the term against the idealism and moralism which his denigrators found in Russian novels in general and George Eliot in particular. "Elle ne connaît l'humanité que par les livres", countered Zola. But Brunetière clearly preferred *le roman à thèse* which she exemplified.[29] Again, this is a matter of taste. Zola's full-blooded portraits of humanity may be nearer to the Russian novelists than the subdued Positivist pictures of George Eliot.[30] But in terms of significant narrative if not in spiritual depth or epic grandeur, George Eliot deserves to be ranked with Tolstoy and Dostoyevsky more than any other Victorian novelist. It is in this area that her strength lies, and it is therefore an appropriate centre of concern for her critics.

Another major contributor to the study of "The Art of George Eliot" is W. J. Harvey, who was prepared at times to be very critical. He discussed the whole process of "idealisation" in her novels in the light of Henry James's complaint

> that she proceeds from the abstract to the concrete, that her figures and situations are evolved, as the phrase is, from the moral consciousness, and are only indirectly the products of observation.[31]

George Eliot's technique of working from the ideal to the real falls short of Harvey's concept of naturalism when a character remains static, isolated or theoretic, when he "cannot bear the weight of value or significance attached to him", when the author is too emotionally involved or "evades certain problems or areas of experience necessary to the full realisation of a character".[32] These are clear criteria, open to debate or disagreement but eminently discussible. F. R. Leavis had actually used the criterion of emotional over-involvement in a character in his criticism of *The Mill on the Floss,* but he failed to acknowledge clearly enough the basis of his position. Instead, he complained of George Eliot's "immaturity" and "sentimentality".[33] It is, of course, possible to unpack these terms for ourselves and to recreate Leavis's methodology. But his strong personal insights would have been more acceptable, at least more openly discussible, had they been placed, like Harvey's, in the context of a clearly articulated set of critical criteria.

In addition to the intellectual and aesthetic approaches, there have been some recent attempts to bring psychological theories to bear upon George Eliot's novels. Of particular interest is Paris's *Psychological Approach to Fiction*, which abjures his earlier intellectual approach. His analysis of "The Inner Conflicts of Maggie Tulliver" actually begins with Leavis, with whom his earlier book disagreed. Now Paris agrees that George Eliot overidentified with her heroine. But he is clearer than Leavis in acknowledging the psychological basis of his criticism. He is deeply suspicious of the novelist's intentions:

> While George Eliot's intuitive grasp and mimetic presentation of Maggie's psychology are flawless, her attitude, values and analyses are considerably less trustworthy.[34]

In spite of her attempts to "cover up" inadequacies which she was unable to appreciate in her heroine, partly because she contained so much of them herself, Paris claims that George Eliot was honest enough to her experience to supply sufficient evidence for the psychoanalysis which he gives in Horneyan terms. He discovers obvious signs of insecurity in her fantasies of being a queen, her need to be recognised for extraordinary attainment, her defensive strategies such as withdrawal into books and punishing her doll-fetish, her morbid dependency on Tom, her masochistic desire for self-sacrifice and martyrdom, and her final "neurotic search for glory" which satisfies her "profound wish for death". Such a bundle of anxieties, Paris argues, could hardly grow into an adult. Although there are obvious dangers in a psychological approach which treats fiction as real life, such an analysis seems capable of fruitful discussion, so long as the basic criteria for judgement are clearly acknowledged.

Ruby Redinger's psychological biography of George Eliot is less satisfactory than Paris's criticism partly because it is less open about the standpoint from which it makes its

29

psychoanalysis and partly because it bases too much upon too little evidence, especially in discussing "The Primal Passionate Store" of her early childhood.[35] Laura Emery is clearer about her methodology in her analysis of *George Eliot's Creative Conflicts*. She disclaims any attempt to be constructing "a neo-Freudian aesthetic" but she does attempt to analyse the "fantasy and defence" elements of the novels from a Freudian standpoint.[36] The trouble is that it is not the characters who are being analysed but their author, which is not literary criticism but biography. But so long as this distinction is clearly recognised and the complexities of "implied authorship" and authorial voice duly observed, such psychological approaches can contribute to our understanding of the novels.

Of the various historical approaches to George Eliot, the Marxist is one of the most interesting. At its worst it merely attacks her for preferring the Positivist to the Marxist solution to the problems of the nineteenth century. David Craig praises her portrait of a real trades unionist at the expense of her ideal working-man in *Felix Holt* convincingly as long as he directs his attention at the text. He has fun with the way in which George Eliot claims that the Duffield men

> were unconciously influenced by the grandeur of his full yet firm mouth, and the calm clearness of his grey eyes, which were yet somehow unlike what they were accustomed to see along with an old brown velveteen coat.

Craig notices the stock "association of 'clear' eyes with moral loftiness" and the untypically blurred "somehow". He points out that George Eliot attempts to introduce "proletarian directness" by "the occasional homely phrase, 'he pours milk into a can without a bottom' and the like" in the same way that Pulcheria laughed at Daniel Deronda's fingering his coat-collar.[37] These are failures in the realisation of character. But he goes on to attack Felix Holt and George Eliot's belief that there was an alternative to the "hard-lipped antagonism" of the trades unions towards early Victorian capitalism. This in itself is quite plausible but makes for unhelpful literary criticism when couched in such general terms as Craig's sneers at "the wishful liberalism of George Eliot's tradition" and its "high-mindedness", which was "only preachifying in mid-air".[38]

This merely reduces criticism to the level of political slogans.

Another Marxist critic, Terry Eagleton, is more subtle in his analysis of George Eliot's position, which he describes as an attempt to resolve the conflict between "a progressively muted Romantic individualism . . . and certain 'higher' corporate idealogies". But he too is over-fond of labels such as "petty-bourgeois liberalism" which only serve to crudify the argument. Again, they reveal more about his position than George Eliot's. Eagleton's own preface anticipates and precludes criticism of his "cryptic and elliptical" language, but his treatment of *Middlemarch* is quite convincing. He sees it in characteristically paradoxical terms as a "triumph of aesthetic totalisation deeply suspicious of ideological totalities." Christianity, Positivism and Romantic individualism all succumb to the entrenched provincial conservatism of Middlemarch. Eagleton conjures up visions of a Marxist *Middlemarch* even more absurd than Harrison's suggestions of a Positivist utopia which provided the initial blueprint for the novel.[39] But his complaints about George Eliot's attempted resolution of her ideological dilemma raise important questions about the nature of the novel:

> what cannot be resolved in "historical" terms can be accommodated by a moralising of the issues at stake. This, indeed, is a mystification inherent in the very forms of realist fiction, which by casting objective social relations into interpersonal terms, constantly hold open the possibility of reducing the one to the other.[40]

It is debatable who is being reductive here. Whether politics or personal relationships hold the answer to all our problems is a matter of belief. But it is important that the implicit assumptions of liberal humanism to be found in the very form of the nineteenth-century novel should be brought into the open and made the subject of discussion.

Since George Eliot's novels are nearly all based on historical events, whether forty or four hundred years before the time of writing, and since she was extremely thorough in her research, there is room for continued work on the accuracy with which she reports these events and the validity of the interpretation she gave them. Valentine Cunningham finds some faults in her portraits of different varieties of nineteenth-century nonconformity. He notices her modification of Methodist hymns to fit the humanist themes of *Adam Bede,* but in general exonerates her from the blame he attaches to many other Victorian novelists for allowing their prejudice to dictate their presentation of dissent.[41] But he is not unpartisan himself as his defensive indignation indicates. It is impossible to describe or to select information without interpretation and any criticism of George Eliot's historical accuracy brings with it an evaluation of her beliefs about the events she records. Many of the studies in this volume examine her treatment of history in an attempt to bring out more clearly the implicit assumptions of her work.

The concern with George Eliot as a woman portraying the plight of women is not new. Elaine Showalter begins her study of "British Women Novelists" with a quotation from George Lewes in the year he met George Eliot in which he argues that women have different physiological "organisations, and consequently different experiences" and that they should therefore stop imitating male writers: "to write as women is the real task they have to perform".[42] This seems to be the underlying assumption of such studies as Patricia Spacks' *The Female Imagination.* Showalter is rightly suspicious, however, of any attempt to erect a biologically determined model of female sensibility and prefers to concentrate on the cultural conditioning for which there is so much more evidence. The analysis of Victorian sexual attitudes has the additional advantage of being as open to men as to women, as Eric Trudgill has shown.[43] Women, of course, have more of an axe to grind, and this gives their work more bite. But the proliferation of histories of downtrodden but resilient women-writers needs to be directed more firmly at the texts themselves before they contribute very much to our understanding of George Eliot not only as a woman but as a writer.

One thing should be clear from this brief survey of possible approaches to George Eliot and that is that there can be no single "right" reading of her novels. Although the principles of "antithetical criticism" as outlined by Bloom are too subjective and obscure to be made into a system, it might be helpful if critics of George Eliot took some of them to heart, in particular his belief that "accurate" interpretations are worse than mistakes and that there are only more or less creative and interesting misreadings. Bloom overstated the case in his anxiety to escape the dilemma of "barren moralising" or formalistic reduction into which he felt that modern criticism was falling.[44] It seems to me to be possible to combine a concern for accuracy with a vigorous commitment to a particular set of beliefs. Certain readings can be dismissed as inaccurate or ignorant and others respected for their acuteness even if they are found unacceptable.

Bad criticism, I have repeatedly said, reveals more about the critic, than the text. But without some active engagement with the text a critic is unlikely to reveal anything at all. Criticism that can combine the vigorous commitment of a Dr Leavis with the careful scholarship of a Professor Haight and the sophisticated self-consciousness of a Terry Eagleton will do justice to the fusion of intellectual precision and emotional profundity which George Eliot attained. It will be objective enough to be discussible and subjective enough to be significant.

NOTES

1 Stephen Hazell, *The English Novel: Developments in Criticism since Henry James* (London, 1978), p.22.
2 Richard Simpson, "GE's Novels", *Home and Foreign Review* III (1863) 522-49, reprinted in David Carroll, ed., *GE: The Critical Heritage* (London, 1971), pp.221-50.
3 Lord Acton, "GE's Life", *Nineteenth Century* XVII (1885), 464-85, reprinted in G.S. Haight, ed., *A Century of GE Criticism* (London, 1965), pp.151-60.
4 M.L. Cazamian, *Le Roman et les Idées en Angleterre: l'Influence de la Science (1860-1890)* (Strasbourg, 1923); E.J. Pond, *Les Idées Morales et Religieuses de GE* (Paris, 1927); Ingeborg Tegner, *GE: En Studie i Hennes Religiösa och Filosofiska Utreckling* (Lund, 1929); Minoru Toyoda, *Studies in the Mental Development of GE in Relation to the Science, Philosophy and Theology of her Day* (Tokyo, 1931); P. Bourl'honne, *GE: Essai de Biographie Intellectuelle et Morale, 1819-1854* (Paris, 1933); Ben Euwema, *The Development of GE's Ethical and Social Theories* (Chicago, 1936).
5 B.J. Paris, *Experiments in Life: GE's Quest for Values* (Detroit, 1965).
6 U.C. Knoepflmacher, *Religious Humanism in the Victorian Novel* (Princeton, 1965,); *GE's Early Novels* (Berkeley, 1968).
7 Felicia Bonaparte, *Will and Destiny: Morality and Tragedy in GE's Novels* (New York, 1975).
8 I.T. Ker, "GE's Rhetoric of Enthusiasm", *EC* XXVI (1976), 134-55.

9   K.K. Collins, "G.H. Lewes Revised: GE and the Moral Sense", *VS* XXI (1978), 463-92.

10   G.S. Haight, "GE", *VN* XIII (1958), 23; William Baker, *Some GE Notebooks: An Edition of the Carl H. Pforzheimer Library's GE Holograph Notebooks, MSS 707, 708, 709, 710, 711,* Vol. I (Salzburg, 1976), pp.1-3.

11   "Italian Notes/ GE/ 1862", i and 51 ff., Bod. MS Don g.8.

12   "GE's Notebook", Nuneaton Public Library.

13   William Baker, *The GE-GHL Library: An Annotated Catalogue of Their Books at Dr. Williams's Library, London* (New York and London, 1977).

14   Haight, *op.cit.,* pp.86, 53 and 80.

15   Leslie Stephen, *GE* (London, 1902), p.206.

16   Virginia Woolf, *The Common Reader,* First Series, (London, [1925] 1945), pp.205-18.

17   David Cecil, *Early Victorian Novelists* (London, 1934).

18   Mark Schorer, *"Fiction and the 'Matrix of Analogy' ", KR* XI (1949), 550-59, partially reproduced in *"Middlemarch": Critical Approaches to the Novel,* ed. Barbara Hardy (London, 1967), pp.19-22.

19   David Carroll, "An Image of Disenchantment in the Novels of GE", *RES* ns XI (1960), 29-40.

20   Brian Swann, "Eyes in the Mirror: Imagery and Symbolism in *Daniel Deronda", NCF* XXIII (1969), 434-45.

21   "Notes, possibly for a projective novel, on the back of one card of a calendar for January, 1876", Yale.

22   *The GE Letters,* ed. G.S. Haight, 9 vols. (New Haven, 1954-55 and 1979), IV 300-1; G.H. Lewes Journal, 23/7/75, Yale.

23   John C. Pratt, "A *Middlemarch* Miscellany: An Edition with Introduction and Notes, of GE's 1868-71 Notebook", Princeton Ph.D., 1965; "Quarry for *Middlemarch",* 2 MSS in Houghton Library, Harvard, ed. with introd. and notes by A.T. Kitchel to accompany *NCF* IV (1950).

24   Jerome Beaty, *"Middlemarch" from Notebook to Novel* (Urbana, 1960), pp.77 and 99-107.

25   A.F. D'Albert-Durade to J.W. Cross, 15/2/85, Yale.

26   Barbara Hardy, *The Novels of GE* (London, 1959), p.116.

27   *Ibid.,* pp.233-38.

28   Georges Lukács, *Writer and Critic,* trans. A. Khan (London, 1970), pp.110-35.

29   J.P. Couch, *GE in France: A French Appraisal of GE's Writings, 1858-1960* (Chapel Hill, 1967), ch.3, "Brunetière, GE, and Literary Cosmopolitanism", pp.86-134.

30   Owen Chadwick, *The Secularization of the European Mind in the Nineteenth Century* (Cambridge, 1975), pp.248-49.

31   W.J. Harvey, *The Art of GE* (London, 1961), p.178.

32   *Ibid.,* p.179.

33   F.R. Leavis, *The Great Tradition* (London, [1948] 1962), pp.39-46.

34   B.J. Paris, *A Psychological Approach to Fiction,* (Bloomington and London, 1974), p.166.

35   Ruby Redinger, *GE: The Emergent Self* (London, 1976).

36 Laura Emery, *GE's Creative Conflict: The Other Side of Silence* (Berkeley, 1976), p.3.
37 Henry James, *"Daniel Deronda:* A Conversation", reprinted in F.R. Leavis, *op.cit.,* pp.249-66.
38 David Craig, *The Real Foundations* (London, 1973), pp.131-42.
39 James Scott, "GE, Positivism, and the Social Vision of *Middlemarch"*, *VS* XVI (1972), 59-67.
40 Terry Eagleton, *Criticism and Ideology: A Study in Marxist Literary Theory* (London, [1976] 1978), pp.110-25.
41 Valentine Cunningham, *Everywhere Spoken Against: Dissent in the Victorian Novel* (London, 1975).
42 Elaine Showalter, *A Literature of their Own: British Women Novelists from Brontë to Lessing* (Princeton, 1977), p.3.
43 Eric Trudgill, *Madonnas and Magdalens: A Study of Victorian Sexual Attitudes,* (Leicester, 1975).
44 Harold Bloom, *The Anxiety of Influence* (London, 1973), p.43.

I should like to thank two of my colleagues, Linda Anderson and Ken Robinson, for their help in discussing some of the issues raised in this paper.

3

The Mill on the Floss and The Unreliable Narrator

by GRAHAM MARTIN

The "classic realist text", a contemporary post-Barthes critic
has argued, is chiefly marked by two features.[1] It presents a
hierarchy of discourses capped by a meta-language which both
settles for the reader the relative weight of all other discourses
and at the same time conceals its own nature as a discourse; and
it directs the story towards a final revelation in whose light the
preceding chain of significations are newly, and for the first time
properly, understood. If the second of these is, except in the
trivial sense that the first reading of a novel differs from all the
rest, hard to accept without radical qualification, the first bears
directly on that familiar topic of George Eliot studies, the
functioning of the authorial voice. We are accustomed to think
of this as a commentary on the substance of the fiction, not of
course separable but distinct enough to mediate between the
actual world where readers struggle with their own moral and
emotional dilemmas, and that hypothetical world where the
characters are pursued by their complicated but known
destinies. This practice allows too little attention to the
intimately-related authorial role, that of arranging without
explicit comment or recognition the hierarchy of discourses
within the fiction itself, granting to characters this or that
connection with each other and with the symbolic discourses
offered by descriptions, authorising as "real" sets of
relationships which conceal ideological choice and unargued
social assumptions. Some of these authorial dispositions can no
doubt be subsumed under the notion of the *donnée*, as in a

36

discussion of a group of texts exemplifying a particular writer's chosen *milieu*. Thus we speak, and perhaps too glibly, of "the world of Graham Greene/Henry James/Jane Austen", or in more portentous mood, of their "vision of the world". But other aspects, if they are not to remain invisible, require attention to single texts, and a pre-eminent case is the relationship between the explicit authorial voice and the narrated fiction where the second is judged to embody or realise with peculiar completeness the values asserted by the first. We have learnt, as a rule, to celebrate this embodiment as a rare and difficult achievement, and perhaps few novelists have been judged to achieve it more impressively than George Eliot in her best work. Her characteristic strength, we say, is to authenticate authorial commentary in a rich and subtly-discriminated variety of instances which nevertheless cohere in a complexly unified effect. It is, in other words, the near-seamlessness of the continuum that has been marked out for the highest praise. Yet precisely in this seamlessness can the commentary, the meta-language, be seen to suppress its own nature most successfully, by turning for its justification to an array of "evidence" that the author has already edited into its convincing shape. It is as if a judge both selected the jury and drafted the brief for its discussion of the case. In such circumstances, consonance between the directions from the Bench and the jury's verdict would hardly be a matter for wonder. On the contrary, shouldn't we here be most energetically on guard?

It is of course, common for first readers of George Eliot to protest against the all-persuasive analysis and appraisal which so effectively works to constrain independent movement within the fictional space. The judge, or to switch to a more suitable metaphor, the Intourist Guide is continuously at our elbow, pointing to the salient details of this or that scene, offering cultural annotation which modifies our untutored responses, steering us past dubious areas where closer inspection might prompt embarrassing questions, or silences. Much brilliant criticism has laboured to persuade us that the maverick impulse to dodge the Guide and explore a bit on our own is fundamentally wrong-headed, a product of ignorance, or at best a conception of the novel wholly at variance with George Eliot's practice. But it is one thing to read her novels in conformity with the principles of their construction, that is, to accept a position vis-á-vis the text which imposes George Eliot's definition of the reading-self; another thing altogether to accept that position without knowing what it is. For it cannot *be* known just by being accepted; it must also be refused. Our untutored-reader's uneasy resistance has, after all, its seed of knowledge, and in what follows I want to suggest that we learn as much about *The Mill on the Floss* by looking at discontinuities between the authorial meta-language and the narrated fiction, as by remarking on their fusion.

U. C. Knoepflmacher has recently pointed out that the narrator of *The Mill* is both intellectually more sophisticated and more learned than those of previous novels.[2]

> In *The Mill* . . . we have the voice of that Victorian sage who was to speak with far greater assurance in *Middlemarch*. Multiple allusions to Greek, Shakespearean and Romantic tragedy, to natural science, history and legend are made by a bookish commentator who even possesses "several manuscript versions" of the history of St Ogg, the city's patron saint. This narrator difers considerably from the limited observer who had pretended to know Adam Bede and Amos Barton personally. Unlike the earlier works, *The Mill* never disguises the fact that its author is a sage eager to influence her own age.

Sage-like aspirations (it is nevertheless worth stressing) are not exactly foreign to these earlier novels, usually realized in a manner that makes the reader uncomfortable. The uneasy didacticism of the often-quoted passage from *Amos Barton* ("Depend upon it, you would gain unspeakably if you would learn with me to see some of the poetry and the pathos, etc.") springs from the narrator's wanting to be a sage, and pretending otherwise. The invitation that the reader join the narrator in a *shared* discovery of hidden poetry is a patent charade. Even in *Adam Bede* where we find a sustained effort to express the narrator's privileged insights in the language of Loamshire, we also hear another voice:

> . . . it is too painful to think that Hetty is a woman, with a woman's destiny before her - a woman spinning in young ignorance a light web of folly and vain hopes which may one day close round and press upon her, a rancorous poisoned

garment, changing all at once her fluttering trivial butterfly sensations into a life of deep human anguish.

(Chapter 22)

Despite the pastoral butterfly metaphor, we are not likely to mistake this for the moral sensibility of Mrs Poyser's kitchen, nor indeed of those graver commentators on the human lot, Dinah Morris or Adam himself. And perhaps it is not surprising that it should take the prospect of Hetty's *"woman's* destiny" to force the narrator to this unmasking. Hetty is the character, as most readers would now agree, who radically questions the narrator's claim to impartiality. What else could account for the judicial savagery of that "rancoured poisoned garment", fixed upon her, after all, not by destiny but by the author's final dispositions for the plot.

Certainly, in comparison with these, *The Mill's* narrator represents a truly striking access of self-confidence on George Eliot's part. We can see this, as it were structurally, in the fact that the narrator is equally at home in Dorlcote Mill, in the business and social activities of St Ogg's and in the cultivated metropolitan world to which the reader is assumed to belong. We notice it also in the unforced assurance of a multitude of passing observations about the characters. Mr Tulliver "had the marital habit of not listening very closely"; Mrs Pullett "sent the muscles of her face in quest of fresh tears as she advanced into the parlour"; Mr Deane had a "tendency to repress youthful hopes which stout and successful men of fifty find one of their easiest duties"—almost any page of the novel yields such examples.

And we notice it in the way the narrator organises impressive stores of learning into a pattern of literary and historical allusions, entertaining in their immediate context, yet also threatening a formidable rhetoric against readers insufficiently disposed to respect the careers of hero and heroine. Indeed, Knoepflmacher's description of the narrator as "a sage *eager* to influence her age" needs modification. This sage has surely progressed beyond mere eagerness. The determination that awkwardly surfaces in earlier novels has strengthened into the conviction that she *will* influence the age, and that potential recalcitrants risk finding themselves dismissed to that trivial realm where Mrs Tulliver frets over her lost linen and china.

Yet in the end, this account of *The Mill* applies more to the way the narrator wishes to be seen, than to the total impression which he finally conveys. It presupposes that we know *who* the narrator is, or rather, that the narrator is in fact knowable as a coherent and unified presence. But is this the case? Take, for example, the opening chapters. The person we meet in Chapter 1 is not so much narrator as *revenant*, flitting amongst scenes from the past in a mood not very distant from Hood's "I remember, I remember".

> How lovely the little river is, with its dark changing wavelets! It seems like a living companion while I wander along the bank and listen to its low placid voice, as to the voice of one who is deaf and loving. I remember the stone bridge.

> And this is Dorlcote Mill. I must stand a minute or two here and look at it.

Further description of the scene is suffused with the same quality of intimate feeling, and at points we seem to have entered upon a journey of self-exploration in the high Romantic manner ("As I look at the full stream . . . I am in love with moistness"). The little girl, unexpectedly discovered on the river-bank, and equally fascinated by the mill wheel, may draw our attention away from the speaker, but hardly disturbs a mood which could quite easily have culminated in a meeting between them. But then, of course, the speaker breaks off. We learn that it has all been a dream. Having wakened to find himself in his armchair instead of leaning on Dorlcote Bridge, the narrator tells us that he had actually intended to recount

> what Mr and Mrs Tulliver were talking about, as they sat by the bright fire in the left-hand parlour, on that very afternoon I have been dreaming of.

This conversation then opens Chapter 2, and at once we hear another voice supposedly that of the person who recounted Chapter 1, but evidently very wide-awake indeed.

> Mr Tulliver was speaking to his wife, a blond comely woman in a fan-shaped cap (I am afraid to think how long it is since fan-shaped caps were worn—they must be so near coming in again.

At that time, when Mrs Tulliver was nearly forty, they were new at St Ogg's and considered sweet things.)

The insinuations working within this seemingly bland fashion-note are quite remarkable. What is the feeling behind the concluding sentence - patronising, catty, or just fond? I find it impossible to decide, though there is nothing uncertain about the distance here marked out between the teller and at least one aspect of the tale. And the reader too is put in his place. In a kind of Swiftian double-turn, the first sentence invites us to join in sly amusement at Mrs Tulliver's old-fashioned attire, only to trap us in the second sentence's implication that we lack the narrator's impressively long perspectives, which far out-reach mere revolutions of fashion. If it was provincial of St Ogg's to admire fan-shaped caps so whole-heartedly, it is in another sense provincial in the metropolitan reader to despise St Ogg's for doing so.

So from the outset, we are presented with a narrator with two conflicting relationships with the story. There is the relationship of the dreamer, the deep self-exploratory reverie, which admits the reader to full intimacy; and there is the relationship of the shrewd, potentially hostile commentator in command of and external to the material, expertly conscious of the reader and how to manage him. This doubling is not only not admitted, it is sealed over by a structural device. The little girl of Chapter 1 who evokes the speaker's (maternal?) solicitude ("it is time the little playfellow went in, I think") is of course Maggie, about to be summoned home by her actual mother in Chapter 2, and to be admonished against the danger of the same water whose fascinations link her directly with the speaker of Chapter 1. Nor can it be argued that this shift from the first to the second relationship articulates in the narrator a progress from sentimental indulgence towards the past (dream/child) to maturely-sardonic observation (reality/parent). That would be to posit a theme of planned self-discovery in the narrator for which the remainder of the novel gives no warrant whatsoever. It is difficult to escape the conclusion the *The Mill* opens with a narrator who is neither altogether dreaming nor altogether awake.

This formal ambivalence certainly disappears after Chapter

41

1, though as I hope to show, it provides an essential clue to the narrator's role, or (perhaps one should really say) personality, in subsequent chapters. But it is first worth noticing a related formal problem arising from the conclusion of the novel. We have seen that the narrator's authority lies in the initial claim to be reviving a store of personal memories. As the novel develops, there is a further claim, that of being a kind of historian both of St Ogg's and more generally of a complex process of social and economic change. But neither of these *personae* can account for the narrator's detailed knowledge of Maggie's final hours, of her rescue of Tom, nor of their intense moment of spiritual reconciliation at the point of death:

> living through again in one supreme moment the days when they had clasped their little hands in love, and roamed the daisied field together.

And even more problematic is the closing sentence:

> The tomb bore the names of Tom and Maggie Tulliver, and below the names it was written — "In their death they were not divided."

It seems necessary to ask: who composed this remarkable epitaph? If we take only its conventional meaning ("they died together"), we need look no further than members of the family. But for the reader who has just completed the penultimate chapter, a quite different meaning is inescapable ("when they died they were spiritually and emotionally at one; Maggie's life-long need that Tom accept her was finally satisfied"). Such a message is available to nobody *in* the novel. It can only have been constructed by the narrator who recounted the final catastrophe, and who has by this point been transformed from the personal and social historian into Maggie's invisible companion, with privileged access to events and meanings closed to all the other characters. In this new identity, the narrator, in effect, uses the epitaph to draw the reader into complicity with these secrets, as if to say "only you and I can write the true epitaph, but we have to express it ambiguously, so that it will seem plausible to the outsiders, the Tulliver family and their friends."

It is, of course, usual to explain these shifts of perspective in biographical terms. Indeed, most of the commentaries on *The Mill* make the author's complex relationship with Maggie a central issue: was George Eliot over-indulgent to her heroine, etc? The objection to such an approach is that it effects a conceptual transformation from "narrator/fiction" to "author/character", which both narrows and distorts. For so central an ambiguity of formal structure cannot be discussed in terms of Maggie alone, as if the novel were a kind of *Villette*. It affects every aspect of *The Mill* with a result that may be put in this way. The narrator's judgements reveal a persistent failure to know what to make of the issues raised by the story. His confident air of authority and knowledge covers deep and extensive uncertainty. It is as if the sealing over and suppression of the double relationship set up in the opening chapters produces a neurotic imbalance in the working of his conscious mind.[3]

If this at first seems an overstatement, consider the basic contradiction in the narrator's attitude towards childhood. Book 2 ends, it will be recalled, with Maggie bringing Tom the news of their father's financial failure and illness, and of Tom's departure from the Stelling household. Maggie and Tom begin walking to the turnpike to get the coach home:

> The two slight youthful figures soon grew indistinct on the distant road — were soon lost behind the projecting hedgerow.

> They had gone forth together into their new life of sorrow, and they would never more see the sunshine undimmed by remembered cares. They had entered the thorny wilderness, and the golden gates of their childhood had for ever closed behind them.

The religiose melancholy of these sentences is hardly less surprising than the strangeness of the prophecy. Would they *never* again see the sunshine "undimmed by remembered cares"? And *is* "thorny wilderness" an adequate image for their future life? There is trouble ahead, but surely this is overdoing it. Even stranger is the contrast between this summary of their childhood and the actual events already set before us. How is it possible to reconcile the pastoral-Edenic vision implied by those shut-for-ever "golden gates" with (to choose at random) Maggie beating her rag-doll, cutting off her hair, or pushing

Lucy into the mud, and Tom scrapping bitterly with Bob Jakin, quarreling with Maggie over jam-puffs, or having his self-esteem regularly assaulted by the Reverend Stelling? We have to conclude that the narrator's final formulation for their childhood belongs to a different novel than the one we have been reading. Or, to revert to the situation of Chapter 1, the narrator who dreams of an ideal childhood seems not to know what his wide-awake *alter ego* has remembered in such convincing wealth of detail.

This is not an isolated case. Edenic idealisation is present in the narrator's account of Tom's and Maggie's deaths (see above), while similar regressive nostalgia affects the following passage:

> Life did change for Tom and Maggie; and yet they were not wrong in believing that the thoughts and loves of these first years would always make a part of their lives. We could never have loved the earth so well if we had had no childhood in it—if it were not the earth where the same flowers come up again every spring that we used to gather with our tiny fingers as we sat lisping to ourselves on the grass—the same hips and haws on the autumn hedgerows—the same redbreasts that we used to call "God's birds", because they did no harm to the precious crops. What novelty is worth that sweet monotony where everything is known, and *loved* because it is known?
>
> (Book 1, Chapter 5)

What begins as an affirmation of Wordsworthian continuity linking every stage of life regresses into a rhetorical appeal against the reality of growth and change. In the same context, we can even interpret George Eliot's remark about lingering too long over the early Books (leaving inadequate space for the development of Maggie's adult life) as an authorial version of the dream-narrator's investment in these idealisations of the childhood state.

Turning now to a more characteristic example of the meta-language of judgement and interpretation, it is easy to notice the suppressed contradictions, the play of unadmitted feelings, which collectively undermine the claim to authority.

> Mrs Tulliver was what is called a good-tempered person—never cried when she was a baby, on any slighter ground than hunger

44

and pins; and from the cradle upwards had been healthy, fair, plump and dull-witted; in short, the flower of her family for beauty and amiability. But milk and mildness are not the best things for keeping, and when they turn only a little sour, they may disagree with young stomachs seriously. I have often wondered whether those early Madonnas of Raphael, with the blond faces and somewhat stupid expression, kept their placidity undisturbed when their strong-limbed, strong-willed boys got a little too old to do without clothing. I think they must have been given to feeble remonstrance, getting more and more peevish as it became more and more ineffectual.

(Book 1, Chapter 2)

The first sentences (as far as "amiability") are well in control, exactly conveying the narrator's case against Mrs Tulliver's brand of good-temper. What follows brings less conscious feelings into play. Consider the confusing "milk and mildness" image: are we to envisage a child fed on sour milk? and from the breast? The real point, of course, is the souring of the "mildness", and the image works to convey a strong sense of unlocated distaste which then covers the failure to show how "mildness" (a moral, not a natural, trait) can turn sour by a mere process of nature. From this tangle of specific feeling, the passage about the Raphael Madonnas seems to offer an escape. In Feuerbachian spirit, the narrator notes the role of Christian iconography in validating an ideal conception of human mothers as stupid good-tempered blondes, and both the allusion and historical perspective signify a claim 'for detachment. But again, other feelings are at work: distinct relish in the notion of the Madonna being shaken out of her placidity by an energetic little boy, even a note of sour triumph over her "feeble remonstrance" and "peevish" ineffectuality. And the implied analogy with Mrs Tulliver, whom we have just seen reduced to "feeble fretfulness" by her energetic little girl, has further consequences. It dignifies Maggie as a version of the Holy Infant (as her mother of course doesn't), and covertly glances at the fact of her sex in determining her mother's attitude towards her. The paragraph, in sum, conceals a hostility against Mrs Tulliver-as-mother and against the society that celebrates her temper as good, of an intensity that the narrator has to take refuge from in irony and allusion.

45

Raymond Williams[4] has already written perceptively of the break in texture in the George Eliot novel "between the narrative idiom of the novelist and the recorded language of her characters; between the analytic idiom and the overwhelming emphasis on emotion". But the above paragraph reveals a further break *within* the narrative idiom itself, between one analyst for whom the language of the reported *milieu* ("what is called good temper") perfectly accommodates the necessary criticisms, and another who needs to elaborate a language from altogether different sources. Moreover the asserted formal continuity between these languages covers markedly different narrator-attitudes. The superior detachment and more learned generality claimed by the second is in truth a mask for an "emotion" absent from the "analytical idiom" of the first, which has the further effect of countering the relatively even-handed presentation of the characters *within* the "fiction".

This particular example, of course, invites the narrower biographical interpretation. We might say, for example, that the author is in competition with Mrs Tulliver for the privilege of mothering a version of her childish self and here demonstrates her superior qualifications. But similar contradictions elsewhere touch on unambiguously general issues. Consider the chapter in which Riley advises Tulliver to send Tom to the Reverend Stelling. From a close analysis of Riley's motives, the narrator moves to an injunction to the reader not to judge him too severely, and then concludes:

> Besides, a man with the milk of human kindness in him can scarcely abstain from doing a good-natured action, and one cannot be good-natured all round. Nature herself occasionaly quarters an inconvenient parasite on an animal towards whom she has otherwise no ill-will. What then? We admire her care for the parasite. If Mr Riley had shrunk from giving a recommen-dation that was not based on valid evidence, he would not have helped Mr Stelling to a paying pupil, and that would not have been so well for the reverend gentleman. Consider, too, that all the pleasant little dim ideas and complacencies—of standing well with Timpson, of dispensing advice when he was asked for it, of impressing his friend Tulliver with additional respect, of saying something, and saying it emphatically, with other inappreciably minute ingredients that went along with the

warm hearth and the brandy-and-water to make up Mr Riley's consciousness on this occasion—would have been a mere blank.

(Book 1, Chapter 3)

Could the severest reader crush Riley more thoroughly than this? If the condescension of the final sentence (from "Consider") isn't evidence enough of the narrator's feelings, we can point to the parasite image. Here again, a specifically learned perspective becomes the means of releasing a quality of contempt which the narrator's analysis has so far kept in abeyance. How far the manoeuvre falls outside the narrator's consciousness is, admittedly, less easy to be sure of. The image can be seen to belong to a pattern of animal analogies recurring throughout the novel, and particularly relevant to Book 1.[5] Moreover, we are faced here with an overall address to the reader clearly intended to dispose of unthinking condemnations of people like Riley and so to allow the narrator's views their full impact. The fact remains that we begin with a primarily analytic idiom inviting the supposedly critical reader to *understand* Riley's behaviour, and we end on the entirely different note of the narrator's powerful contempt for the object of analysis. If this is less than a break within the narrative idiom, it is certainly an unexpected development. Nor, on consideration, is it an accident that Riley should provoke it. In more dilute form, so does the Reverend Stelling on account of the inadequacy of his educational provision for Tom. Faced with this all-important impoverishment in the culture available to Tom and Maggie, the narrator is evidently struggling between the necessity of setting it before the reader as an indisputable fact of the place and period, and a warm, if always suppressed, indignation at the consequences. Riley, as initial catalyst in this process of mis-education, can hardly be forgiven.

Such contradictions within the narrator's attitude might be plotted along a scale marking the degree of consciousness they appear to suggest. Of the dual relationship with the story as a whole, and of the contradictory handling of childhood, the narrator seems unaware to the point of schizophrenia. With Mrs Tulliver, there is an uneasy mixture of conscious irony and suppressed animus, pointing to an unconscious manipulation of what has already been presented. With Riley and the

47

Reverend Stelling, we have a borderline case. The play of feeling includes unexpected bursts of intensity, but may be seen as a conscious rhetoric aimed at disturbing the reader's conceivably routine attitudes (though as with Swift, there remains the suspicion that the narrator is directing at the reader a complex of hostilities whose source lies elsewhere.) Two later extensive pieces of authorial commentary show the emergence into full consciousness of the narrator's divided feeling about a major aspect of the novel, and to these we can now turn.

The first opens Book 4, the well-known chapter entitled "A Variation of Protestantism Unknown to Bossuet". We are now more than half-way through *The Mill*, approaching Maggie's adolescence, and the question raised by the narrator is radical.

> It is a sordid life, you say, this of the Tullivers and Dodsons—irradiated by no sublime principles, no romantic visions, no active, self-renouncing faith—moved by none of those wild, uncontrollable passions which create the dark shadows of misery and crime—without that primitive rough simplicity of wants, that hard submissive ill-paid toil, that child-like spelling out of what nature has written, which gives its poetry to peasant life . . . You could not live among such people; you are stifled for want of an outlet towards something beautiful, great or noble; you are irritated with these dull men and women, as a kind of population out of keeping with the earth on which they live—with this rich plain where the great river flows for ever onward, and links the small pulse of the old English town with the beatings of the world's mighty heart. A vigorous superstition that lashes its gods or lashes its own back, seems more congruous with the mystery of the human lot, than the mental condition of these emmet-like Dodsons and Tullivers.
>
> (Book 4, Chapter 1)

We notice at once that though the narrator imputes this view of the Tulliver-Dodsons to the reader,[6] it is also his own. "I share with you this sense of oppressive narrowness", he goes on, and this is no mere tactic. The preceding contrast of the two great Continental rivers, the Rhine and the Rhone, which has already set up the terms of reference, leaves us in no doubt where the narrator's preferences lie. On the one hand, the landscape of the Rhine symbolises "the grand *historic* life" of mankind where passion and belief, adventure and romance produce lasting

48

achievement; on the other, the ruins along the Rhone represent "a narrow, ugly, grovelling existence", whose traces "will be swept into the same oblivion with the generations of ants and beavers". Life along the Floss, we are given explicitly to understand, resembles the mean and trivial scenery of the Rhone, and the seriousness of the point lies not so much in the standard Romantic contrast of poetically-feudal past with prosaic present, as in the assertion that only the first merits attention as a genuinely *human* life. Riley, we have seen, can fairly be compared to a parasite on an animal-like Stelling. It now appears that, in a longer European and historical perspective, the Tulliver-Dodsons appear as emmets scurrying endlessly to and fro at the bidding of nothing beyond an impulse of self-preservation. We have to conclude, then, that the narrator here confronts openly and for the first time his central anxiety whether such people *really deserve to be written about in the first place*. This is the anxiety whose earlier reverberations we have been noticing. How is the anxiety met? Not, it has to be stressed, by appeals to the reader to look for "the poetry and the pathos" hidden within these apparently tedious and obscure lives, though in respect of Tulliver at least, this is precisely what "the fiction" has done and will continue to do. The argument which will become familiar in George Eliot's later novels, involves "history". We are to think of the Tulliver-Dodsons as the historically-constraining *milieu*, the determining context within which Tom and Maggie, as carriers of a more developed human type, must struggle for their true development. We must attend to the Tulliver-Dodsons and feel "their oppressive narrowness", because otherwise we will fail

> to understand how it acted on the lives of Tom and Maggie—how it has acted on young natures in many generations, that in the onward tendency of human things have risen above the mental level of the generation before them, to which they have been nevertheless tied by the strongest fibres of their hearts. The suffering, whether of martyr or victim, which belongs to every historical advance of mankind is represented in this way in every town, and by hundreds of obscure hearths.

At best a negative argument, this might do well enough if it were convincing. Yet it applies not at all to Tom, so thoroughly caught in the rigidity of an inherited Dodson culture that it is hard to believe the narrator is seriously thinking about him at this point. Maggie, of course, fits the bill rather better. She *is* more mentally adventurous than her parents, and she suffers a great deal through her determined, and touchingly solitary, struggle towards a more "human" existence. On the other hand, can she be claimed as a martyr in the cause of the "historical advance of mankind"? This is certainly debatable, and good arguments can be proposed both for the notion that she gains a heroic, if private, victory over the commonplace judgments of the "world's wife", and for the opposite view that she dies a victim to her own failure to break with the dead morality of her upbringing. But there is a deeper problem. Though moral changes have their place in the process of "historical advance", they are never the whole of it, and their relations with other factors are enormously complex. Where are these relations expounded or represented? And more generally what is the "historical advance" within which Maggie's situation might have a place? Looking back to the first three Books, we find so little to help us answer these questions that the whole "historical" thesis about the Tulliver-Dodsons becomes very hard to accept. And though aspects of the remaining Books *are* more germane, I hope to show that the "historical advance" remains little more than an intellectual gesture of the narrator's, given only the most shadowy and ambiguous realisation. We are left with the suspicion that this view of the Tulliver-Dodson clan involves a strong element of rationalisation. The narrator has tried to come to grips with his basic conflict of feeling about them. What he actually expresses is the strongest possible case against their claim to a truly "human" dignity.

The second example of extended commentary comes towards the end of the same Book, the often-quoted paragraphs about "the emphasis of want" in explaining Maggie's developing interest in Thomas à Kempis. We are faced here not so much with evidence of the writer's divided feelings about the story, as an attempt to generalise its significance, which is hardly more successful than the example just discussed. The narrator directs an unambiguous contempt against the obtusely luxurious life of "good society" for whom religious enthusiasm of Maggie's kind would seem positively grotesque. We are given a glimpse of

> a wide and arduous national life condensed in unfragrant
> deafening factories, cramping itself in mines, sweating at
> furnaces, grinding, hammering, weaving under more or less
> oppression of carbonic acid—or else, spread over sheep-walks,
> and scattered in lonely houses and huts on the clayey or chalky
> corn-lands, where the rainy days look dreary.

(Book 4, Chapter 3)

In such circumstances, people develop an imperative need for belief in

> something that will present motives in an entire absence of high
> prizes, something that will give patience and feed human love
> when the limbs ache with weariness, and human looks are hard
> upon us—something, clearly, that lies outside our personal
> desires, that includes resignation for ourselves and active love for
> what is not ourselves.

Yet despite points of analogy with Maggie's situation, what this argument highlights is the fact that her deprivations are *not* harshly material, but emotional and cultural, and the question then arises of the real bearing of *this* national context to her case, or indeed to any aspect of life by the Floss as it has been set before us. We can see that in evoking the larger perspective, the narrator is aiming, as it were in the spirit of the opening of Book 4, to lend Maggie's personal history a representative character. But the link is fragile. Indeed, far from connecting her with "the historical advance of mankind", the analogy threatens the opposite. It identifies Maggie's effort at meaningful self-suppression with a widely experienced and understandably *a-historic* impulse to withdraw from conditions of severe oppression felt to be beyond challenge. And with no further application to events in *The Mill*, we can only take these paragraphs as a digressive attack on metropolitan readers tempted to dismiss the "history of unfashionable families" as beneath their notice.

Enough has now been said about the ambiguity of the relationship between the meta-language of the narrator and the story upon which it is offered as authoritative commentary. It now only remains to ask why the "historic" thesis advanced to justify close attention to the Tulliver-Dodsons and

51

representative character to the lives of Tom and Maggie is insufficiently convincing. I have suggested already that Books 1-3 offer no preparation for this thesis, that Tom's life seems wholly unrelated to the "historical" claim made for it, and Maggie's only to some degree. What support for the thesis does the rest of the novel give? There is an irony in the fact that if we turn from the narrator to the fiction, we can see that by means of the events that lead to Tulliver's bankruptcy and to Tom's career with Guest & Co, the novelist underpins the development of the story with a specific historic process: the movement of economic power from rural to urban conditions, the enlargement of trading markets, and the more ambitious disposition of capital which these necessitated. This process is, in effect, symbolised in the narrative shift from Dorlcote Mill to St Ogg's, from the traditional milling process that so fascinates the Tulliver children to the warehouses and counting houses where Tom starts his career, and from Tulliver's local journeyings round and about the Mill to Tom's journey to York and perhaps even those of the Dutch vessel which picks up Maggie and Stephen on its journey to Mudport. But this process needs hardly to be sketched before we notice how little Tom could be said to be its "victim or martyr", and how Maggie has no relation to it whatsoever.

Latent within this history, there is of course an inherent contradiction between "commerce" and "culture" which is a familiar theme of Victorian social criticism, and of considerable interest to the later George Eliot (as, for example, in *Daniel Deronda*). But this has no bearing on Maggie's tragedy in *The Mill*. We may also advance a more fundamental reason for the extremely tenuous relationship of this underlying history to Tom's and Maggie's personal careers, and that is the conception of history which appears within the narrator's meta-language. In Book 1, Chapter 12, the narrator first presents himself in his character of historian of St Ogg's, informing us that

> it is one of those old, old towns which impress one as a continuation and outgrowth of nature, as much as the nests of the bower-birds or the winding galleries of the white ants: a town which carries the traces of its long growth and history like a millenial tree . . .

This organic analogy renders the complex process of historical change as a continuous *growth*, a product of nature's mysteriously inaccessible forces. The same organic conception underlies the role of the river and its attendant floods in symbolising those changes that cannot be easily subsumed as gradual and continuous. "The mind of St Ogg's," we are told, "did not look extensively before or after. It inherited a long past without thinking of it" and had forgotten what the narrator has not: the legend connecting its origins with the visitation of the floods.

This symbolism is, of course, usually given a psychological interpretation in relation to Maggie and the powerful inner emotions which she struggles to control. But the old legend connects it clearly enough with St Ogg's as a human community, and from a comment we have already glanced at (see p. 48), we learn that the river connects "the small pulse of the old English town with the beatings of *the world's* mighty heart". (My italics.)

The problem about such analogies is that they tend to conceive history as merely happening, as distinct from being made to happen, one way and not another, by the deliberate choices of men and women. This point comes over with considerable force later in the passage about St Ogg's from which I have quoted, when we meet references to "the troubles of the civil war" in the seventeenth century when Puritans and Loyalists fought for its control. Such events, whatever else they were, cannot be seen as "growth". Or we can take central examples from the novel itself. Tulliver does not grow into bankruptcy, and his appointment as manager to the man he hates in the mill he had once owned comes about not through any natural process, but—as the narrator is careful to tell us— because Wakem resembles other successful men in choosing to humiliate an old enemy. In the same way, the development of Guest & Co and the resulting changes in St Ogg's (and no doubt elsewhere) follow from the specific application of human decisions and human energies embodied in such as Mr Deane and his enterprising and determined nephew. The novel presents the same paradox throughout. On the one hand, the fiction details a series of actions propelled by human choice; and on the other, the narrator conceives the sum of these actions, the imagined history they make up and the larger real history to which he refers them, as resembling organic processes of nature. Such a conception of historical change makes it impossible to connect the lives of the characters with "the historic advance of mankind", or indeed to give that phrase the concrete significance it deserves. That Maggie's personal struggles take place in, as it were, a separate moral compartment of the novel, sealed off from other than mechanical connections with the under-pinning historical process, should not after all surprise us.

This essay has only been able to touch on the more obvious discontinuities in the relationship between narrator and fiction in *The Mill on the Floss*. But perhaps it may suggest the usefulness of this approach to George Eliot's novels as a whole, and in particular to her later work, where the narrator assumes with increasing aplomb the role of "historian". In *The Mill* itself, we see the evidence of conflicts which are subsequently suppressed, only to re-emerge as significant evasions and silences affecting every aspect of the formal structure of the novels. To read these conflicts in a biographical light is to ignore these more general results. What we might call Maggie's case against her family is never thoroughly aired principally because the narrator has failed to clarify his own, and that absence of clarification remains one of the most significant aspects of *The Mill* which we can explore.

NOTES

1   Colin McCabe, *James Joyce and the Revolution of the Word* (1978), Chapter 2.
2   *George Eliot's Early Novels* (1968), p.184.
3   For an extremely interesting psychoanalytic account of *The Mill* see L.C. Emery, *George Eliot's Creative Conflict* (1976), Chapter 1.
4   *The English Novel from Dickens to Lawrence* (1971), pp.79-80.
5   See Reva Stump, *Moment and Vision in George Eliot's Novels* (1959), Chapter 5.
6   Correctly, judging by the review of *The Mill* which appeared in *The Times*, 19 May 1860. See *A Century of George Eliot Criticism* (ed. Gordon S. Haight, 1965).

4

Adam Bede and "the Story of the Past"

by CHARLES PALLISER

The question why George Eliot wrote only historical novels—
with the exception of *Daniel Deronda* at the end of her life—is of
particular interest and importance at the start of her career as a
novelist. When, after writing *Scenes of Clerical Life* set in the
period of her childhood and earlier, she decided to locate her
first novel in the late 1790s, it was because she conceived of a
necessary connection, in a certain sense, between the writing of
fiction and the exercise of the historical imagination—a
connection whose complexities she was to explore in all her later
novels. An understanding of how she set out to investigate this
connection in *Adam Bede* will take us to the very centre of her art.

A number of critics have argued that George Eliot is not
concerned in this novel with history, with the specific
intellectual, religious, and political issues of her chosen period.
In a sense they are right: what she is interested in is not so much
the truth about the past, as the way in which we understand it.
The novel is certainly not about history in the way that, for
example, Charlotte Brontë's *Shirley* is—set in the period about
ten years later than that of *Adam Bede* and written a few years
earlier in 1848 and 1849. Yet as far as George Eliot's novel does
depict a specific society it does so very accurately, recon-
structing a community that is credible in socio-economic
terms. However, it does not attempt to explore the complexities
of the rise of Methodism or the breakdown of rural feudalism in
the way the *Shirley* tackles the moral and political implications
of the war-time economic crisis, or *Middlemarch* illustrates the

paradoxes and contradictions inherent in the linked notions of Reform and Progress. Whereas in other of her books— *Middlemarch, Romola,* and even *Scenes of Clerical Life* which, although it preceded *Adam Bede,* seems in this respect more adventurous than it—George Eliot tries to go beyond the widely received view of a particular subject to arrive at the complex reality, in *Adam Bede* she employs a commonly accepted view of the recent rural past, a myth, of the kind discussed by Raymond Williams in *The Country and the City.* However, it is because she adopts this strategy in full awareness of its implications, that it is possible to see her attitude towards the rural past as conservative—or even reactionary, sentimental, and lacking in sympathy for the working class, as Williams does—and yet still defend the complexity and intelligence of her treatment of history in the novel.[1] For the book is not so much about the 1790s as about the question of what it means to write a historical novel. George Eliot builds into the book an awareness of the dangers of hindsight and the temptation to nostalgia that lie in wait for a writer who makes up "a story of the past", but also of the advantages of setting one's action in the past. What she demonstrates is that the very act of simplifying and mythologizing by which we interpret the past in terms of an easily comprehensible and reassuring "myth" is an analogy of the way we interpret our own experience, and, further, of the way the artistic imagination itself functions.

We ourselves face the problem that we read *Adam Bede* in the light of what we know was to come and therefore, tempted to apply a crudely progressive model of development to George Eliot's career, we see it as only partially successful anticipation of the later novels. In doing this we acknowledge its strengths, but we see as successful those elements that we admire in the later novels, and see as weaknesses those that are apparently much better done in the subsequent books. The most common charge made against the novel is of a certain maladroitness in such things as the use of the narrator, the characterization, the treatment of the Methodist theme, and the construction of the plot. George Eliot is often seen as having progressed towards greater literary polish, as if her famous parallel with Dutch genre painting in Chapter 17 were to be taken as an apology in this first novel for clumsy sincerity instead of an argument for highly-wrought artifice. In fact, as that chapter itself shows with its discussion of the nature of realism, *Adam Bede* is in many ways her most literary, though not her most accomplished, book and the one in which she most self-consciously discusses her artistic intentions.

So in *Adam Bede* George Eliot sets out to examine the nature of fiction and its peculiar kind of access to the truth, asking what the differences are between the way we read fiction and the way we "read" actual experience, and in what sense, following on from this, a novel can claim to offer its readers advice on how to conduct their lives. Since *Adam Bede* is a historical novel this issue is more specifically related to the question of how fiction's method of insight into the truth about the past compares with that of the discipline of history. George Eliot is asking whether, if literature can only be historically truthful by dealing with the representative, with what is already accepted as historically true —an assumption which she does not make in other books—it is then necessarily trapped inside such preconceptions and limited by them? What she does is to integrate into the book, in both the commentary and the very structure, a demonstration of the relation between myth and reality.

We can see that the novel appealed, at least for most of its length, to conventional ideas about village life in the late eighteenth century, and that its tragic plot was at the same time accepted—whether rightly or wrongly is a question which is not at issue here—as historically plausible, by considering an unsigned contemporary notice in the *Saturday Review*. Its author saw in the novel a conflict between these two—historical reality and literary preconceptions about the rural past—that many later readers have found: "The degree of horror and painfulness is [. . .] out of keeping with the calm simplicity of rural life."[2] The question is: where does that notion of "the calm simplicity of rural life" come from? The answer is that it is a literary myth, a cliché, which is not necessarily "true", for the reviewer at the same time recognizes that the novel's grimmer events were— and still are—also historically accurate: "Of course, every one knows that every sin under heaven is committed freely in agricultural villages, and if any one chooses to insist that pretty dairymaids are in danger of being seduced, he at least keeps within the bounds of fact." The objection is that a discordant sense of reality has intruded into what until then has seemed to be a much safer kind of literary treatment of the subject, and the reviewer revealingly goes on to protest that there is "no reason why a picture of village character and village humour should be made so painful as it is by the introduction into the foreground of the startling horrors of rustic reality." The reviewer means that he is forced grudgingly to acknowledge that both are "true"—the literary cliché and the harsher "reality". It is in this sense that his rosier veiw of the rural past constitutes a myth: it can survive even in the face of an awareness of its variance from the truth, because it is held as a matter of faith and belief rather than fact and reason. As we shall see, the reviewer is correct in seeing the novel as deliberately appealing, at first anyway, to its reader's preconceptions about village life in the past, but he is wrong in asserting that the book is then damaged by the intervention of "reality".

One way to approach *Adam Bede* without being misled by our knowledge of what came later is to consider the book, as its first readers did, in the light of *Scenes of Clerical Life,* and in this event we will probably be struck by several similarities betwen these two apparently dissimilar works. The three stories in the collection have roughly the same theme and structure: they start by telling us the generally accepted view, in a circle of small-town gossips, of a central character or characters, and then gradually reveal that the truth is very different. Each is thus about the difficulty of understanding from the outside the real complexity of a situation and is a study of the unknowableness of other people and their mysteriousness to those around them.

Adam Bede works in rather the same way: we start from outside a situation which we probably think we understand, and then slowly we are shown a more complex reality than the assumptions we have made. So far this does not sound like anything but a conventional novelistic procedure, but there is a difference which is related to the sense in which *Adam Bede* might seem to be a step backwards after *Scenes of Clerical Life.* In that collection George Eliot shows us how strange and paradoxical reality is: Amos, in "The Sad Fortunes of the Rev. Amos Barton", is not the wife-abusing adulterer that his parishioners imagine but an obtuse yet devoted husband; the central character in "Mr Gilfil's Love-Story" conceals a passionate heart beneath a very unremarkable exterior; and Mr Tryan, in "Janet's Repentance", is not the expected canting Evangelical he at first appears. In *Adam Bede*, however, we do not find an increasing complexity the closer we get to Dinah and Adam, or to Arthur and Hetty, and although the reader probably misunderstands in certain respects, it is not because he has been misled by the characters but because he has not understood correctly the relation of *Adam Bede* as a fiction to the reality it portrays. What happens is that the reader is first encouraged, partly by the nostalgic narrator, and partly because of the nature of the subject he is introduced to, to make a stock response in the way that the reviewer in the *Saturday Review* did, and then, in a strictly literary manoeuvre the perspective is suddenly enlarged and he realizes how much he has allowed himself to forget.

The opening of the novel raises certain literary expectations about the subject—an apparently idyllic village in the past— which are initially satisfied. In the first chapter describing in a leisurely, slightly patronizing tone the scene in Burge's workshop, Adam emerges as a model artisan: conscientious, intelligent, God-fearing—though a little limited as far as imagination and a sense of humour are concerned. It is as an idealized figure of this kind that he appears to the unnamed horseman who sees him at the end of this chapter: "As [Adam] reached the foot of the slope, an elderly horseman, with his portmanteau strapped behind him, stopped his horse when Adam had passed him, and turned round to have another long look at the stalwart workman in paper cap, leather breeches, and dark-blue worsted stockings." With what seems like an ingenuous clumsiness the narrator hands over to this horseman, and the village of Hayslope is now introduced to us through the eyes of this figure: the main street, the delightful old inn, its comic landlord, and the picturesque village green. So far all that has been described has been conventionally charming, and at this point there occurs a long evocation of the village and the beauty of the scenery surrounding it. With a single parenthetical exception to which we shall return, this passage evokes all the qualities traditionally associated with the English countryside—

its richness, peace, and sense of social harmony—in a way which deliberately appeals to the reader's expectations of the pastoral idyll. It ends with an appeal to our sense of nostalgia and an almost shameles attempt to involve us in a sentimental response in the last sentence: "It was that moment in summer when the sound of the scythe being whetted makes us cast more lingering looks at the flower-sprinkled tresses of the meadows." The focus then moves to the Green and the evocation of the conventionally rustic continues in the description of the villagers listening to Dinah preaching. The horseman listens intently to her sermon—which is given at length—and at the end of the chapter he rides on his way without comment. He has been used as a kind of distancing "frame" by means of which we are introduced to a village which we will take as charming without the narrator having to endorse this judgment directly, for the very act of framing it in this way makes it seem an idyllic picture that is being presented to us. Similarly, Dinah is introduced through her sermon without direct commentary so that the Christian values which she enunciates are simply presented to us in all their untested idealism. The relevance of the themes of her sermon emerges only much later: in the midst of these incongruously charming surroundings she evokes Christ's "great agony in the garden" and insists that, even though we may not see him, he is always near us in our sufferings. The idea of a failure to perceive what is before our eyes—either because of an act of wilful concealment on the part of the observed, or, as here, because of the observer's inability to see immediately what is not obvious—is a recurrent motif in the novel.

The horseman, too, introduces an important motif in the book: that of the journey through countryside which one interprets correctly or incorrectly. Holding his counsel, he now travels on—to reappear later—and the narrator takes over again and introduces us to the world of the novel through representative institutions and areas of village life: the workshop, the prosperous farm of the Poysers, the church, the big house, and the night-school. In a series of "set-pieces" centring on each of these institutions, we are shown in a very deliberate way what appear to amount to celebrations of the past. However, the authorial commentary establishes a complex attitude towards the fact that the story takes place in the past, balancing a recognition of its apparent simplicity, charm, and stability against an awareness of the prevalent ignorance, superstition, and injustice. At times, though, the narrator goes so far in praising the past that we may suspect either confusion on George Eliot's part or the conscious creation of a compromised narrator whose judgement we are intended to reject. There is, however, a third possibility.

The Poysers' farm is presented as a warm, secure community in which everyone has and knows his place. The narrator describes Adam visiting there on winter evenings "when the whole family, in patriarchal fashion, master and mistress, children and servants, were assembled in that glorious kitchen, at well-graduated distances from the blazing fire" (ch.9). George Eliot uses the word "family" here in its old sense meaning the whole household which was already archaic by the time she was writing. Later, though, it becomes clear that there is another way of seeing the farm. Again, the account in Chapter 18 of the Poyser family going to church is a wonderful evocation of the past which also serves the important function of showing the relation of these people to their environment, for the attitude of the novel's characters to the countryside is an important theme. Interwoven with the children's excitement at the countryside and the gossip of their parents is the sense—in Mrs Poyser's comments on the milch-herd or her husband's regret that the Sabbath is preventing him from making hay—that the countryside through which they are passing is not merely beautiful scenery but is also their working environment. The description of the church-service again seems to be an unequivocal lament for the old certainties: the piety of the congregation, the musical ability of the parish-clerk, and the sense of the whole community sharing in the Bede family's grief for the death of Thias. But then the narrator comments: "none of the old people held books—why should they? not one of them could read. But they knew a few 'good words' by heart, and their withered lips now and then moved silently, following the service without any very clear comprehension indeed, but with a simple faith in its efficacy to ward off harm and bring blessing" (ch.18). The implication seems to be that the old people are just as well off, if not better, with their "simple faith" as they would be if they could read and so think for themselves.

However, it could be argued that on the contrary these words have to be taken in connection with the description of Bartle Massey's night-school and George Eliot's sympathetic treatment of working-men learning to read, and that she is very far from saying that ignorance is better than education. If this is the correct way to read this passage then it could be said that the manner in which she balances the advantages of the past— here the sense of a community linked by shared faith—against its drawbacks—the widespread illiteracy—is an aspect of the historical objectivity that she is trying to achieve.

In fact, my argument is that George Eliot is not interested in *Adam Bede* in historical objectivity in this sense, and that instead, by means of a deliberate ambivalence, the narrator intends to leave with us the question of whether things are better or worse than sixty years before, or, indeed, whether they are any different. A characteristic example of this occurs when, after Arthur's visit to Hall Farm during which he arranges to meet Hetty in the wood, the narrator comments on her foolish preoccupation with him in these terms: "Foolish thoughts! But all this happened, you must remember, nearly sixty years ago, and Hetty was quite uneducated - a simple farmer's girl, to whom a gentleman with a white hand was dazzling as an Olympian god" (ch.9). The implication is surely that things are just the same at the moment of writing, and this is characteristic of an irony which works both against the past and against any assumption of superiority on behalf of the present.

Incidentally, the question of literacy and the idea of reading are, as we shall see, of great importance in the novel. Bartle Massey's night-school figures at a length which is not justified by its relevance to the plot; we are told about Adam's reading in some detail; and we see Dinah consulting her Bible for guidance by lots—with unfortunate consequences on the occasion when she goes to offer Hetty her assistance and is rebuffed. Partly, George Eliot is using literacy and the attitude towards books as a measure of progress, but she is also asking: in what sense can books tell us how to live? In this larger sense the theme is related to the idea of interpretation—of interpreting one's own experience, of "reading" the countryside, and, finally, of reading *Adam Bede* itself. The equation of understanding reality with the act of reading is made explicit several times. When Adam sees

Arthur kissing Hetty in the wood his realization of the truth is described in these words: "a terrible scorching light showed him the hidden letters that changed the meaning of the past" (ch.27). The idea of a concealed—or, rather, not perceived— fact changing the way a story is to be interpreted is central to the novel. The idea occurs in a slightly different sense when, in the context of her naivety in relation to Arthur, the narrator remarks: "Hetty had never read a novel; if she had ever seen one, I think the words would have been too hard for her; how then could she find a shape for her expectations?" (ch.13). *Adam Bede* itself is about exactly this: the shaping of expectations in life as well as in fiction.

The same ironic ambivalence towares the "pastness" of the novel's setting that we have found in the narrative voice is built into the way in which the characters in it make assumptions about an imagined and idyllic future based on their certainty of the stability of their environment. The novel exploits, that is to say, a kind of proleptic nostalgia in which the characters project into the future the happiness and security that they have always known. Their assumptions are wrong, for the future they imagine is in fact precluded by Arthur's seduction of Hetty. It is as if in reading their future they were making the same assumptions that the unwary reader makes in reading the novel, and, like him, they misread it and have to revise their expectations. Moreover, these alternative futures which open up briefly to show us "what might have been" and are then closed out, stress the chanciness of life which, contrary to the allegation of determinsim which is often made against her, George Eliot is always keenly conscious of. So she remarks of Arthur that he might not have revealed the selfishness he was capable of if circumstances had been different (ch. 12), and makes Adam exclaim that if Hetty had not been seduced he would have married her and might never have known what she was capable of (ch. 46). At each point innumerable alternative novels are generated by these glimpsed possibilities.

Very early in the novel, in the midst of an evocation of the security represented by the Poysers' farm, an example of this false proleptic nostalgia occurs when Arthur makes a joke by pretending to Mrs Poyser that he might decide to take over the farm himself: "I think yours is the prettiest farm on the estate, though; and do you know, Mrs. Poyser, if I were going to marry and settle, I should be tempted to turn you out, and do up this fine old house, and turn farmer myself" (ch.6). In alarm, Mrs Poyser hastens to tell him how unsatisfactory the house is, and he then reassures her: "I'm not likely to settle for the next twenty years, till I'm a stout gentleman of forty; and my grandfather would never consent to part with such good tenants as you." Immediately after this comforting vision of the future, Arthur makes an assignation with Hetty in the wood—thus initiating the chain of events which ultimately brings about a very different future. George Eliot is anxious to make clear this tendency in Arthur to take his future for granted, and in the same scene, while he is flirting with Hetty by trying to get her to promise him a dance at the feast to celebrate his birthday, he insists: "you must bring all your children, you know, Mrs. Poyser; your little Totty, as well as the boys. I want all the youngest children on the estate to be there—all those who will be fine young men and women when I'm a bald old fellow" (ch.7). Similarly, at the start of Chapter 12 in which he tries, and fails, to avoid the temptation to keep his assignation with Hetty, George Eliot relates the lack of moral rootedness in his good intentions to his fantasising concept of the future which allows him simultaneously to plan for a popular career as squire and to intrigue in secret with the niece of one of his tenants:

> He was nothing, if not good-natured; and all his pictures of the future, when he should come into the estate, were made up of a prosperous, contented tenantry, adoring their landlord, who would be the model of an English gentleman—mansion in first-rate order, all elegance and high taste—jolly housekeeping, finest stud in Loamshire—purse open to all public objects—in short, everthing as different as possible from what was now associated with the name of Donnithorne. (ch. 12)

The future yields only too easily to the self-indulgent will of the generous egoist.

The coming-of-age celebration brings together most of the themes touched upon. The feast is a celebration of continuity, community, stability, social harmony, mutual trust, and interdependence—all the values against which Arthur is secretly offending. It is also the moment in the book when the sense of nostalgia most clearly conspires with the sense of history to license ill-founded assumptions about the future, for it links past and future in a number of ways, and the humblest person present becomes both historian and prophet. The celebration has been looked forward to for a long time: the ale is now to be drunk which was brewed after Arthur's birth; old people are present whose memories stretch far back; and Martin Poyser senior actually feels young in comparison with an old man—"the Hayslope partiarch, old Feyther Taft"—who went out to fight the Scots in the 'Forty-Five.

Arthur responds to the mood when he projects himself into the future in his ironic words to Irwine: "I was determined to have the children and make a regular family thing out of it. I shall be the 'old squire' to those little lads and lasses some day, and they'll tell their children what a much finer young fellow I was than my own son" (ch.22). Unless Arthur is particularly unfortunate as a parent, this is unlikely to be true. Similarly, when Martin Poyser comments that Hetty will boast when she is an old woman that she danced with the squire on his twenty-first birthday (ch. 26), the imagined future and the actual present ironically collide since at this moment Hetty is in fact regretting that Arthur has not publicly paid more attention to her. The same kind of dramatic irony about the future informs the after-dinner speeches made by Martin Poyser, Arthur himself, Irwine, and Adam. Consequently, at the climax of the part of the book which most appears to invite and license notstalgia, there is an ironic contrast between the pleasant fiction in which the characters participate here and the actual future which is very different.

These false glimpses of the future are central to George Eliot's discussion of the way we imagine the past. In showing us the dangers of allowing the will to dominate over reality and construct comforting fictions of the future by a misreading of the present, she is offering us a lesson on how to read not only the past but the novel itself. The characters in the book, misreading their present, imagine the future in the self-gratifying way that we are always tempted to imagine the past, and this is particularly true in the case of the historical novel which so often rests on a sentimentalization of the past and the exploitation of a sense of its "safeness" that a novel set in our own time does not have.

We have seen that the narrator's apparent nostalgia for the past is to be interpreted ironically. My argument is that this irony is built into the structure of the book which first invites the reader to make certain assumptions about what is revealed—specifically, the idyllic nature of the world presented—and then forces him to revise them. Moreover, this act of revision parallels the experience of the central character. The idea of an act of revision, of "looking again", occurs frequently in the novel as one of the images of sight which have often been noticed. It is related to the theme of concealment and secrecy and the difficulty of judging people correctly from their appearance which George Eliot discusses in connection with Arthur and Hetty in particular. For example, the arrogant and imperious Mrs Irwine—who is mistaken in her estimation of her godson Arthur—argues in opposition to her wiser son that appearances do reveal the inner reality:

> You'll never persuade me that I can't tell what men are by their outsides. If I don't like a man's looks, depend upon it I shall never like *him*. I don't want to know people that look ugly and disagreeable, any more than I want to taste dishes that look disagreeable. If they make me shudder at the first glance, I say, take them away. (ch. 5)

The distinction is between those characters who are content with a "first glance" and those who, like Adam above all, have the wisdom to profit from a "second look".

Much of this is made clear in a complex and important passage in which George Eliot exploits the idea of the journey as an analogy for experience, and relates it to the idea of interpretation and the "second look"—specifically in relation to the idea of "reading" the countryside. The passage occurs in Chapter 54 in the account of Adam's journey to Snowfield to ask Dinah if she will marry him. As he rides along he remembers his first journey to Snowfield to fetch Hetty back—as he mistakenly believed—before their marriage:

> What keen memories went along the road with him! He had often been to Oakbourne and back since that first journey to Snowfield, but beyond Oakbourne the grey stone walls, the broken country, the meagre trees, seemed to be telling him afresh the story of that painful past which he knew so well by heart. But

no story is the same to us after a lapse of time; or rather, we who read it are no longer the same interpreters: and Adam this morning brought with him new thoughts through that grey country—thoughts which gave an altered significance to its story of the past.

In this passage there are actually three relevant journeys: Adam's first expedition to collect Hetty when he travelled in joyful anticipation; his return to Hayslope in alarm when he guessed that she had gone to find Arthur; and his present journey in full knowledge of what had really happened and its consequences. The motif of the "second look", or the repeated journey, raises the question of whether one has learned from experience. The titles of the chapters describing Hetty's search for Arthur and its aftermath—"Journey in Hope" and "Journey in Despair"—suggest that, incapable because of her egoism of learning from experience, Hetty makes her return from Windsor a tragic repetition of her outward journey.

Adam, however, learns from his journeys, and his experience, now seen objectively and therefore understood, becomes a "story", for in this passage George Eliot makes explicit the association of the journey-as-life with the story itself. The relationship between Adam's three journeys becomes an image not only of the story of his life but also of the way we should read *Adam Bede* itself. One of the functions of this passage is to prepare us for Adam to put behind him the "story" of his involvement with Hetty and begin a new one with Dinah, and the author has here to overcome the problem of the appearance of a possible callousness in Adam's closing that chapter of his life. Her solution is one that reminds us that this is a historical novel: she stresses that the passing of time itself creates an objectivity which allows one a "second look" which will be more truthful, more perceptive, than the first: "no story is the same to us after a lapse of time; or rather, we who read it are no longer the same interpreters." So the "new thoughts" that Adam carries with him on this third journey are part of the necessary and inevitable process of development—or progress on the historical level—which will lead him to a new life with Dinah, and they so distance him from his own experience that George Eliot can say that they "gave an altered significance to [the] story of the past." Adam, therefore, reads his own story in the way in which the author herself reads her historical period, and in the way in which her reader should read the novel itself—as an objective and unsentimental study of a historical period. But there are other lessons about the way to read *Adam Bede* that this passage, with its image of the journey-as-experience-as-story, contains.

One of these is related to the question of George Eliot's alleged determinism and, specifically, the charge that at the end of the novel she rewards Adam too neatly and heartlessly with marriage to Dinah, consigning Hetty off-handedly to transportation and death. A journey is always made towards a destination although one may not fully understand this during its course. Similarly, the individual's life moves towards events in the future, and we have seen how far *Adam Bede* is about the way in which this is not understood by those who try to comprehend and predict the course of their lives. Finally, a novelist creates a plot which progresses towards an end which must both arise naturally out of events and yet conclude with a satisfying inevitability. In the paragraphs that follow the passage quoted above George Eliot stresses that, perceiving now the shape which his life is to have, Adam does not rejoice that out of Hetty's suffering has come the possibility of his own happiness with Dinah. Adam's freedom from the egoism of Arthur and Hetty makes him reflect in the next paragraph: "Other folk were not created for my sake, that I should think all square when things turn out well for me." His sympathy has been enlarged by his own suffering, George Eliot goes on to say, in a characteristic assertion of her belief in the humanizing power of suffering. And now she makes explicit another aspect of the parallel between the journey which Adam is now making and the idea of the journey-as-experience: "His feeling towards Dinah, his hope of passing his life with her, had been the distant unseen point towards which that hard journey from Snowfield eighteen months ago had been leading him."

This is an extraordinary statement: from the moment when Adam learned that Hetty was not at Snowfield with Dinah and rode home in alarm at the thought that she had gone to join Arthur, he had been thinking of Dinah—though only unconsciously—as his future wife. This is part of the answer to those critics who have objected to the way in which George

Eliot makes Adam apparently transfer his affections from Hetty to Dinah in a way that is convenient both to himself and to her own interests as a novelist: Adam and Dinah's love for each other is one of those many alternative futures which are opened up in the course of the novel and which might have remained only an unexplored possibility. The sense of poignancy and irony suggested by the tenuousness of the chain of events that has brought Adam and Dinah together is important, although this is not to say, of course, that George Eliot's actual handling of the ending is wholly successful.

Finally, Adam's understanding of his own story comes to him through his correct interpretation of the landscape, as George Eliot is at pains to point out twice in the passage quoted: "beyond Oakbourne [. . .] the broken country [. . .] seemed to be telling him afresh the story of that painful past." It is important to notice that what instructs him is the contrast between the lush countryside of Loamshire and the landscape of Stonyshire: "Adam this morning brought with him new thoughts through that grey country—thoughts which gave an altered significance to its story of the past." This awareness that outside the limited world in which most of the novel is set there is another and harsher environment is of central importance and is the final lesson about how to read the novel that the passage holds.

For most of the novel's length we are allowed to forget the selective nature of the frame that has been imposed on the historical reality depicted. However, we will perceive it by means of the more penetrating "second look" to which the novel eventually prompts us. For example, in the introductory description of the village in Chapter 2, the beauty of Loamshire is contrasted with the harshness of neighbouring Stonyshire in the experience, significantly, of a hypothetical traveller:

> That rich undulating district of Loamshire to which Hayslope belonged, lies close to a grim outskirt of Stonyshire, overlooked by its barren hills as a pretty blooming sister may sometimes be seen linked in the arm of a rugged, tall, swarthy brother; and in two or three hours' ride the traveller might exchange a bleak tree-less region, intersected by lines of cold grey stone, for one where his road wound under the shelter of woods, or up swelling

hills, muffled with hedgerows and long meadow-grass and thick corn.

We are reminded occasionally in the course of the novel that Hayslope and Loamshire represent only one aspect of England in the 1790s because, suggestively, it is from Stonyshire that Dinah comes. When she discusses it with Irwine he says: "It's a dreary bleak place. They were building a cotton-mill there; but that's many years ago now" (ch. 8). She acknowledges the prosperity that the mill has brought but admits: "it's still a bleak place, as you say, sir—very different from this country." It would be an oversimplification and a distortion to suggest that Stonyshire represents merely the coming of industrialization which has intervened between the world of Hayslope and the present in which George Eliot is writing, for its significance is part of a larger and subtler contrast than this. The more important contrast is suggested—rather than defined—by the contrast between the bleakness of the landscape of Stonyshire and the lushness of Loamshire.

The landscape figures largely in the novel. All the important characters are brought into a relation with the countryside—frequently in the course of a journey—and their perception of it constitutes a kind of moral test. The landscape appears at first to embody all those positive values which we have seen are associated with the past: rootedness, peace, charm, and social harmony. But, like the view of the past of which it is a part, it is increasingly seen ambiguously, and what is important is whether each character perceives this ambiguity or not. As Arthur, for example, rides home after hearing of the death of his grandfather he thinks about taking possession of the estate and reflects at the same time on his affection for his native countryside in a way that reveals his general and characteristic failure of perception (ch. 44). His sense of the countryside's charm is linked to his sense of his own future, and he misreads both in the same way. At this moment he feels an acute sense of continuity, and has a vision of his place historically: "Poor grandfather! and he lies dead there. *He* was a young fellow once, coming into the estate, and making his plans. So the world goes round." Arthur does not realize yet how far his actions have disrupted that continuity and therefore how very different things are from their appearance. So when he arrives home he

70

thinks: "Here was dear old Hayslope at last, sleeping on the hill, like a quiet old place as it was, in the late afternoon sunlight." His sense of the place's safeness and charm—secure in his nostalgic memory—is broken in upon by the revelation of Hetty's arrest for the murder of his child. In contrast Adam, in the passage discussed above, now understands the lesson that the countryside has to offer him—that outside Hayslope there are suffering and harshness—and this is a measure of the spiritual progress he has made on his journey through life.

It is in relation to Hetty that the idea of understanding the true nature of the countryside is most relevant. George Eliot describes her in Chapter 35 walking through the countryside, unaware of its beauty as she broods on some secret unhappiness. Then, in a passage which uses the idea of the traveller through beautiful countryside failing to perceive at first the hidden suffering concealed within it, the author comments:

> What a glad world this looks like, as one drives or rides along the valleys and over the hills! I have often thought so when, in foreign countries, where the fields and woods have looked to me like our English Loamshire—the rich land tilled with just as much care, the woods rolling down the gentle slopes to the green meadows—I have come on something by the roadside which has reminded me that I am not in Loamshire: an image of a great agony—the agony of the cross.

"I am not in Loamshire," George Eliot writes, meaning first, of course, that since Loamshire is in a Protestant country one would not expect to find a symbol of Catholicism, but also meaning that such a reminder of suffering would be anomalous in so charming a place. And yet the rest of this paragraph and, indeed, the remainder of the novel itself, goes on to show us that exactly the "anguish" of which the crucifix is a reminder does indeed exist even here, although it is concealed from a first glance:

> It has stood perhaps by the clustering apple-blossoms, or in the broad sunshine by the cornfield, or at a turning by the wood where a clear brook was gurgling below; and surely, if there came a traveller to this world who knew nothing of the story of man's life upon it, this image of agony would seem to him strangely out of place in the midst of this joyous nature.

The "story" that the traveller "reads" in the figure of the crucified Christ amid the beauty of the countryside is the central image of Dinah's sermon: the agony in the garden. The point of her sermon was that Christ "is upon this earth too; he is among us" although we may fail at first to see him. Both aspects of what the crucifix represents—the suffering that Hetty undergoes and the hope that Dinah brings her—are concealed, the one through guilt and the other because undervalued. The need for a more penetrating effort of perception is referred to in what George Eliot goes on to say of the traveller:

> He would not know that hidden behind the apple-blossoms, or among the golden corn, or under the shrouding boughs of the wood, there might be a human heart beating heavily with anguish; perhaps a young blooming girl, not knowing where to turn for refuge from swift-advancing shame; understanding no more of this life of ours than a foolish lost lamb wandering farther and farther in the nightfall on the lonely heath; yet tasting the bitterest of life's bitterness.

At this precise point, with the revelation of Hetty's pregnancy, the book begins dramatically to force the reader to revise many of the expectations he has formed, as the hypothetical traveller here is forced to revise his conception of the beauty of nature. The point is, George Eliot is saying, that if we look more closely we will see these things, and a reproach is implied to the reader who can be surprised by this revelation:

> Such things are sometimes hidden among the sunny fields and behind the blossoming orchards; and the sound of the gurgling brook, if you came close to one spot behind a small bush, would be mingled for your ear with a despairing human sob. No wonder man's religion has much sorrow in it: no wonder he needs a suffering God.

The idea raised by the image of the crucifix—that of hidden anguish amid the beauty of nature—is directly related to Hetty, who is herself trapped by an inexorable law of nature of which she is a part and in whose fertility she unwillingly participates.

Adam has been as guilty as the hypothetical traveller or the unwary reader of failing to perceive this concealed and harsh dimension of reality, and so in "misreading" Hetty by refusing to take her seriously as an adult moral agent. So when he hears

72

the news that she has been arrested for infanticide he exclaims to Irwine: "It *cannot* be! [. . .] It is not possible. She never had a child" (ch. 39). He cannot yet accept that evil—the ability to commit murder—may exist in someone so beautiful and apparently innocent. And when he has to recognise the truth, he revealingly laments: "she can never be my sweet Hetty again [. . .] I thought she loved me . . . and was good" (ch. 41).

Adam's sense of shock is paralleled on the literary level by the early reviewer already quoted. His expectations have been outraged, he protests, for: "We do not expect that we are to pass from the discreet love of a well-to-do carpenter to child-murder and executions, and the shock which the author inflicts upon us seems as superfluous as it is arbitrary."[3] The point is that the sudden shift from pastoral idyll to rural tragedy in the latter part of the novel is intended to be exactly that: a shock. Yet it calls for a revision of the reader's expectations which is not arbitrary but has been signalled from the beginning of the novel.

This is the central strategy of the book: the mistakenness of the assumptions which the reader has been allowed to make is exposed by means of a more penetrating "second look" and the essential complexity of the situation is made clear by a reminder of what has always been present in the novel but which the reader has been allowed to ignore. We have already seen, for example, that when Hayslope is first described, mention is made of the harsher environment of the neighbouring county of Stonyshire, and this is recalled in the suggestive name of the town where Hetty is tried—Stoniton. Similarly, the farm of the Poysers which has been presented as a centre of warmth and security is revealed—for example, in the scene in Chapter 20 in which Mrs Poyser harasses a servant girl — to be an authoritarian hierarchy ruled over by a comical but grossly unjust mistress. More important, however, the farm is shown, in the account of the second visit by a Donnithorne, not to be as secure as it at first appears. The old Squire's visit echoes that of his grandson, and he even repeats Arthur's praise in very similar terms: "I like these premises, do you know, beyond any on the estate" (ch. 32). But this time there is a note of menace in the Squire's compliments to Mrs Poyser since he has come to put to the family a rearrangement of the land which is to their disadvantage but which he can force upon them with the threat of ending their tenancy. Here again, the implications of the hierarchical nature of this society and the realities of absolute power are made clear.

It is in relation to Hetty above all that the "second look" is important. When Dinah arrives at the prison where she is being held she encounters the anonymous horseman of Chapter 2 who is now named as Captain Townley and revealed to be a magistrate of the town where the prison is. The discovery now that the man was impressed by Dinah's preaching—he says to her: "I know you have a key to unlock hearts"—and will therefore let her into the prison, is evidence that the values propounded in her sermon in that opening scene may be efficacious even here, and this they are revealed to be in Dinah's "conversion" of Hetty which follows. The encounter is one of those moments in the novel when an apparent clumsiness—the arbitrary coincidence that brings these two together again at this point—in fact justifies itself because of the resonances it creates. When Dinah addresses the man he stares at her for some moments:

> "I have seen you before," he said at last. "Do you remember preaching on the village green at Hayslope in Loamshire?"
> "Yes, sir, surely. Are you the gentleman that stayed to listen on horseback?"
> "Yes. Why do you want to go into the prison?" (ch. 45)

The bringing together in the memories of the speakers of these two areas of experience—the Green and the prison, the garden and the agony—is an adroit reminder of the distance we have travelled.

It is Hetty who experiences the cost of that distance, for once she leaves the safety of Hayslope—the selective segment of historical reality which has been "framed" by the novel—she is in the real world. Here George Eliot shows Hetty encountering— not cruelty, for that would be melodramatic—but something that is both more chilling and historically more convincing: indifference. There is, for example, the encounter with an old man who finds her after she has spent the night in a hovel of furze. Their exchange makes clear the extent to which she is now outside the safe world she has always taken for granted, for, accused by him of resembling "a wild woman", she tries to give him money in order to assert her social superiority and meets with this response: "He looked slowly at the sixpence, and then said: 'I want none o' your money. You'd better take care on't, else you'll get it stool from yer, if you go trapesin' about the fields like a mad woman a-that-way" (ch. 32). Hetty is now in a situation in which her social position cannot be taken for granted as "given" to her by the people among whom she lives, as a consequence of the sense of community and stability which the earlier part of the novel has celebrated. Instead it has to be earned on the basis of her appearance and behaviour, and by these criteria she has deserved the man's curtness and the "hard wondering look" he gives her. There are exceptions to this rule, among whom the most important is the woman who shelters her while she gives birth.

The fact that, having found kindness and assistance, Hetty chooses to leave this woman's house and then to kill the child so that the forces which drive her to murder are not part of the social, political, and economic circumstances of the period but are the product of her own sense of guilt and shame is, it might be argued, an evasion on the author's part of the historical realities of the period. However, my argument has been that George Eliot is not interested in *Adam Bede* in this kind of historical verisimilitude. It is enough that she has reminded the reader of the existence of another area of experience outside that which is "framed" by most of the novel and where there exist both widespread suffering in society and the capacity for evil in the individual. She does not need to analyze the relation between them—it is sufficient for her purposes to have shown that they exist alongside the "myth" of the rural past which also has its own kind of truth.

In doing this she has shown how, in the writing of a historical novel, the temptation to nostalgia and oversimplification can be overcome in the interests of historical truth and yet at the same time the past be legitimately exploited as a reassuring fiction of the kind that we inevitably create in the process of interpreting our own lives. In first presenting a selective and "safe" version of reality which the reader is then forced to recognise as only a partial view of historical truth, she is putting forward an analogy for the concept of realism which the novel both defines and demonstrates: the attempt to reconcile the conflicting claims of history/reality and art by an ironic alternation between reassuring and disconcerting the reader. *Adam Bede* is the starting-point for George Eliot's exploration in all her later fiction of the relationship between the historical and the artistic imagination.

NOTES

1 See Chapter 16 of *The Country and the City* (London, 1973), pp. 165-81.
2 Unsigned review, *Saturday Review*, 26 February 1859, pp.250-51; rpt. in David Carroll, ed., *George Eliot: The Critical Heritage* (London, 1971), pp.73-6.
3 Carroll, ed., pp.75-6.

5

Romola and the Myth of Apocalypse

by JANET K. GEZARI

1

Most recent critics of *Romola* have agreed that the novel is a failure. It is an agreement which contradicts George Eliot's own assertions. "There is no book of mine about which I more thoroughly feel that I could swear by every sentence as having been written with my best blood, such as it is, and with the most ardent care for veracity of which my nature is capable," she wrote her publisher more than fifteen years after the appearance of the novel.[1] Perhaps even her assurances provide a clue to the uneasiness most readers feel in confronting *Romola*. The mournful remark to John Cross that she began the novel as a young woman and finished it an old one, is often adduced as evidence of something intrinsically wrong with the novel; if we remember that it robbed its author of her youth, we may want to take the reference to her "best blood" in all its literal unsavouriness: writing *Romola* must have been a painful experience for Eliot, one which drained her of life. But the inescapable fact about *Romola* is not really its failure; it is its seriousness. Even Henry James, a reader fundamentally unsympathetic to Eliot's art, believed that *Romola* was "decidedly the most important" of Eliot's works, "not the most entertaining nor the most readable, but the one in which the largest things are attempted and grasped."[2]

Romola commands attention by its very peculiarity in relation to the rest of Eliot's fiction. Although all of her novels are set in the recent past, *Romola* is George Eliot's only historical novel and her only novel to have characters who are not English but

Italian. *Romola* is perhaps still more interesting for what it tells us about three important aspects of the development of Eliot's mind and her art. First, it is evidence of her relaxation of the realist posture so stiffly struck in *Adam Bede* and so deliberately maintained in *The Mill on the Floss:* the novelist's task in these books is seen in terms of her ability to portray our fellow-parishioners who are, like ourselves, "more or less ugly, stupid", and "inconsistent".[3] There are very few characters who play a significant role in *Romola* who are, in this sense, ordinary, and the decision to recreate the life of Savonarola which is the seed of *Romola* marks a new interest in the extraordinary personality, the hero and leader. Then, *Romola* is the novel in which Eliot can be seen working out the complex relationship between Christian faith and the political and social life of the community; the importance Eliot attached to religious feeling in the moral life of the community is evident in all of her novels and, of course, in her commitment to Feuerbach. Finally, *Romola* is an early attempt to express the "stealthy convergence of human lots" by means of separate plot lines;[4] although Savonarola's role in the novel has often been minimized, his story is as important as Romola's and bears the same kind of relationship to it that Lydgate's does to Dorothea's.

George Eliot is not, as of course she might be, entirely wrong about the quality of *Romola*. The novel has been undervalued because Eliot happened to write *Middlemarch*, one of the greatest novels of the nineteenth century, and because many modern readers cannot accept the sub-genre to which *Romola* belongs, the historical novel, as an important form.[5] It has been disparaged at least partly because it demands of its readers a comfortable familiarity with Renaissance Florence. Thus, one early reviewer criticized the novel because its "allusions [were] half-riddles", while another asserted that "a twentieth part of the erudition . . . would have given us the feeling and colour of time."[6] Implicit in both these assertions are assumptions we may question: that novels should not demand specialized knowledge of their readers, or that the historicity of a novel is a matter of generalized mood and ambience. The second, more famous reviewer, Henry James, went on in his essay on *Romola* to make what I take to be another commonly held (at least since

James) but questionable critical assumption: that there is an absolute divorce between the intellect of the thinker and the imagination of the artist. Since *Romola* is the novel which engaged the mind of George Eliot more than any of the others, it must have engaged the imagination least.But surely the close companionship of intellect and imagination is one of the defining attributes of Eliot's art.

Any revaluation of *Romola* has to begin with a consideration of the role of Savonarola, since both Romola's story and Tito's are related to his and since the turbulent life of the prophet and preacher is the most powerful expression in the novel of the life of Florence itself. More than one recent critic has argued that the "historical apparatus" of *Romola* "may probably be ignored for all but its Victorian connotations"[7] and that Eliot must have been attracted by the idea of a novel set in late fifteenth-century Florence because of "apparent similarities between the Florence of Savonarola and the England of Cardinal Newman".[8] Although Eliot probably did see a relationship between her own time and Savonarola's, any effort to transform Renaissance humanists into Victorian rationalists and Renaissance religious reformers into Victorian religious revivalists forces the main themes of *Romola* out of focus.

As a prophet with a compelling vision of the perfected human community, Savonarola is more closely related to other Eliot characters than to Eliot's contemporaries and is a fitting hero for a novel about imaginative vision. In the novel, his millenarian vision has its opposite in Romola's brother Dino's vision of Romola's deathly marriage to "the Great Tempter", for according to Dino's vision, the consequence of this marriage is a stony world where there is "no water" and "no trees or herbage". Romola's actual marriage to Tito, who is carefully associated with the forces of evil in the historical world of the novel and in the world of the human imagination, is an important expression of the frustration of moral yearnings and spiritual needs, a familiar subject for readers of Eliot's novels. But *Romola* treats this subject more fully and more uncompromisingly than any other Eliot novel. The historical setting of *Romola* has less to do with any romantic attraction to the "colour of the time" than with Eliot's determination to face, for once, the yawning gap between the world of historical or political experience and the world of fulfilled human desire.

2

A look at the historical events which are part of the plot of *Romola* should help to put Eliot's image of Savonarola and the main themes of the novel back into focus. *Romola* begins on 9 April 1492, the day after Lorenzo the Magnificent's death. Much later in the novel, Eliot reminds us that "Italy was enjoying a peace and prosperity unthreatened by any near and definite danger" when Lorenzo died.

> Altogether this world, with its partitioned empire and its roomy universal Church, seemed to be a handsome establishment for the few who were lucky or wise enough to reap the advantages of human folly,—a world in which lust and obscenity, lying and treachery, oppression and murder, were pleasant, useful, and when properly managed, not dangerous. And as a sort of fringe or adornment to the substantial delights of tyranny, avarice, and lasciviousness, there was the patronage of polite learning and the fine arts, so that flattery could always be had in the choicest Latin to be commanded at that time, and sublime artists were on hand to paint the holy and the unclean with impartial skill. The Church, it was said, had never been so disgraced in its head, had never shown so few signs of renovating, vital belief in its lower members; nevertheless it was much more prosperous than in some past days. The heavens were fair and smiling above; and below there were no signs of earthquake.[9]

It is no wonder, then, that the main subjects of conversation in Florence on the day after Lorenzo's death are the strange portents which seem to threaten evils to come. Several chapters later, Monna Brigida, Romola's foolish but well meaning aunt, gives some shape to these evils when she reports having heard Fra Domenico, one of Savonarola's closest associates and most dedicated disciples, preach the three doctrines of his master: the scourge of Florence and the Church; the regeneration of Florence and the Church; and both soon. A little more than two months later, in September 1492, Romola is called to the bedside of her dying brother Dino, who had, like Savonarola himself, become a Dominican friar against the wishes of his family. Romola's parting visit with Dino is the occasion for her meeting with Savonarola, who is the prior of the Dominican convent of San Marco.

Between the end of the first volume of the novel and the beginning of the second, eighteen months pass unrecorded. During this time, Lorenzo's son, Piero de Medici, has been ruling Florence with considerably less tact and success than his father, and Romola has married Tito. The second volume of the novel begins about a week after the revolution which resulted in the expulsion of Piero de Medici from Florence. The date is 17 November, memorable because the city is preparing for the entry of Charles VIII and his troops. The French had been invited by Ludovico Sforza, acting duke of Milan, to invade Italy and assert the claims of the House of Anjou to the Neapolitan throne. For complicated reasons, Charles had the support of the people of Florence and of Savonarola, who was by now preaching regularly to large crowds in the Duomo. On the day that the French arrive in the city, Romola is among those listening to Savonarola, as is Baldassarre, the adoptive father Tito has betrayed, brought as a prisoner by the French and freed in the streets by excited Florentine youth. On 24 November, Charles consents to sign a treaty with the city, and the French leave Florence on 28 November.

During the winter of 1494, Florence is debating the kind of government the city ought to have, and Savonarola, as Eliot reminds us, is taking an important role in these debates by expressing his own ideas on good government in his sermons. On 23 December, Florence decides to create a Great Council on the Venetian model. This Great Council placed the government of the city on a broader political base than ever before, although membership in it was still restricted, and only those citizens whose ancestors had served in one of the three major magistracies of the republic were eligible for it. Savonarola had vigorously supported the establishment of the Council in his sermons, and, according to at least one of his biographers, these sermons mark the real beginning of his career as a politician.[10] On the same day that the Great Council is approved, the last of Romola's father's library, sold by Tito without her knowledge, leaves Florence.

There are three important political factions in Florence during the period of the popular republic: the supporters of the

Medici, sometimes called Bigi; the supporters of Savonarola and the popular government, variously identified as Popolari, Frateschi, or Piagnone; and the supporters of an aristrocratic government in opposition to the Medici, called Arrabbiati. On the evening before the approval of the Great Council, Tito attends a supper at the Rucellai gardens, a place where prominent Florentine men often met to discuss political and literary subjects. There he accepts the Medici commission to ingratiate himself with both Piagnone and Arrabbiati, and discredits Baldassarre, who has slipped into the house to accuse Tito publicly of abandoning him to slavery. On 24 December, Romola sets out from Florence disguised as a nun and intending to leave Tito and disown her marriage. She meets Savonarola on the road, is recognized by him, and, by means of exhortations to duty and fellow feeling, is dissuaded from her course of action and turned back to the city.

The third volume of the novel begins on 30 October 1496, after an intermission of about twenty-one months. The situation of the Florentine republic by now seems desperate. The city, which has been debilitated by famine and the plague, is being attacked by Pisa, which has the support of Venice and Milan. A Holy League, with Pope Alexander VI at its head, has been formed in opposition to Florence's French allies. There is even talk of a new attack on the city to be led by the German Emperor Maximillian. A few days before, French ships bringing food to Florence were driven from the coast by strong winds. For more than a month, Savonarola has refrained from preaching in order not to increase the anger of the Pope against him, but on 28 October, he preached in the Duomo at the request of the Signoria, the supreme magistracy of the Florentine republic. In the hope of further encouraging the people and of placating the divine powers who seem to have forsaken Florence, the city government organized a procession of the Madonna dell'Imprunetta for 30 October. The procession is in progress when news of the arrival of the French ships, carrying corn and men, comes.

From then on, important events occur rapidly. Tito is instrumental in an abortive plot to send Savonarola out of Florence so that he can be captured by his enemies and, in the beginning of 1497, Francesco Valori, the head of Savonarola's party, is elected to the highest public office, that of Gonfaloniere. The ascendency of Savonarola's forces is marked by the Carnival celebrations, in particular the Pyramid of Vanities, a ritual bonfire which reduces rouge, ornaments, false hair, and the works of "indecent" poets like Petrarch to the same ashy residue. On 28 April, Piero de Medici tries to enter Florence with a band of 1,300 men, but this new attempt to overthrow the popular government fails. By the end of May, the Pope's brief excommunicating Savonarola on suspicion of heresy arrives in Florence. In June, the excommunication is publicly proclaimed, but Savonarola responds by declaring it invalid and retains the support of the people of Florence.

The "arrest of Lamberto dell'Antella with a tell-tale letter on his person, and a bitter rancour against the Medici in his heart" (III, 57) results in revelations about Medici conspirators within the city and in information about a new plot to reinstate Piero. These revelations provide a reason for arresting five important Florentines including Romola's godfather, Bernardo del Nero, a long-time loyal Medicean and the elected Gonfaloniere at the time of Piero's attempt to enter the city. Bernado is accused of having known about Piero's plans and of having remained silent. In *Romola*, Lamberto dell'Antella is not the only informer. Tito, who is himself implicated in Piero's plot because of his dealings with the Medici, secures his safety from prosecution by revealing to Francesco Valori a new plot to bring Piero into Florence in the middle of August and by promising to obtain documentary evidence of it to be used in the trial of the five accused men. Late in August, Romola, who is ignorant of her husband's part in supplying evidence against the accused men, visits Savonarola in his cell to beg him to intercede in favour of her godfather who, along with the others, may be condemned to death. At issue is the right to appeal a decision of the Signoria to the Great Council, a right Savonarola had supported when it was originally legislated. According to Pasquale Villari, author of *Life and Times of Girolamo Savonarola* and one of Savonarola's most ardent defenders, Savonarola remained, during the turmoil over the trial of the five,

> secluded in his convent, without taking any share in the excitement, and wholly absorbed in revising the proofs of his

"Triumph of the Cross". Neither in the histories, memoirs, correspondence, or biographies of the period do we find one single word to indicate whether Savonarola was favourable or unfavourable to any of the accused.[11]

In Eliot's version of the story, Savonarola clearly has the opportunity to influence Bernardo del Nero's fate but refuses, for reasons that I will consider in more detail later, to support any plea for clemency. The five men, including Bernardo del Nero, are sentenced to death and denied an appeal to the Great Council. Romola watches her father bravely face his execution and leaves Florence.

After a lapse of about six months, the novel returns to Florence for the last morning of Carnival and another bonfire of Vanities. In the middle of March 1498, the Signoria had finally acceded to the commands and blandishments of the Pope and forbidden Savonarola to preach. Along with the excommunication of Savonarola the previous May had come the threat of a general interdict against Florence if the government did not take steps to silence him. In fact, Savonarola had remained silent for several months after the excommunication but had preached in his own church of San Marco on Christmas day of 1497 and, on command of the city government, in the Duomo in February of 1498. Those who supported the continuation of Savonarola's sermons feared civil war if he were stopped. Those who opposed him argued that the Pope had the power to return Pisa to Florence, that the continued preaching of an excommunicated friar signalled ecclesiastical chaos, and that the Pope was liable any day to interdict the entire city and seize Florentine merchants and their goods outside the city.[12]

At the end of March 1498, a Franciscan friar, Fra Francesco di Puglia, challenges Savonarola to test the truth of his prophecies by walking through fire; if Savonarola survives the fire, in which Fra Francesco himself expected to be consumed, the miracle would attest to his innocence of any heresy. At about the same time, Savonarola's conflict with the Pope is moving toward crisis and providing Eliot with an opportunity to involve Tito very personally in Savonarola's fall. By the end of March or the beginning of April, Savonarola had prepared letters to the rulers of France, Spain, England, Hungary, and

Germany. In them, he called for a General Council which would reform the abuses of the Church, beginning by deposing Pope Alexander, "who was not rightfully Pope, being a vicious unbeliever, elected by corruption and governing by simony" (III, 64). "Now, I hereby testify," Savonarola wrote,

> *in verbo Domini*, that this Alexander be no Pope, nor can be held as one; inasmuch as, leaving aside the mortal sin of simony, by which he hath purchased the Papal Chair, and daily selleth the benefices of the Church to the highest bidder, and likewise putting aside his other manifest vices, I declare that he is no Christian, and believes in no God, the which surpasses the height of all infidelity.[13]

In *Romola* it is Tito who visits Savonarola in the guise of a devoted follower and takes from him his letter to King Charles. He also conveys information "in cipher, which was carried by a series of relays to armed agents of Ludovico Sforza, Duke of Milan" (III, 64), and which results in the interception of Savonarola's letter. Sforza forwards the letter to the Pope, providing him with final proof of the seriousness of Savonarola's opposition to him.

In Florence, Savonarola repeatedly refuses to submit to the trial by fire, but his disciple, Fra Domenico is eager to be his proxy. Finally, Savonarola, by now badly in need of a miracle to reactivate the faith of Florence in him, agrees to allow Fra Domenico to enter the fire with the Franciscan. The day set for trial is 7 April, and a large crowd assembles for the spectacle. After considerable hesitation on the part of the Franciscans, including strong objections to Fra Domenico's costume and to his intention to enter the fire bearing the crucifix or the Host, a rainstorm wets the fuel and makes the trial impossible. The crowd, "hungry in mind and body" (III, 65), is disappointed of its miracle and suspicions of Savonarola, who after all could have entered the fire himself at any time, are aggravated. On the following day, Palm Sunday, an angry mob lays seige to San Marco and murders the leader of Savonarola's party, Francesco Valori. From this point on, Savonarola's fate seems determined. Together with Fra Domenico and another friar closely associated with him, Fra Salvestro Maruffi, the friar whom Savonarola had appointed as Romola's confessor,

Savonarola is put to the torture and certain confessions are extracted. Romola returns to Florence on 14 April, after an absence of almost eight months, in time to witness the hanging and burning of Savonarola and his companion friars on 23 May 1498. The novel is over, except for an epilogue in which we see Romola, eleven years later, commemorating the suffering and death of Savonarola.

3

If this is the historical ground of *Romola*, the pattern Eliot traces on it is bold and, insofar as it involves Savonarola, more original than has yet been recognized. According to Villari, who comments on the books on Savonarola which appeared in the time between the publication of the first and second editions of his biography, *Romola* is an "admirable work of art" which "added no new facts to history, because, as was only natural, [Eliot] accepted unquestioningly the conclusions already arrived at."[14] Villari surely has in mind Eliot's dependence on his own work, the first edition of which we know she read, but her vision of Savonarola is, in fact, different from Villari's in ways he may have found it difficult to perceive. Villari is mainly interested in Savonarola as a political hero, the champion of the liberty of republican Florence against Medici tyranny. He is a little embarrassed by Savonarola's faith in his prophetic powers, but he argues for a recognition of his hero's consistent personal integrity and of the originality of his thinking. For Villari, Savonarola is "essentially Catholic",[15] but Eliot would also have been aware of the representation of Savonarola by his nineteenth-century German biographers as a precursor of the Reformation. This view had behind it the authority of Luther, who had canonized Savonarola as a Protestant martyr.

Eliot's interest in Savonarola is at once more universal and more particular than that of previous biographers. The comparison of Savonarola with Thomas à Kempis, Maggie Tulliver's saintly mentor in *The Mill on the Floss*, is instructive. Like Thomas à Kempis, Savonarola was a man who "ages ago, felt and suffered and renounced";[16] unlike Thomas à Kempis, Savonarola was a man who has to be described repeatedly as "power-loving". In her portrait of Savonarola, Eliot confronts the essential paradox of the philosophy of renunciation so unperplexedly articulated in *The Mill on the Floss:* the impossibility of not enlarging, nourishing, and rewarding the self even in the performance of the most arduous acts of self-sacrifice. But if Eliot's Savonarola is a man who is deeply flawed, he is heroic because his love of right is equal to his love of power and because his vision is equal to his ambition. In *Romola,* Savonarola emerges neither as the architect of Florentine liberty nor as the Protestant reformer whose cause is the transformation of the Church but as a prophet with a compelling imaginative vision of the perfected human community. It is Savonarola's promise of punishment for Florence that causes Baldassarre, fresh from his spurning of Tito, to sob with agitated sympathy as he stands among the crowd in the Duomo, but it is the promise of the imminent regeneration of Florence, Italy, and, ultimately, the world, that accounts for Eliot's sense of Savonarola's larger significance in human history.

The formal introduction of Savonarola into the novel does not occur until the first chapter of its second volume, when Florence is awaiting the entry of Charles VIII and his soldiers. Eliot is cynical about Florentine expectations of Charles VIII, who is imagined both as Charlemagne and as Cyrus, "liberator of the chosen people, restorer of the Temple", but not about the "moral emotions" which the convictions about Charles's part in the larger divine plan satisfy. These emotions are most satisfyingly expressed in Savonarola's sermons. Eliot reminds us that Savonarola (who had preached on Genesis every Advent and Lent with one exception since 1490)[17] saw as a proof of divine guidance his not having arrived at the chapter on the flood, the text "Behold I, even I, do bring a flood of waters upon the earth", until the entry of the French army into Italy. The flood was both punishment and promise, an "emblem at once of avenging wrath and purifying mercy" (I, 20).

In his book about Savonarola, Donald Weinstein has argued persuasively that Savonarola began as a preacher of repentance and divine wrath and only gradually became the prophet of Florentine millenial glory and republican liberty. Moreover, he attributes Savonarola's tremendous popular appeal to his appropriation of the apocalyptic, imperial, and republican themes already present in the ideology of Florence, themes which he gave the "stamp of his own powerful, prophetic personality".[18] Savonarola is the charismatic leader required to complete the characteristic pattern of millenarian episodes, and Florence's apocalyptic vision is not merely a response to the crisis at the end of the century but "one of the ways in which Florentines habitually regarded their city."[19] The apocalyptic vision required a French emperor who would purify Italy and the Church, convert the infidels, and bring the New Zion into being. For Weinstein, Savonarola's "prophecies mirrored Florence's yearning for security, riches, and power."[20] Eliot's perception of how easily moral yearnings, in her terms religious needs, were blended with more worldly appetites is nicely represented in a scene, late in the novel, when Tito passes a crowd assembled before a placard which bears an account of Savonarola's doctrines in Latin. "Florence also, after the scourging, shall be purified and shall prosper," Tito translates for them.

> "That means we are to get Pisa again," said the shopkeeper.
> "And get the wool from England as we used to do, I should hope," said an elderly man, in an old-fashioned berretta, who had been silent till now. "There's been scourging enough with the sinking of the trade." (III, 63)

The complexity of Eliot's feelings about Savonarola is suggested in her description of how he developed his millenarian vision. The first impulse comes from the Bible itself and is confirmed by visions, "a mode of seeing," Eliot tells us, "frequent with him from his youth up."

> But the real force of demonstration for Girolamo Savonarola lay in his own burning indignation at the sight of wrong; in his fervent belief in an Unseen Justice that would put an end to wrong, and in an Unseen Purity, to which the lying and uncleanness were an abomination. To his ardent, power-loving soul, believing in great ends, and longing to achieve those ends by the exertion of its own strong will, the faith in a supreme and righteous Ruler became one with the faith in a speedy divine interposition that would punish and reclaim. ((II,21)

Later, Eliot will recreate the mood of one of Savonarola's sermons, emphasizing the force of emotions aroused and exposed as well as the pure drama of Savonarola's delivery:

> Every changing tone, vibrating through the audience, shook them into answering emotion. There were plenty among them who had very moderate faith in the Frate's prophetic mission, and who in their cooler moments loved him little; nevertheless, they too were carried along by the great wave of feeling which gathered its force from sympathies that lay deeper than all theory. A loud responding sob rose at once from the wide multitude, while Savonarola had fallen on his knees and buried his face in his mantle. He felt in that moment the rapture and glory of martyrdom without its agony. (II, 24)

Eliot's vision of Savonarola is always double, always ironic, but the irony undermines without eliminating other, very different responses to Savonarola. In the first passage, he is described as both "ardent" and power-loving", both idealistic and ambitious for himself. If the faith in God too easily becomes a faith in apocalypse, this faith is still the expression of a "burning indignation at the sight of wrong" and a belief in justice. In the second pasage, the irony is less subtle. The "rapture and glory of martyrdom without its agony" sounds like a self-deceiving bargain with divinity, but the "wave of feeling" gathers its force from "sympathies that lay deeper than all theory". The novel shows us that these sympathies, which respond to sympathies in Savonarola himself, are the channels for all moral deeds.

Eliot's Savonarola is essentially Catholic, but his program for Florence emphasizes the sacraments less than the active practice of Charity, the love of good works which he justifies to Romola as the debt a man owes to his fellow-citizens. The renovation of Florence is seen as an act of God, but one requiring the participation of men. Thus the novel pays some attention to Savonarola's creation of new ceremonies like the burning of the Pyramid of Vantities which can symbolize the commitment of the community to its own purification.

The crisis for Savonarola in *Romola* is not, as any history of his life might lead us to think, the trial by fire or the experience of torture and humiliation which culminates in the public execution. It is instead Savonarola's final confrontation with Romola and, in specific, his rejection of mercy for vengeance, moral principle for political expediency, and love for faith. The scene, which is of course Eliot's invention, occurs about halfway through the third volume of the novel, after the plot to reinstate Piero de Medici has failed and Bernardo del Nero, Romola's godfather, has been implicated and imprisoned for trial. Romola requests the interview with Savonarola because she knows he is powerful enough to change the minds of the men of his own party, who are loudest in calling for the death of Bernardo del Nero and the other four. She offers him two motives for intercession: the love of mercy and the commitment to the right of a prisoner condemned by the Signoria to appeal the decision to the Great Council. As Romola does not fail to remind him, Savonarola had supported the right of appeal at a time when the identities of those who might claim its protection were unknown. "Do you, then, know so well what will further the coming of God's kingdom, father, that you will dare to despise the plea of mercy,—of justice,—of faithfulness to your own teaching?" Romola asks Savonarola in what is surely her angriest moment in the novel. "Take care, father, lest your enemies have some reason when they say that in your visions of what will further God's kingdom you see only what will strengthen your own party." "And that is true!" Savonarola answers her, identifying Romola's voice with "the voice of his enemies". "The cause of my party *is* the cause of God's kingdom" (III, 59).

The text which helps us most in understanding the nature of the issue here is Feuerbach's *The Essence of Christianity*, the book which most influenced Eliot's understanding of religious ideas.[21] In his last chapter, Feuerbach explores the contradiction between faith and love, a contradiction which is of primary importance to his argument as a whole:

> Thus faith is essentially a spirit of partisanship. He who is not for Christ is against him. Faith knows only friends or enemies, it understands no neutrality; it is preoccupied with itself. Faith is essentially intolerant; essentially, because with faith is always associated the illusion that its cause is the cause of God, its honour his honour.[22]

Romola rejects Savonarola because she discovers that his faith is fundamentally inconsistent with the vision of the perfected human community which has made her his disciple. But when Eliot describes "half the tragedy" of Savonarola's life as "the struggle of a mind possessed by a never-silent hunger after purity and simplicity, yet caught in a tangle of egoistic demands, false ideas, and difficult outward conditions, that made simplicity impossible" (III, 59), she argues for a separation of a judgement of the essence of Savonarola's religion, his millenarian vision of a perfected human community founded on love and virtue, from a judgement of the necessarily flawed individualities of personality and circumstance. The epilogue of the novel, which shows us Romola worshipping Savonarola, dressing an altar to him and about to light fresh tapers in commemoration of his death, makes no sense at all unless we read it as an expression of the essential Feuerbachian revelation, that the secret of religion is atheism, the worship of man as God, or the worship of the divine predicates in man.

4

The overriding theme of *Romola* is imaginative vision, and the novel is full of seers and prophets, both true and false. Representative of the false seers are minor characters like Camilla Rucellai, "chief among the feminine seers of Florence" (III, 32) and Fra Salvestro Maruffi, Savonarola's "confidential and supplementary seer of visions" (III, 52). Both are described by Eliot as "shallow", and Romola shrinks instinctively from both, yet neither is properly a hypocrite. Fra Salvestro lacks Savonarola's capacity for a sustained, unifying vision; his mind is "unable to concentrate itself strongly in the channel of one great emotion or belief" (II, 41). The limitations of Camilla's visionary capacities are even plainer; her "faculties seemed all wrought up into fantasies, leaving nothing for emotion and thought" (III, 52). For both these characters, vision seems to be mechanical, a kind of nervous reflex associated with other aberrant behaviour, excessive excitability or insomnia, but independent of the waking self. The consequence is that these visionaries, like the members of the dreamer tribe described by Moneta in Keats's "The Fall of Hyperion", do not "pour[s] out a balm upon the World" but only "vex" it.

There is some difference between these false visionaries and a visionary like Dino, Romola's brother. Dino's dying vision, a vision he has seen three times, each time with increasing clarity, is a warning against Romola's marriage to Tito in the shape of a very naive allegory.

> And you stood at the altar in Santa Croce, and the priest who married you had the face of death; and the graves opened, and the dead in their shrouds rose and followed you like a bridal train. And you passed on through the streets and the gates into the valley, and it seemed to me that he who led you hurried you more than you could bear, and the dead were weary of following you, and turned back to their graves. And at last you came to a stony place, where there was no water, and no trees or herbage . . . And my father was faint for want of water, and fell to the ground; and the man whose face was a blank loosed thy hand and departed; and as he went I could see his face, and it was the face of the Great Tempter. (I, 15)

By a curious coincidence, Dino did meet Tito, without knowing him to be the man Romola was about to marry. Two months before his death, Dino recognized Tito as the man to whom Baldassarre had sent a confirmation of his having been sold into slavery and a plea for liberation. Indeed, Dino's visions of Romola's deathly wedding only begin after this chance meeting with Tito, when Dino delivers Baldassarre's message to him. Eliot makes a point of reminding us that Dino might have prevented Romola's marriage simply by revealing to her Tito's denial of Baldassarre's claim on him: "the revelation that might have come from the simple questions of filial and brotherly affection had been carried into irrevocable silence" (I, 15). Still, Dino's vision has a precision which the visions of Fra Salvestro and Camilla Rucellai lack. Moreover, since it follows Dino's meeting with Tito, the vision seems to be motivated by genuine, human sympathies, though they are sympathies which have been almost entirely transmuted into the fundamental spiritual drama of his own life. Dino's vision, though not as helpful as ordinary concern for his sister would have been, is redeemed from entire falseness by being tied, even with the finest threads, to his thinking and feeling self.

These three nervous visionaries can be contrasted with Piero di Cosimo, a painter who lived and worked in Florence at the end of the fifteenth century and whose apparent importance in *Romola* is hardly justified by any contribution he makes to the novel's plot. Eliot's Piero is phlegmatic and saturnine as well as perceptive and tender-hearted. If his paintings do not at first strike us as visionary expressions which are related to those others I have so far considered, it is mainly because Piero's vision is thoroughly dependent upon his human intelligence and feelings. It is Piero who chooses Tito first as his model of the "perfect traitor", Sinon deceiving Priam with his tale of the Trojan horse (I, iv), then as his model of a man under the influence of fear, telling Tito that he has "a face that expresses fear well, because it's naturally a bright one" (I, 18), and finally as a "a good model for a coward" (II, 28). Piero's responses to Tito are the more remarkable because he is the only character in the novel whose first impressions of the young Greek include intimations of weakness and treachery. Tito is only interesting to Piero as a model; otherwise, he sees him as a man to be as much as possible avoided. When Tito first visits Piero's studio to commission a painting showing himself in the character of Bacchus and Romola in the character of Ariadne, Piero not only acts disgruntled but also refuses to accept the payment Tito offers him. Piero clearly finds Tito as repulsive as the rest of Florence is finding him attractive: "I'd rather not have your money: you may pay for the case," he tells him (I, 18).

Tito's response to Piero's portrait of him as a man under the influence of fear argues for both its power and its insight. He "saw himself with his right hand uplifted, holding a wine-cup, in an attitude of triumphant joy, but with his face turned away from the cup with an expression of such intense fear in the dilated eyes and pallid lips that he felt a cold stream through his veins, as if he were being thrown into sympathy with his imaged self" (I, 18). The painting has an allegorical quality, dependent on the purity of the emotion it expresses and, perhaps, on the raised wine-cup itself, which seems to symbolize pleasures poisoned by guilt. If it makes no prophecy, it at least looks forward to Tito's two public confrontations with Baldassarre, the one on the steps of the Duomo, the other at Bernardo Rucellai's supper. In both cases, Baldassarre's appearance interrupts scenes of complacent triumph for Tito. When Piero happens to witness the confrontation with Baldassarre at the Duomo, he understands intuitively the relationship between the two and is able to complete his painting by making Baldassarre the spectre of Tito's fearful imaginings.

Piero also paints a portrait of Oedipus and Antigone, using Romola and her father Bardo as his models. It is easy to see that Piero's vision of Romola as a strong-willed and faithful Antigone, the sole support of her blinded father and the champion of her family's honour, is truer than Tito's premarital image of her as a sporting Ariadne, companion of Bacchus, though Romola is, like Ariadne, abandoned early on by her lover. But the two paintings of Piero's own devising, the one of Tito and Baldasarre and the one of Romola and Bardo, have a more important purpose in the novel: they provide us with the clearest single expression of the essential opposition between Romola and Tito. It is appropriate that this opposition should be imaged in terms of the first human relationship, that between parent and child. These two portraits of parent and child can be set beside the first work by Piero which is mentioned in the novel, a somewhat puzzling sketch which hangs in the shop of Nello the barber and makes a prophecy of comparable comprehensiveness. It shows three masks, "one a drunken, laughing Satyr, another a sorrowing Magdalen, and the third . . . the rigid cold face of a Stoic"; the masks rest on the lap of a cherubic child (I,3). As Barbara Hardy points out in her careful discussion of Piero di Cosimo in *The Novels of George Eliot*, the three masks are "a faint image of the three faces of Tito, Romola, and Savonarola". She follows Tito's lead in seeing the child as "the hope" or the Golden Age.[23] The child may be the promise of a future beyond the lives of satyr, stoic, or Magdalen, or, more simply, an image of human possibility which embraces sensual extravagance, spiritual sorrow, and self-denying endurance. In any case, the sketch supports Piero's own idea of his pictures as "an appendix . . . to the universe" (I,3) and contributes to our sense of his special, visionary role in the novel. Though Piero di Cosimo and Savonarola don't meet in *Romola* and don't show any sympathy for each other, the novel presents them to us as men whose visions are companionable. They see their world accurately, the one in order to reveal it, the other in order to transform it. The sources of their visions are very different, but seeing is for both dependent upon thinking and feeling.

Even in its debased forms, the visionary capacity seems to be evidence of the sympathy with others that, in the world of

George Eliot's novels, always requires imagination. It would be hard to find a better illustration of the absence of imagination than Maggie Tulliver's mother in *The Mill on the Floss*. Because Mrs Tulliver has no imagination, she is permanently locked within the narrow cage of her own experience; her selfishness when her husband becomes a bankrupt is a consequence of her inability to imagine anyone's situation but her own. The blindness of Romola's father Bardo has its significance mainly in relation to this metaphorical dimension of the novel.[24] His selfishness, like Mrs Tulliver's, is a consequence of a limited imagination; thus he sees Tito only in relation to himself, as he has always seen Romola and, we may imagine, Dino. If Romola imagines what marriage to Tito will be like with an innocence which breeds false dreams, Bardo never imagines the marriage at all. His welcome of Tito as a son who can work with him is the preface to Tito's formal proposal for Romola, and both Romola and Tito speak to Bardo of the marriage as if its purpose were mainly to secure him a son and helper. Eliot's treatment of Bardo should make us question what many readers of *Romola* have taken for granted, the ideality of Romola's relationship with her father and the perfidy of Dino's abandonment of him for the life of a wandering friar. In the chapter called "Blind Scholar and his Daughter", Romola is weary of her perpetual service to her father and feels the injury of his valuing her less than the son he has lost. Later we discover that Tito is relieved to be separated from Baldassarre, who was "exacting, and had got stranger as he got older" (I, 9). Clearly, there is more virtue in Romola's performance of her duty to her father because the father is often unattractive. But Dino's rejection of Bardo is one more expression of the theme that Eliot saw in the lives of both Savonarola and Romola. In a letter to R. H. Hutton, she says that "the great problem of [Romola's] life . . . essentially coincides with a chief problem in Savonarola's."[25] What she means is clearest in the novel when Romola finally determines to dissolve her marriage to Tito:

> The law was sacred. Yes, but rebellion might be sacred too. It flashed upon her mind that the problem before her was essentially the same as that which had lain before Savonarola,— the problem where the sacredness of obedience ended, and where the sacredness of rebellion began. (III, 56)

In the end, both Bardo and Dino turn out to have cut themselves off from the living, the father acknowledging that "the living often seemed to [him] mere spectres" (I, 5) and the son seeking to "live with [his] fellow-beings only as human souls related to the eternal unseen life" (I, 15). The threat of Dino's vision of Romola's deathly wedding is that she too will be cut off from the living. In the context of the novel as a whole, the vision comes to have a meaning beyond its immediate applicability to Romola's aproaching marriage to Tito. It is the antetype of Savonarola's vision, the demonic parody of apocalypse.

Tito is, of course, the most seriously selfish character in the novel; he is also, despite his cleverness, one of the least imaginative characters in the novel. In his first colloquy with himself about the use to which he should put the money gained from the sale of Baldassarre's jewels, Tito does not imagine that Baldassarre is alive or that he will return to exact punishment for Tito's betrayal of him. He comforts himself with the rationalization that if it were certain that his father were alive and in slavery, he would surely go to his rescue. Since it is not certain, he is free to believe him dead. Similarly, Tito does not imagine what marriage to Romola will be like, as he does not imagine what Romola herself is like. He does not make a clear distinction between Romola and Tessa, though he is always aware that the woman he has chosen to marry legally is nobly born, not foolish, and proudly beautiful. He does not imagine that Romola will come to know him, or that knowing him she will cease to be a loving and unquestioningly supportive wife. Finally, Tito does not imagine his death at the hands of either the Florentine mob or Baldassarre. In two of these instances, Tito fails to gauge the force of the emotions he arouses in his father and wife, for despite his easy sensuality, Tito is incapable of powerful feeling. In all of these instances, his imagination seems incapable of conceiving eventualities which are unpleasant for him. The novel expresses Piero di Cosimo's idea of Tito as a coward less by showing him buying the chain mail to guard himself from Baldassarre's dagger than by showing him repeatedly without the courage to imagine his future.

From the beginning, the portrait of Tito has been recognised by readers as one of the successful aspects of *Romola* and as the expression of an important moral theme.

"Our deeds determine us," George Eliot says somewhere in *Adam Bede*, "as much as we determine our deeds." This is the moral lesson of *Romola*. A man has no associate so intimate as his own character, his own career,—his present and his past; and if he builds up his career of timid and base actions, they cling to him like evil companions, to sophisticate, to corrupt, and to damn him.[26]

The moral idea which Tito illustrates is so basic to Eliot's understanding of human psychology that she works several variations on it in her novels. But there are at least two important differences between Eliot's treatment of Tito and her treatment of characters in other novels who are morally related to him.

Because the public world has more importance in *Romola* than it does in the other novels, we see how dependent the morality of politics is on the morality of private life. Tito is instrumental in bringing about the deaths of Bernardo del Nero and Savonarola as a result of having left his father in slavery and having been unfaithful (in the largest sense) to his wife. In the important scene in the Rucellai Gardens, when Tito accepts his commission to spy for the Medici on both the Arrabbiati and the popular party, meanwhile planning to spy on the Medici in order to ingratiate himself with the two other parties, the narrator reminds us that "all the motives which might have made Tito shrink from the triple deceit . . . had been slowly strangled in him by the successive falsities of his life" (II, 39).

Because Eliot feels the pressure to see actions in *Romola* under their most universal aspect, Tito is not only an ordinary, pleasure-seeking creature, whose weakness corrupts him, but the very embodiment of evil. Thus, early in the novel when Tito learns that Dino, who had delivered Baldassarre's message to him, is dying in Fiesole and feels relieved, we may recognize the recapitulation of an earlier scene, when Tito's decision not to try to ransom Baldassarre with the proceeds from the sale of Baldassarre's jewels makes it "impossible that he should not from henceforth desire it to be the truth that his father was dead" (I, 9). The psychological point of both scenes is that "the contaminating effect of deeds often lies less in the commission than in the consequent adjustment of our desires" (I, 9). But the narrator's comment after Tito wishes that Dino were dead reminds us of the symbolic significance of his action: "He had sold himself to evil, but at the present life seemed so nearly the same to him that he was not conscious of the bond" (I, 12).

The narrator's remark about Tito's bargain with the Devil occurs at the beginning of the chapter in which he and Romola exchange pledges of love and reveal to Bardo their desire to marry. It not only places Tito's proposal in its proper context but prepares us to receive Dino's dying message with reduced scepticism. Dino's vision of Tito as "the Great Tempter" is, after all, shared by the narrator, though the forms in which the two visions find expression are different. Tito is also associated with two other more than human figures in the novel, explicitly with Bacchus and implicitly with Cupid. The association with Bacchus depends mainly on the painting of himself and Romola that Tito commissions Piero di Cosimo to make. Its function is to emphasize the theme already expressed in the image of Tito as the Great Tempter. His appeal to Romola is the appeal of a life of sensation, and this life is seen in all of Eliot's novels as an escape from "real" life, which involves our thoughts and feelings. "I wish we lived in Southern Italy," he tells Romola before their marriage,

> where thought is broken, not by weariness, but by delicious languors . . . I should like to see you under that southern sun, lying among the flowers, subdued into mere enjoyment, while I bent over you and touched the lute and sang to you some little unconscious strain that seemed all one with the light and warmth. (I, 17)

Romola's response to Tito's romantic fancy establishes the unbridgeable distance between them: "it seems to me as if there would always be pale sad faces among the flowers, and eyes that look in vain" (I, 17). The association of Tito with Cupid is more casual than the association with Bacchus and belongs not to his relationship with Romola but to his relationship with Tessa. Several times Tito warns Tessa that "nobody must know that you ever see me, else you will lose me forever" (I, 20). He keeps his real identity a secret, and after he has established Tessa in her own house, he only visits her during the night. But Tessa is no Psyche, only a foolish, trusting contadina whose innocence protects her as much as Romola's innocence harms her. The idea of Tito as Cupid works to underline his commitment to pleasure and his evasion of the responsibilities more human characters undertake. As Tito's opposite in the novel, Romola has an especially difficult role to play. More than any of Eliot's heroines, she is the prototype for Dorothea Brooke, proud, wilful, and full of moral needs. Both are associated with Ariadne and Antigone, and both are seen as latter-day Christian saints. Both choose to dedicate their lives to older men whose scholarly pursuits create no illumination, and both marry men whom they have idealized in their innocence and whom they learn to know, painfully, only when it is already too late. But Eliot's idealization of Romola is more extreme than her idealization of Dorothea. If Dorothea is like Saint Theresa, Romola is the "visible Madonna", the saint who, in the chapter with that title, is more of a blessing to her worshippers than the "unseen Madonna" to whom the Church pays homage. She not only feeds the sick and rescues the meek but performs these actions in a clearly symbolic way. When she rescues Tessa from the Florentine zealots who are trying to force her to consign her silver necklace and clasp, presents from Tito, to the Pyramid of Vanities, Tessa hears "a soft, wonderful voice, as if the Holy Madonna were speaking" (II, 50). When she restores Baldassarre's life with bread and wine, it is as if she is actually administering the sacraments to him. When she finally abandons Tito and Florence toward the end of the novel, we find her succouring a whole village nearly depopulated by the plague. The young boy who sees her approaching the well to draw water for the sick knows her immediately: "It is the Holy Mother, come to take care of the people who have the pestilence," he thinks (III, 68).

A number of explanations for Romola's failure to engage the sympathies of readers of the novel have been tried out. Early on, readers felt that she was too perfect to be fully human, or really likeable.[27] Recently, George Levine has argued that Romola belongs to the tradition of romance or moral fable, while Tito belongs to the tradition of the realistic novel, so that *Romola* as a whole embodies an irresolvable tension.[28] But Tito's story is full of fabular elements. He is as complete a study of evil as Romola is a study of good. The problem with Romola is at least as much a product of her isolation in the novel as of her idealization.

What Eliot provides for Tito and denies to Romola is simply personal relations. W. J. Harvey has rightly seen Romola as "the best example [in Eliot's novels] of a character who, while more or less continuously soliciting our attention, is inadequately placed in any real contact with the network of other characters in the novel."[29] She is always seen in isolation from these other characters, from her father, who cannot see her, from Tito, who does not know her, and from Savonarola, with whom her contacts, although decisive, are always impersonal. In the meeting on the road after Romola has left Tito for the first time, Savonarola convinces her to return to her husband by means of arguments which are general, not particular, and which Romola lacks the conviction or experience to oppose. In the much later meeting in Savonarola's cell, when Romola pleads for mercy for Bernardo del Nero, her arguments are abstract rather than concrete, and Savonarola reveals a far more personal response to the situation than Romola. In addition, we never see Romola acting without restraint, naturally, as Dorothea is natural with her sister Celia in the early scenes of *Middlemarch*. Romola is always acting a role, and the reader is never permitted to glimpse the gap between individual and role which is so productive of fine ironies in Eliot's other novels. Romola is full of ideas and needs but does not display a personality and so, for readers of the novel, must have none. She remains a responsive presence in the world of the novel, a vibrating sensibility rather than a fully developed consciousness.

The seriousness of *Romola* is largely a result of Eliot's assumption of the task of working out in it ideas about the religious feelings and moral needs of men and women like Romola and Savonarola in relation to the progress of human history. In contrast to Romola, Savonarola is a fully developed consciousness. He shares Romola's moral elevation and her readiness for personal sacrifice but possesses, in addition, the capacity to focus his generous impulses and moral yearnings to produce a larger vision. This vision is shadowed, but not obscured, by the faith that is, for Eliot as for Feuerbach, ultimately exclusive of love. The vision of a perfected human community never plays a more prominent role in Eliot's novels than it does in *Romola*, but no other novel so thoroughly denies the possibility of realising it. In *Romola*, the historical world, which includes Tito and, with increasing complexity, Savonarola himself, cannot coexist with the world of human imagining. In the end, only Romola remains to be faithful to the vision, but the vision has been reduced to what Eliot understood was its real substance, a moral yearning and a spiritual need.

NOTES

1 *The George Eliot Letters,* ed. Gordon S. Haight, 7 vols. (New Haven, 1955), VI, 335-36.
2 Henry James, "The Novels of George Eliot", *Atlantic Monthly,* 18 (October, 1866), 479-92, rpt. in *A Century of George Eliot Criticism,* ed. Gordon S. Haight (Boston, 1965), p. 52.
3 George Eliot, *Adam Bede,* Bk. II, ch. 1.
4 I have taken the phrase from *Middlemarch,* Bk. I, ch. 11.
5 Joan Bennet expresses this view most clearly in *George Eliot: Her Mind and Her Art* (Cambridge, 1962), pp. 139-51.
6 R. H. Hutton, "Romola", *Spectator* (18 July 1863), 2265-267, rpt. in *George Eliot and Her Readers,* ed. John Holmstrom and Laurence Lerner (Oxford, 1966), pp. 56-64. Henry James, "George Eliot's Life", *Atlantic Monthly,* 55 (May 1885), 668-78.
7 Carole Robinson, "*Romola:* a Reading of the Novel", *Victorian Studies,* 6 (September 1962), p. 32.
8 Bennett, p. 148.
9 *Romola,* Bk. II, ch. 1. References to book and chapter for subsequent quotations will appear in paretheses in the text.
10 Pasquale Villari, *Life and Times of Girolamo Savonarola,* trans. Linda Villari, 2 vols. (1888; rpt. St. Clair Shores, Mich., 1972), I, 259-60.
11 Villari, II, 219.
12 Richard C. Trexler, *The Spiritual Power: Republican Florence Under Interdict* (Leiden, 1974), pp. 173-77.
13 Quoted in Villari, II, 293.
14 Quoted in Guido Biaggi, ed., *Romola,* 2 vols. (Chicago, 1906), p. xxxvii.
15 Villari, I, xlvii.
16 *The Mill on the Floss,* Bk. IV, ch. 3.
17 Donald Weinstein, *Savonarola and Florence: Prophecy and Patriotism in the Renaissance* (Princeton, N. J., 1970), pp. 69-70.
18 Weinstein, p. 374.

19   Donald Weinstein, "The Myth of Florence", in *Florentine Studies: Politics and Society in Renaissance Florence*, ed. Nicolai Rubinstein (Evanston, 1968), pp. 19-20.
20   Weinstein, *Savonarola and Florence*, p. 374.
21   For a full discussion of Eliot's religious ideas and the influence of Feuerbach on her, see Bernard J. Paris, *Experiments in Life* (Detroit, 1965) especially Chapter 5.
22   Ludwig Feuerbach, *The Essence of Christianity*, trans. George Eliot (New York, 1957), p. 255.
23   Barbara Hardy, *The Novels of George Eliot: a Study in Form* (New York, 1959), pp. 170-75.
24   For a different interpretation of the significance of Bardo's blindness, see Lawrence Poston III, "Setting and Theme in *Romola*", *Nineteenth-Century Fiction*, 20, 355-66.
25   *Letters*, IV, 97.
26   Henry James, "The Novels of George Eliot", in Haight, p. 53.
27   See, in particular, Sara Hennell's letter to Eliot ("in Romola you have painted a goddess, and not a woman") and Eliot's response. *Letters*, IV, 103-4.
28   George Levine, *"Romola* as Fable", in Barbara Hardy, ed., *Critical Essays on George Eliot* (New York, 1970), pp. 86-8.
29   W. J. Harvey, *The Art of George Eliot* (New York, 1962), p. 182.

6

Law, Religion and the Unity of *Felix Holt*

by NORMAN VANCE

Felix Holt, the Radical has not been fully appreciated. Commentators have complained of the needlessly complicated legal plot, the apparently disappointing issue of the radical promise of hero and title, and a lack of overall imaginative coherence.[1] This essay seeks to review these criticisms against the background of the 1830s and of the 1860s, the historical setting of the novel and the intellectual climate of the decade in which it was written.

The most obvious link between the two periods is the question of parliamentary reform. After the novel was published in 1866 George Eliot was induced to make explicit its implied topicality, the connection between the treatment of the 1832 Reform Bill and the political excitement which was to culminate in the second Reform Bill in 1867. In November 1867 she wrote "Felix Holt's Address to Working Men" which applied to the 1860s the essentially gradualist and ethical approach to political and social change put forward in her novel about the 1830s.[2] But *Felix Holt* is much more than a political novel in the narrow sense. It presents a comprehensive view of English society at a critical moment of transition from aristocratic and agrarian values to the new leadership offered by the middle classes in the towns created or transformed by the Industrial Revolution. The law relating to land-ownership and the social and political status of the new urban Dissenters are two important aspects of the transition on which the novel focuses, but George Eliot begins by drawing attention to the general history of the late 1820s and early 1830s.

This historical moment is brilliantly captured in the Introduction to the novel, which was written independently of the early chapters, as the manuscript indicates,[3] to provide a general statementof the social theme of the whole book. After some general description the total vision of society crystallizes in the perceptions of the coachman travelling through a now changing countryside, uneasily aware of riot and disturbance and "Reform" in town and country, sensitive to the violent beginnings of a railway age which threatened his own livelihood and provided a comprehensive metaphor of dislocation:

> the recent initiation of railways had embittered him: he now, as in a perpetual vision, saw the ruined country strewn with shattered limbs, and regarded Mr. Huskisson's death as a proof of God's anger against Stephenson.[4]

These terrible new railways were an important sign of the times. Huskisson, a former President of the Board of Trade, had been killed on 15th September 1830, at the opening of the Liverpool-Manchester line. Tennyson had been on the first train on this railway and took from it an image of progress for his poem "Locksley Hall".[5]

But George Eliot's coachman was more interested in the land than in railways. Like the radical William Cobbett on his rural rides in the 1820s, he always knew whose the land was wherever he went. He was familiar with the traditional patterns of prosperity and dissipation, extravagance and game-preserving on the land, but was disturbed and disoriented by the new dimension of Reform in the early 1830s, a phenomenon which had been observed by John Stuart Mill in his articles on "The Spirit of the Age" (1831)[6]. The disputed ownership of Transome Court can be seen as a symptom of this new instability in an era of Reform. With old families fallen on evil days and new fortunes being made the coachman opined darkly that "property didn't always get into the right hands". The Transomes were poor, but lawyer Jermyn had grown rich in their service. Durfey the heir had been feeble-minded and dissipated, as if to suggest that the older gentry had had its day, and Harold, the more energetic second son, was in a position to improve the family estates after the depredations of litigation about title only because he could bring a new, commercial fortune to the task. Harold's businesslike energy and efficiency, and his radical politics, are out of keeping with the traditions of the old landed gentry, more in keeping with the entrepreneurial skills of the new men like lawyer Jermyn who set out to make Treby Magna into a commercially successful spa. The plot symbolically demonstrates this by disclosing that Harold is in fact Jermyn's natural son and not a Transome at all. The illegitimacy is compounded in that it turns out that the Transome family have lost their title to the estates Harold was to inherit.

George Eliot was not alone in seeing problems of land-ownership as an important index of social change in the 1820s and 1830s. William Cobbett, mentioned in passing in the novel, deplored the supplanting of the old landed gentry by commercial interests and observed everywhere how estates had passed into the hands of the "new men". Spicer the Stockbroker now drove a much better carriage then the once-great magnate Lord Onslow, and the Baring brothers, from the banking family, had acquired the lands of the Duke of Bedford and Lord Northington.[8] The elaborate inheritance-plot of *Felix Holt*, with its dependence on the law as an institution for furnishing ultimate title or warrant for land-ownership in conditions of social change, is not merely appropriate to the economic conditions of the period: it functions as an extended metaphor for problems of moral and political warrant in a novel concerned with the relationship between personal integrity and social position. The politico-religious theme of the novel relates to this as well. It is not merely that political and religious radicalism have gone together since the seventeenth century and that the 1832 Reform Bill gave political power to Dissenting shopkeepers, as Wellington ruefully acknowledged:[9] the heroine is (ostensibly) the daughter of a Dissenting preacher with tastes and insticts and, as it turns out, an inheritance above and beyond her humble social station, but in the end she eschews the position among the landed gentry and the socio-religious establishment which could be hers. Morally as well as politically this is less unique, less worthwhile than it might once have been, and in her love for Felix Holt and his moral reformism she finds a better resting place.

The themes of social change and the social status of Dissenters were still current and controversial in the 1860s. Matthew Arnold's *Culture and Anarchy* began to appear in article form in July 1867, a year after *Felix Holt* was published. Its concern not so much with aristocratic Barbarians as with the newly powerful middle-class Philistines reflects the same sense of a changing society. Six years previously, in the Introduction to *The Popular Education of France,* Arnold had raised the same issues, noting that

> The time has arrived, however, when it is becoming impossible for the aristocracy of England to conduct and wield the English nation any longer . . . the masses of the people in this country are preparing to take a much more active part than formerly in controlling its destinies.[10]

In retrospect the Reform Bill of 1832 seemed to represent an important phase of this transition, the beginning of the end of the old order which had been much more drastically terminated in France with the Revolution. In the period between the two Reform Bills many advanced thinkers brooded on the political power conferred by the ownership of land and the inappropriateness of this in an increasingly democratised society. In 1851 Herbert Spencer, George Eliot's friend and mentor, published his *Social Statics,* which was enthusiastically reviewed by Lewes in *The Leader.* Some of Spencer's most radical ideas, partly repudiated in later life, were introduced in the ninth chapter on "The Right to the Use of the Earth", which Lewes half-teasingly described as a "terrible chapter".[11] Spencer advocated a kind of joint-stock public ownership of the land on moral grounds, claiming that private ownership led to landowning despotism. He argued, ingeniously, that the legal fiction that all land in England was vested in the crown had a certain literal force:

> After all, nobody does implicitly believe in landlordism. We hear of estates being held under the king, that is, the State; or of their being kept in trust for the public benefit; and not that they are the inalienable possessions of their nominal owners.

From this he concluded that claims to private, ancestral ownership of land were ultimately ill-founded, "constantly denied by the enactments of our legislature".[12] By resting his case on the law, or rather on a fundamental principle of law cutting deeper than the superficial legitimacies of land ownership, Spencer provided George Eliot with a hint of the plot of *Felix Holt.* Through this the novelist elaborately contrived to undermine the legitimacy of the Transomes' position in the country by permitting underlying legal principle, allied with the moral principle of Esther and Felix Holt, to dispossess them morally if not materially.

Henry Fawcett, Professor of Political Economy at Cambridge, was as concerned as Spencer about the manifestly unjust distribution of landed property. In his *The Economic Position of the British Labourer,* which George Eliot read in November 1865 in preparation for writing *Felix Holt,*[13] he stoutly maintained that any law which affected land ownership should immediately be altered if it failed to promote the welfare of the whole community. Fawcett was particularly opposed to the entailing of estates on eldest sons as this prevented land from being brought into the market and caused stagnation by discouraging proper development and efficient cultivation: income and capital often had to be diverted from this to provide for the other children who could not inherit the estate.[14] In *Felix Holt* the contrast between the eldest son Durfey, an effete wastrel who is only a drain on the estate, and the vigorous Harold Transome who has had to seek an independent fortune, is a sufficient illustration of the unfairness of the principle of primogeniture which Fawcett attacked.

But Fawcett had a more fundamental point to make: like Spencer he was sensitive to a changing social and political climate in England and did not see why there should be anything sacred about the traditional association of political power and ownership of the land, or indeed why land should continue to be regarded as inalienable private property. Some might claim that

> the existence of the House of Lords depends upon the maintenance of the large landed estates of our peers. Educated people will rebel against such opinions . . . [15]

Like Spencer, he felt that the traditional rights of private property, the liberty to do what one likes with one's own, simply did not apply to the land, which had always involved social responsibilities. The innovations of the Industrial Revolution made this the more apparent: in cases of necessity the private land owner had to yield to Parliament and give up some of his land, perhaps for a new railway passing through his property, "because public convenience requires it". Spencer had used the same argument and the same example, adding the further examples of canals and turnpike roads.[16] Harold Transome's attempt to graft a new radical politics onto a traditional power-base of land which is not inalienably his is bound to fail, for there is a truer radicalism indicated by Spencer and Fawcett which locates political legitimacy in responsibility to society in general and in moral principle rather than in land-ownership as such. The empty and unhappy life of Mrs Transome on her neglected estate is a private tragedy which is also a symbol of the bankruptcy and decay of the old order challenged by the 1832 Reform Bill.

The law in *Felix Holt* threatens to pull down the mighty from their seats and to exalt the humble and meek, but it does not actually do so as in the end Esther waives her inheritance and marries Felix. Law is the book's central mechanism, but more importantly it emerges as one of its central metaphors. It is possible to see the story in terms of an opposition of Byronic and Wordsworthian romanticism: the aristocratic world of Transome Court and the exoticism of Harold's past life and marriage with a slave-girl from the Levant, contrast with the obscure dignity of Felix's educational endeavours in the spirit of Wordsworth's *Excursion*.[17] Esther rightly chooses Felix and Wordsworth rather than Harold (perhaps hinting at *Childe Harold*) and Byronism, so her rewards are moral rather than material and the law becomes an image of moral legitimacy rather than a prize-giving instrument.

Rufus Lyon, who shares with Felix Holt the responsibility for the novel's moral positives, hints at this additional meaning of "law" in a discussion of the prospects of society with Felix. There is a sense in which the underlying principle of social harmony, imperfectly realised at present, represents the Law behind legalisms, the Law which is more important than lawyer Jermyn. Rufus sees in this the final solution to the political and social unrest of the time:

I apprehend that there is a law in music, disobedience whereunto would bring us in our singing to the level of shrieking maniacs or howling beasts . . . And even as in music, where all obey and concur in one end, so that each has the joy of contributing to a whole whereby he is ravished and lifted up into the courts of heaven so will it be in that crowning time of the millenial reign, when our daily prayer will be fulfilled, and one law shall be written on all our hearts, and be the very structure of all thought, and be the principle of all action.

The writing is brilliantly concise. George Eliot strengthens the reader's sense of the seventeenth-century matrix of Rufus's thought by recalling Milton's *L'Allegro* with its "hidden soul of Harmony" ecstatically revealed by soft Lydian airs. But Rufus's rhetoric is firmly linked to a non-classical millenarian vision which recalls traditions of radical political thought associated with Milton and seventeenth-century puritanism. For the man of faith the realisation of "one law" is coterminous with the second coming and the realisation of the Kingdom of Christ, but for the nineteenth-century agnostic like George Eliot the words can carry a purely secular meaning. There was a kind of secular millenarianism associated with Comte's positivist "religion of humanity" which formed part of George Eliot's intellectual background, and it is not difficult to substitute for the prospect of "one law . . . written on all our hearts" Comte's vision of present activity as "but a preparation for the final science of Humanity".[19] Reasoning from different premises the novelist's friend Herbert Spencer arrived at a similar confidence in an ultimate future when, on condition of "search[ing] out with a genuine humility the rules ordained for us", men might eventually come to an epoch "when there is perfect sincerity— when each man is true to himself—when every one strives to realize what he thinks the highest rectitude . . .".[20]

George Eliot deliberately leaves the content of Rufus's apocalyptic vision of "one law" rather vague, because at that point positivist and Puritan would begin to part company, but the general idea of underlying Law is put forward, in different contexts, by Felix and Esther as well. Felix's assault on the constable during the Treby election riot was technically in breach of the law but was in fact a calculated action in support of a more fundamental notion of law and order, the only stratagem available to save the mob from itself and from anarchy. At his trial Felix tactlessly defended his action in terms of general principle, distinguishing between the idea and the imperfect reality of law:

> I reverence the law, but not where it is a pretext for wrong, which it should be the very object of law to hinder.[21]

He does himself no good by proceeding to argue that his hatred of disorder does not mean he would never fight against authority, for moral principle represents a higher court of appeal than legally constituted authority. The unfavourable verdict despite convincing evidence of Felix's purity of motive in the riot, a verdict influenced by the manifest prejudice of the judge, indicates all the more clearly the distinction between law properly understood, fundamental justice, on which Felix takes his stand, and the legal mechanisms which secure his conviction.

Poor old Tommy Trounsem is only a helpless cipher in the legal plot but his death in the riot (which was promoted by Transome's agent) has the morally satisfying consequence of destroying Transome's title to his estate, and this demonstrates the operations of fundamental moral law in the novel, working through the mechanisms of the law of the land. Tommy's uncomprehending words to Christian, as he loyally sticks up Transome election posters, are rich in irony:

> For there's no man can help the law. And the family's the family . . . [22]

In fact, the family is not the family, for Harold is not a Transome at all. But the law is still the law. Its inexorability and pervasiveness are a moral metaphor. If Tommy does not realize this, Esther does, for her growing love for Felix brings with it an irresistible personal intuition of underlying moral principle, the "one law" of which her father had spoken:

> [Felix] had seemed to bring at once a law, and the love that gave strength to obey the law.[23]

This contrast of superficial mechanisms and underlying Law is at the very heart of the novel, the meaning and perhaps the justification of the complicated legal plot, the fundamental insight which George Eliot maintains will sustain "Reform" and preserve a troubled society through major social change. Mrs Transome's tragedy is that she has never fully confronted this ultimate Law, and public and private themes intersect in the moral compromise which has poisoned her life, encumbered the estate, and involved Harold in the toils of corruption associated with Jermyn his natural father. As George Eliot observes:

> She had never seen behind the canvas with which her life was hung. In the dim background there was the burning mount and the tables of the law; in the foreground there was Lady Debarry . . .[24]

So Mrs Transome contrives to keep up appearances and cherishes a morally worthless and outmoded aristocratic ideal of social position and display. The sheer complication of the plot, the almost physical effort the reader must make to disentangle the problem of the ownership of the Transome estate, represents the devious paths by which the Transomes and their kind have departed from the original and ultimate sanction of power and position, the enlightened and socially responsible moral integrity preached and practiced by Felix Holt. With an excellent sense of etymology Rufus commends Felix's radicalism as seventeenth-century "root and branch" perception of underlying principles,[25] and this perception constitutes the radicalism of the novel. Cautiously gradualistic in outlook, *Felix Holt* is a radical novel in a precise though not in a popular sense.

But politics and society require institutions as well as principles. The era of "Reform" represented a phase of institutional adjustment, which was supposed to purify and preserve the principles of the great British Constitution derived from the seventeenth century and the "Glorious Revolution" of 1688. The political propaganda of the 1830s claimed that the fourth William would complete the work of the third and that consititutional monarchy would come to rest on a surer foundation than before.[26] The 1860s registered the same concern for innovation which would yet preserve eternal values and principles, and Matthew Arnold spoke for his contemporaries when he urged that "Human thought, which made all institutions, inevitably saps them, resting only in that which is absolute and eternal".[27]

In *Felix Holt* the vision of the absolute and eternal, represented by the idea of fundamental Law, is not fully realised in the ephemeral antagonisms of Tory and Radical, Church and Dissent, vested interest and "Reform" whether in quack medicines or in politics. But it is part of Rufus Lyon's dream of heaven and Felix and Esther's agenda for the future. No existing institution, no present system of ideas could fully comprehend it. But Rufus Lyon has the heart of the matter in him, and the reader's small smile at his quaint idiosyncracy is chastened by the warning that "none of our theories are quite large enough for all the disclosures of time".[28] The plot of the novel, like the march of history from the 1830s to the 1860s and beyond, has plenty of disclosures to make, and Rufus's ideas survive better than most people's in the book. Both Mrs Transome and he have unexpected past histories, but his love has been purer and more unselfish than hers and has ennobled rather than embittered him, and his human instincts are sounder than his Puritan theology as a result of it. He could not consign his beloved Annette, or Esther, or Felix Holt, to the limbo officially prepared for those who have not professed their faith in the Dissenting fashion, and in the court scene his praise for Felix despite his heterodoxy redounds to the credit of both men. George Eliot laconically notes that he is a greater little man than his church can appreciate: after his departure they appoint a successor "whose doctrine was rather higher", for the "one law" is not yet written in their hearts.[29]

George Eliot makes a fundamental distinction between underlying Law and the law as it is actually used and abused by lawyer Jermyn, or by the Durfey cousin, also a lawyer, who originally purchased the entail from the Transomes and founded the line of Durfey-Transomes. This distinction is symptomatic of the reforming spirit of the 1860s, which extended to the law. New ideas about the law were abroad, even if there was little actual change. Frederic Harrison, a former pupil of the positivist Richard Congreve and himself a leading positivist and barrister, helped out with the legal complexities of the plot. It was Harrison who furnished George Eliot with the concepts of base fee and remainder man by which the Transome entail could be purchased and yet revert quite unexpectedly to someone outside the family more than a hundred years later.[30] Harrison was a radical theorist and reformer by temperament, associated with two of the keenest legal minds of the day, Sir Henry Maine and Westbury the Lord Chancellor.

Harrison had been one of Maine's law-pupils in the 1850s, and had attended the lectures on jurisprudence in the Middle Temple which ultimately became Maine's epoch-making book *Ancient Law* (1861).[31] Using the historical method and the techniques of comparative philology, Maine had put forward an evolutionary theory of law tracing continuities of the past and present as well as organic growth and development. In an address delivered in 1865, the very moment George Eliot was writing *Felix Holt* with the help of his pupil, Maine declared his conviction that

> if indeed history be true, it must teach that which every other science teaches, continuous sequence, inflexible order, and eternal law.[32]

This extreme positivist assertiveness has been compared with the outlook of Herbert Spencer,[33] and it seems likely that George Eliot's central image of underlying Law owes something to both thinkers. Both were among her luncheon guests.[34] Harrison had a unique opportunity to put some of Maine's insights into the essential nature of law into practice when Westbury, a family friend and like Harrison a former Fellow of Wadham College Oxford, appointed him secretary to a Royal Commission for Digesting the Law in 1869.[35] This was after the publication of *Felix Holt*, but the project had been close to Westbury's heart since the 1850s when he had begun his career as a legal reformer in the posts of solicitor-general and attorney-general, and the two men must often have discussed it. Westbury wanted nothing less than the codification of English law, and his Statute Law Revision Act of 1863 advocated the framing of a digest of laws which was finally attempted by the 1869 commission. In the nature of things, codification or a digest of existing laws draws attention to legal principle, the fundamental law on a given subject underlying the accumulated case-law. Land-law was a particularly complicated area of the law, and one of Westbury's special interests was in the simplification of the proof of title and conveyance of land.[36] By consulting Westbury's friend Harrison about the land-law of *Felix Holt* George Eliot put herself in touch with some of the most important legal thought of the time, and her thematic deployment of the idea of fundamental Law can be seen as a metaphorical extension of contemporary ideas about legal principles.

There is an obvious conceptual difficulty with any unitary notion of underlying Law which attempts to be comprehensive, and the different uses of the term "law" in *Felix Holt* are perhaps a verbal device to hint at a greater unity than the novel actually achieves. Rufus Lyon's politically alert religion, Esther's sympathetic emotion, Felix's political and educational ideas all converge on the same word "law", enshrining the eternal principle of moral order which alone can harmonise the discords of the Reform era. But this almost mystical veneration for a slightly nebulous comprehensive category described as "Law" can be traced back to the constitutional excitements of the seventeenth century.

It is no accident that Rufus Lyon constantly harks back to the religious controversies of this epoch, for these were political controversies as well: the inferior social and political status of Dissent, increasingly resented in the 1820s and 1830s, stemmed directly from seventeenth-century reactions to the successful assault on the Church and King of the Civil War period. George Eliot's positivist friends Harrison and Congreve were both interested in Cromwell and the "English Revolution" of the seventeenth century,[37] and her favourite novelist Sir Walter Scott stimulated her imagination with his romantic vision of the politics of religion in *Old Mortality* and *Woodstock*. Almost her first juvenile exercise in fiction was a tale of the Civil War in England, partly derived from Scott, and in a sense it is Scott's sympathetically treated Puritans like Peter Poundtext and Ephraim McBriar in *Old Mortality,* or the worthy Holdenough in *Woodstock,* that provide the imaginative matrix of George Eliot's "rusty old Puritan" Rufus Lyon.[38] At one point in *Felix Holt* the Debarry daughters vaguely describe Dissent as Holdenough and what happens in *Woodstock* .[39] But Scott's seventeenth-century Puritans represented religion at its best for George Eliot: in a review of Harriet Beecher Stowe's novel *Dred* the highest praise she could bestow on its religious fervour was to claim it was reminiscent of the best bits of *Old Mortality*.[40] Like George Eliot, Scott had been brought up in the shadow of an austere religious commitment he no longer fully shared, but like her he retained a generous sympathy and respect for the humanity, dignity and moral seriousness of old-fashioned religious notions he resisted intellectually. For George Eliot the "old-fashioned Puritan" Rufus Lyon was essentially no more ridiculous than his great predecessor "Mr. John Milton".[41]

This fascination with Milton's century is entirely appropriate in a novel about the comparable political and religious excitements of a later century, and the parallel was often drawn in the 1830s. But seventeenth-century constitutional turmoil also stimulated interest in the law. Sir Edward Coke, James I's chief justice of the common pleas, challenged the royal prerogative on the grounds that it encroached upon the immemorial continuities of the English common law. Sir Matthew Hale, half a century later, compiled an epoch-making *History of the Common Law of England* critical of and yet in some sense stemming from Coke's pioneer work. Hale wrote after the Restoration, but he had collaborated with the Cromwellian regime "to steady the ship of the law through a tempest" as one commentator puts it, and this helped to give him a profound sense of the English common law as a vital principle of continuity in a changing world. Both he and Coke maintained that because of this "formal" continuity of the law from remote times even the disruptions of the Norman conquest need not be regarded as a constitutional break.[42] There was an historical precedent for George Eliot's invocation of Law as a source of continuity and moral legitimacy in rapid social and political change, and Rufus Lyon provides the reader with a route back to it, but the imaginative metaphorical extension of the term "law" is idiosyncratic, a function of George Eliot's attempt to give unity to her novel.

At least one critic has complained that George Eliot loaded Rufus Lyon with too much significance, anachronistically making him both a seventeenth-century puritan and a political dissenter of the 1860s without due respect for the nature and concerns of Dissent in the late 1820s and early 1830s.[43] But this is both to mis-state the nature of Dissent at the period of the novel and to misunderstand the role and function of Rufus Lyon. It is known that Rev. Francis Franklin, minister at Cow Lane Baptist Chapel in Coventry 1798-1852, provided a model for many aspects of Rufus Lyon and was very much an "old-fashioned Puritan" in the same mould. His lack of interest in the political questions which exercise Rufus Lyon might seem to suggest that George Eliot went beyond her historical evidence at this point, in the interests of strengthening the links between the political and Dissenting themes of her novel.[44] This would be important in the 1860s as political Dissent and protest against the Established Church were particularly strong, spearheaded by Edward Miall's paper *The Nonconformist* which took its stand on "The Dissidence of Dissent and the Protestantism of the Protestant religion". The 1832 Reform Bill had given Dissenters a voice in parliament, which was one reason why in 1867 Arnold took exception to their manifest lack of sweetness and light in relation to parliamentary business such as a Bill to legitimize marriage to a deceased wife's sister. Miall of *The Nonconformist* is one of the villains of *Culture and Anarchy*. Lyon's political concerns do have this topicality for the 1860s, but they are closer to the concerns of the 1830s than has been realised, for in a sense political Dissent of the Miall variety grew out of the late 1820s and early 1830s when Dissenters worked for Catholic Emancipation.

It is perhaps a mistake to pay too much attention to specific models for Rufus Lyon. Francis Franklin obviously supplied some details, but Franklin was a Baptist, and George Eliot makes it clear that Rufus was an Independent, in a chapel built by the Presbyterians. Independents and Presbyterians were characteristically among the best educated and most enlightened of the Dissenters. Joseph Priestley, Presbyterian minister, pioneer scientist and Jacobinical radical had been a case in point thirty years before. Baptists like Franklin might well have been politically inert in 1832, but not so the Independents, for this was the year in which many of them decided to join together to form the Congregational Union as a better way of opposing the tyrannical monopoly of the Anglican State Church in which they had to marry and to which they had to pay Church rates. The campaign had begun about 1827, and had involved political action from the outset. Catholic

Emancipation was in the air, and in this liberal climate of opinion Whigs and Dissenters formed a political alliance. In return for their support for Catholic Emancipation the Dissenters gained improved civil rights with the repeal of the Test and Corporation Acts in 1828.[45]

Catholic Emancipation in 1829 was the first major indication that things would never be quite the same again, that to be English was no longer to be either Anglican or some kind of second class citizen, which had been the case since the seventeenth century. In Scotland one Andrew Marshall, a Presbyterian minister, bitterly attacked church establishment as a "yoke of bondage" which the recently enfranchised Catholics could not be expected to tolerate or to support financially as the law required,[46] and the controversy this sparked off had repercussions among the Dissenting clergy in England as well. Rufus Lyon's frustrated debate with the nervous Sherlock (the name ironically recalls a great Anglican divine of the seventeenth century[47]) was brilliantly topical for the 1830s as well as the 1860s and also self-consciously modelled on a seventeenth-century episode recounted in Daniel Neal's *History of the Puritans*.[48] George Eliot hinted that the debate raised questions of universal principle and could even be seen as "part of the history of Protestantism". Rufus wanted to inquire into the "constitution of the true church", hinting fairly broadly that this was not the Church of England. In George Eliot's day Miall was robustly proclaiming "The Establishment a Counterfeit Church - An image carved with marvellous cunning", but in 1832, with a quiet dignity and solemnity more like Lyon than like Miall, Rev. Thomas Binney affirmed that

> It is with me, I confess, a matter of deep, serious religious conviction, that the Established church is a great national evil; that it is an obstacle to the progress of truth and godliness in the land . . .

Binney takes the highest ground, and so does Lyon, convinced that nothing less than the "welfare of England" is at stake.[49] It has been argued that the political temper of Congregationalism in the 1830s was "conservative", so that Lyon's support for Transome's radical politics and Felix Holt's

117

would be unusual.[50] But deep-seated hostility to Church Establishment is hardly conservative, and in any case the point is surely that George Eliot intends Rufus to be an unusual man, penetrating, original, learned and with human sympathies and instincts beyond the ordinary and well beyond his congregation. For them the debate with Sherlock is a social occasion and an opportunity for sectarian knockabout, but for Rufus it is an occasion of the utmost solemnity. Despite his disappointment when Sherlock fails to appear he offers to address some improving words to his flock, but his high seriousness is not for them. His politics take the same high ground, for the legitimacy of the State Church is but one aspect of the problem of the legitimacy of a political and religious Establishment closely connected with aristocracy and the land which had ruled the country since the Civil War. The highest Tory in the novel, Sir Maximus Debarry, who presides over an old-fashioned and inefficient household, is symbolically the brother of the beneficed clergyman with whom Lyon had sought to debate, and the failure of nerve of both Rev. Augustus Debarry and the tremulous Sherlock indicates that in religion as well as in society the old order has lost the initiative in the Reform era. It can no longer defend itself against the attack of Puritan and Dissenter which Rufus is aware has continued in an unbroken tradition of high principle and moral indignation almost since the Reformation. It is significant that Sherlock tries to nerve himself for the fray by aspiring to the polemical fame of a Philpotts,[51] for Henry Philpotts, Bishop of Exeter, was one of the most notoriously conservative bishops on the bench. In October 1831 the Archbishop of Canterbury had claimed in the Lords that the Reform Bill, which could give many Dissenters the vote, was "mischievous in its tendency and dangerous to the fabric of the constitution". The Bill was defeated partly by the hostility of the bishops, and when the Lord Chancellor criticised them it was Philpotts who complained that they were "vilified and insulted".[52]

Rufus Lyon's function in the novel is to ask unanswerable fundamental questions about the legitimacy of the Church and the Establishment which included Philpotts and the Debarrys and to suggest that there might be a higher warrant than custom and tradition for the institutions of the age. His vision of one law transcending and harmonising present turmoil and division is founded in a cleverly presented religious politics imaginatively enriched by Sir Walter Scott, deriving from the seventeenth century yet closely relevant to the situation in the 1830s and of topical interest in the 1860s. Intellectually and imaginatively, this is a *tour de force*. This continuity of principle converges upon the idea of Law illustrated in the land-law which takes away the Transomes' title to their estate after a century. In religion as well as in society, among the disruptions and dislocations of the Reform Era, the way forward is located in an imperfectly realised underlying Law or moral order.

Unfortunately, this does not quite take care of the problem of the unity of the novel. The "message" that human beings must be enlightened moral beings before they can legitimately exercise political power is somehow a meagre response to the vividly presented confusions of 1832. Felix's educational programme is a perfectly legitimate response to the challenge of his times. Though it is essentially a positivist specific[53], it has a radical pedigree in that it is strongly recommended by Samuel Bamford in *Some Passages in the Life of a Radical,* which George Eliot read in preparation for her novel.[54] Bamford's essential gradualism and conservative caution as he reviews his early and less prudent career is reflected in the novel in Felix's respect for law and order. In fact, Felix's family background among Lancashire weavers (such as Bamford), his harking back to the ideas of Sir Francis Burdett whom Bamford met, and even his sense that peddling quack medicines is a poor advertisement for morally indignant radicalism all derive from Bamford.[55]

But this is not the real centre of interest in the novel. Felix himself is a pillar of uninteresting righteousness, with few crucial choices to make and almost nothing important to learn from experience. This makes him useless as a sympathetic unifying focus of the book's personal and social concerns. The radical politics, the election riot, the electoral malpractice and the legal plot are all conscientiously worked up from books, the files of *The Times* and childhood memory of a Reform Bill election in Nuneaton, but the histories of Esther, Rufus Lyon and Mrs Transome are the emotional and imaginative core of the book. It might much more appropriately be called *Esther's Choice,* for public and private themes coincide in her choice between the glittering but effete and compromised old world of Transome Court and marriage with Harold, and the prosaic self-denying high-thinking reformist world of her father and Felix Holt. The old and the new are most graphically presented not in terms of Debarrys and radicals but in the dignified desolation of Mrs Transome's tragedy and in Esther's moral education in sympathetic insight and social responsiblity which liberates her from inane class-consciousness.

Sympathy and moral duty emerge as the real positives of the novel, domestic qualities applicable to but separable from the condition of society at large. The reader is more interested in Felix's affection for little Job Tudge, shared by his otherwise thoroughly tiresome mother, than in what Felix plans to teach him, and it is the affectionate rather than the severely didactic Felix that wins Esther's love. Philip Debarry, sophisticated scion of an old Tory family, contributes to the theme of massive social disruption by evincing a modern dissatisfaction which is to lead him out of the established church and into the Church of Rome,[56] but he engages our momentary interest and respect chiefly because he tries hard to keep his word to Rufus Lyon, where his less scrupulous father and uncle would have arrogantly disregarded a Dissenter.

Felix Holt the Radical presents a comprehensive and authoritative picture of society in the throes of political and social change. With brilliant conceptual originality it deploys the intricate legal plot as an extended metaphor for the underlying Law of human sympathy and moral order which is the only possible source of social stability. The themes of moral and political warrant and legitimacy which convey the novelist's radical insight stem from this central image of Law and link the public and private worlds of the novel. But private emotion has an independent life which may leave the rest of the world to its own devices, and this is what tends to happen in *Felix Holt.* Sympathy and duty are the abiding moral imperatives in George Eliot's fiction, and it is only when these, rather than the condition of England, are her starting-point that full imaginative as well as conceptual unity is possible. *Middlemarch,* set in the same period, is a greater book because it is less self-consciously a history of the times. Both novels triumphantly vindicate George Eliot's quiet confidence in one of her letters seeking information from Frederic Harrison:

On a few moral points, which have been made clear to me by my experience, I feel sufficiently confident,—without such confidence I could not write at all.[57]

NOTES

1 See, e.g., Leslie Stephen, *George Eliot*, 1902, pp. 150, 155; Peter Coveney, ed., *Felix Holt* (Harmondsworth, 1972), p.629; G. J. Holyoake, *Bygones worth Remembering*, 2 vols., 1905, I,92; David Craig, "Fiction and the Rising Industrial Classes", *Essays in Criticism* XVII (1967), 64-74; F.C. Thomson, "The Genesis of *Felix Holt*", *P.M.L.A.* LXXIV (Dec. 1959),577.

2 *Blackwood's Magazine* CII (January, 1868), 554-60; see Coveney *op.cit.*, p.607.

3 Unlike the rest of the MS this is on unlined paper, and the leaves are separately numbered. See British Library Add. MS 34030, ff.1-10.

4 *Felix Holt*, "Introduction".

5 H. Martineau, *History of England during the Thirty Years' Peace: 1816-1846*, 2 vols., 1860, II,6; "Locksley Hall" 1.182: see C. Ricks, ed., *The Poems of Tennyson* (1969), p.699n.

6 *Examiner*, 6 January-29 May 1831; extracts are reprinted in G.L. Williams, ed., *John Stuart Mill on Politics and Society* (1976), pp.170-78.

7 Ch.3.

8 W. Cobbet, *Rural Rides* (1830) (Harmondsworth, 1967), pp.33f, 44.

9 Letter to J.W. Croker, 1833, quoted in David M. Thompson, ed., *Nonconformity in the Nineteenth Century* (1972), p.83f.

10 R.H. Super, ed., *Complete Prose Works of Matthew Arnold*, vol.II (Michigan, 1962), pp.6, 15.

11 G.H. Lewes, "Spencer's Social Statics", *The Leader*, II (8 March 1851), 248-50.

12 H. Spencer, *Social Statics* (1851), p.122.

13 J.W. Cross, ed., *George Eliot's Life as Related in her Letters and Journals*, 3 vols. (Edinburgh and London, 1885), II,413.

14 H. Fawcett, *The Economic Position of the British Labourer* (Cambridge and London, 1865), pp.17-23.

15 *Op. cit.*, p.14f.

16 *Op. cit.*, p.17; Spencer, *op. cit.*, p.122.

17 Specifically mentioned in the text, "Introduction".

18 Ch.13.

19 A. Comte, *A General View of Positivism* (1848 etc.), tr. J.H. Bridges, 1865, p.47.

20 Spencer, *op. cit.*, p.476.

21 Ch.46.

22 Ch.28.

23 Ch.27.
24 Ch.40.
25 Ch.27.
26 See, e.g., "The Reformers of England" (ballad), *Times*, 11 March 1831, p.3 col.c; 11 April 1831, p.1 col.e (election report).
27 *The Popular Education of France*, Super, *op. cit.*, II,29.
28 Ch.6.
29 "Epilogue".
30 G.S. Haight, ed., *The George Eliot Letters*, 7 vols. (New Haven and London, 1954-55), IV, 215-40; see also F. Harrison, "Reminiscences of George Eliot", *Memories and Thoughts* (1906), pp.146-48. I am deeply indebted to Raymond Cock for his help with legal-historical matters in what follows.
31 F. Harrison, *Autobiographic Memoirs*, 2 vols. (1911), I,152. Harrison enthusiastically reviewed both the 1861 and the 1906 (revised) editions of Maine's *Ancient Law:* see *Memories and Thoughts*, pp.118-22.
32 H. Maine, "Address to the University of Calcutta", reprinted in *Village Communities in the East and West* (1871), p.205f. Compare *Ancient Law*, 1906 ed., ch.5, p.119f. See G. Feaver, *From Status to Contract. A Biography of Sir Henry Maine, 1822 - 1888* (1969), ch.5.
33 See J. Burrow, *Evolution and Society* (Cambridge, 1966), Ch.5, esp. p.165.
34 Both men also attended her funeral. See G.S. Haight, *George Eliot: a Biography* (Oxford, 1968), pp.463,550.
35 *Who's Who*, 1910 ed., s.c. "Harrison". Oddly, there is no Harrison D.N.B. entry.
36 W. Holdsworth, *A History of English Law*, 16 vols., XVI (1966 ed.), 74-86; D.N.B.
37 Harrison wrote a popular biography of Cromwell (1888) and three articles reprinted in *Memories and Thoughts*. Congreve lectured on the seventeenth century and planned a book (never completed) to be called *Cromwell, Milton and the English Revolution: [A] Positive or Positivist History of the English Revolution* (c.1890). Bodleian Library MS Eng. Misc. d. 484, f.77ᵛ; MS Eng. Misc. d. 485, f.l.
38 G.S. Haight, *George Eliot*, Appendix I, pp.554-60. See also the rather sketchy pamphlet by A.J. Craig, *Notes on the Influence of Sir Walter Scott on George Eliot* (Edinburgh, 1923).
39 Ch.14.
40 *Westminster Review* LXVI (October, 1865), 572f.
41 Ch.6.
42 See C.M. Gray, in his introduction to Matthew Hale, *The History of the Common Law of England* (posthumously published 1713 etc.), (Chicago and London, 1971), esp. pp.xxxi, xxvi-xxix.
43 V.D. Cunningham, *Everywhere Spoken Against: Dissent and the Victorian Novel* (Oxford, 1975), pp.182-89.
44 Discussed in Cunningham, *loc.cit.*
45 See H.S. Skeats, C.S. Miall, *History of the Free Churches of England 1688-1891* (1891), ch.10.
46 In his 1829 "Voluntary Sermon" reprinted in J.D. Marshall, ed., *Memoir of Andrew Marshall, D.D., LL.D.* (Glasgow, 1889), pp.125ff.

47 William Sherlock, 1641? - 1707, nonjuring Dean of St Paul's who opposed prayerbook alterations that might win back Dissenters. His son Thomas (1678-1761, Bishop of London) and Richard Sherlock (1612-1689, Royalist divine) were also prominent Anglican controversialists. D.N.B.
48 Daniel Neal, *The History of the Puritans . . . an Account of their Principles* (1732-38), 3 vols. (1837), I,420-2, referred to implicitly in ch.15; discussed by Coveney, *op.cit.*, p.661; *Felix Holt*, ch.23.
49 Miall quoted in Clyde Binfield, *So Down to Prayers. Studies in English Noncomformity 1780-1920* (1977), p.111; Binney quoted in Skeats and Miall, *op.cit.*, p.479; *Felix Holt* ch. 15.
50 Cunningham, *op.cit.*, p.176.
51 Ch.23.
52 See Rev. W.N. Molesworth, *The History of the Reform Bill of 1832* (London and Manchester, 1865), pp.257-65.
53 A. Comte, *A General View of Positivism*, pp.180-94.
54 Cross, *op. cit.*, II,404; S. Bamford, *Some Passages in the Life of a Radical*, 2nd ed., 2 vols. (1843), I,12,29.
55 Bamford, *op.cit.*, I, ch.1; I, ch.5; I, pp.47,52; compare *Felix Holt*, ch.5; ch.30; ch.3.
56 Ch.14.
57 Cross, *op. cit.*, II,421.

7

Origins, *Middlemarch,* Endings: George Eliot's Crisis of the Antecedent

by JAN GORDON

> What was the primitive tissue? In that way Lydgate put the question—not quite in the way required by the awaiting answer; but such missing of the right word befalls many seekers.
>
> (ch. 15, p. 178)

Lydgate joins a number of *Middlemarch* residents who attempt to locate a single point of Origin from whence re-form—political, physiological, ontological, fictional—might be understood to have begun. His quest for the primitive tissue, Casaubon's circuitous search for a Key to All Mythologies, Ladislaw's infatuation with the pre Pre-Raphaelite art of the Nazarenes,[1] even George Eliot's setting the novel "back" to the eve of the First Reform Bill all testify to an ardent willingness to believe in some pure Origin of events prior to the corruption by "circumstances" that transform those obsessions to an interest in mere Endings. This imagined Origin was to be sure a fixation of the Victorian mind with its fascination for tracing various lines of succession, whether it be Darwin's *Origin of the Species,* Newman's apostolic succession, remounted in order to discover some presumably original Church, or the project to compile an *Oxford English Dictionary* that would trace the lineaments of linguistic origin and descent. The very figure of the orphan itself, as J. Hillis Miller has argued, bespeaks an interest in the fear of discontinuity which prompts so many of the age's novelistic children to commence the pilgrimage that might

124

bring them into some confrontation with their Origin-as-parent.[2] The Victorian orphan figure can typically make his vocational choice only after he has ascertained his private history, which is but another way of saying that he is his Origin He goes through life under the assumption that the structure of the journey is dependent upon the clarification of his point of departure. Conceived of in such a manner, the Origin is never transitive insofar as it has no object other than its continual clarification. Its model is self-consciousness. Ever so gradually, however, the awful truth emerges: that Origins, "Keys", primitive tissues, sources, historical "background"—the Ur-texts of an epoch—are arbitrary and fictional rather than real, mere attempts to individually appropriate that metaphysical absence which is every Origin.

Those motivated by the quest for some identifiable Origin at the outset of *Middlemarch* tend to share a similar metaphoric world. Perhaps its most salient characteristic is a belief that any source embodies a wholeness and purity which is fragmented and refracted in all descendants. For Casaubon, "the genuine mythical product" has a purity diluted by the "fable of Cupid and Psyche" (ch.20, p. 229) which he sees as only a mere romantic invention, i.e. corruption. And the difficulty is that of somehow getting beyond the various corruptions, filling those interstices which separate the scholar from truth. The world appears as a cluster of fragments which simultaneously obscures yet reveals some originally "given" condition, a prior status. And, in order to enforce any *a priori* wholeness, Casaubon must multiply their fragmented nature "made difficult by the interference of citations, or by the rivalry of dialectical phrases ringing against each other in his brain" (ch.29, p.315), in order to assure himself of the presence of sufficient "evidence". His is the unenviable psychological position of having to create obstructive refractions in order that the true light might appear brighter. Revelation and distancing are mutually re-enforcing, producing an incredible circularity rather than any origin which might serve as a commencement.

Hence the predominance, and significance of the water imagery which Reva Stump has so carefully catalogued;[3] in order to find the elusive Key to All Mythologies, Casaubon must get beyond the tributaries of knowledge, those shallow rivers where lurk Carp, Pike and Tench, and into the clearer reservoirs which they share as a common source of life. The irony of Casaubon's plight lies in the fact that, although he thinks himself on some tortuous journey of connection, his own language reveals symptoms of a discontinuity that belies his life's purpose. Mrs Cadwallader's judgement that he is "all semicolons and parentheses" (ch.8, p. 96) seems borne out by his circuitous marriage proposal. In order to create the illusion of connection, he must rely upon the verbal reservoirs of parenthetical expression that force us to lose sight of any Origin:

> For in the first hour of meeting you, I had an impression of your eminent and perhaps exclusive fitness to supply that need (connected, I may say, with such activity of the affections as even the preoccupations of a work too special to be abdicated could not uninterruptedly dissimulate); and each succeeding opportunity for observation has given the impression an added depth by convincing me more emphatically of that fitness . . .
>
> (ch.5, p. 66)

Even as he tries to arrive at an Ending (the proposal), he betrays "need" as an Origin which replicates itself as connective "successions". Given his perception of the relation between a shared ontic Origin and the descent of myth into the mass of *parergae*, Casaubon's language has its own logic. He either overwrites in order to fill in all gaps so as to create his own meaning at the core of a linguistic labyrinth or, conversely, he underwrites, using a kind of shorthand to point to the metaphysical truth which he assumes to lie beyond the visible. For example, he never refers to content, but only dates in summarizing previous correspondence, convinced that a *"vide supra* could serve instead of a repetition" (ch.3, p. 49). He is always at pains to make clear to Dorothea the nature of "received" opinion during their honeymoon in Rome, as if the meaning of history were present in the footprints of the *cognoscenti*.

To be sure, such assumptions have a puritan bias. If all truth is revealed, then existence in the ordinary world centres about locating and identifying fragmentary "evidence" so that all objects and opinions eventually come to assume the status of clues. But, simultaneously, such a conviction entails a corollary belief that "all the mythical systems or erratic mythical fragments in the world were corruptions of a tradition originally revealed" (ch.3, p. 46). Little wonder that a phenomenology of the "clue" eventually brings Casaubon to a suspicion of human as well as object infidelity. For Casaubon the world is a corrupted text, and his every effort is restorative insofar as it attempts to locate some single authority which lies behind the multiplicity of meanings and systems. In one sense, what Casaubon does do is to make a distinction between a primary source and secondary literature, or between a unified Original and its limitations. Such is the space in which traditional hermeneutics operates and depends for its efficacy upon the closed and hence "sacred" nature of the Origin. As the nineteenth century applied interpretation to scripture in order to consider it as a mode of fiction, so Casaubon applies hermeneutics to fictions in order to restore the difference between an Origin and a lapsed text![4] When in Chapter 22 Ladislaw reminds us that Casaubon, unlike the German, Otfried Muller, "is not an Orientalist", he is pointing out the futility of the effort. Muller's *Prolegomena to a Scientific Mythology*, published in 1825, had ruled out the so-called etymological proofs that had attempted to relate diverse myths to a common Hebrew origin by showing conclusively that mythologies develop independently and arbitrarily, to serve the totemic needs of different societies. Unlike her Casaubon who reads no German, George Eliot knew of Muller's research, having mentioned it in her review of R.W. Mackay's *The Progress of the Intellect* in the *Westminster Review* of January 1851.[5] Perhaps as a consequence of this inability to resolve the many into the One, Casaubon exhibits other rigidly puritan behavioural attitudes. If he is not engaging life (spending) and also getting no nearer the goal (quest achievement), then it follows that Casaubon must be "saving". He comes to believe that "his long studious bachelorhood had stored up for him a compound interest of enjoyment" (ch.10, p. 111). It is but another reservoir in his life, waiting to be tapped. Such is a life lived totally in the conditional; that is to say that Casaubon, like so many Middlemarchers, comes to believe that one decision, one act, will make him. And, as Fred Vincy with old Featherstone's will, only then will he begin to "live". Such a dynamics of dependency, as we shall see, instantly converts life to a gamble that feeds postponement.

Dorothea, somewhat similarly, creates in Casaubon an Origin out of an absence:

> Dorothea's faith supplied all that Mr. Casaubon's words seemed to leave unsaid; what believer sees a disturbing omission or infelicity? The text, whether of prophet or poet, expands for whatever we can put into it, and even his bad grammar is sublime.
>
> (ch. 5, p. 74)

Just as Casaubon's shorthand involves the use of "touchstones" of critically respectable opinion, so Dorothea somewhat similarly begins to see even emptiness—Casaubon's deep-set eyes, for example—as signs which point beyond themselves. She, too, is compelled to create continuities out of the obviously discontinuous. Paralleling Casaubon's attempt to posit the category of the *subauditum* to account for a missing word from the text of the quotation of some French king in Chapter 9, Dorothea

> filled up all blanks with unmanifested perfections, interpreting him as she interpreted the works of Providence, and accounting for seeming discords by her own deafness to the higher harmonies.
>
> (ch. 9, p. 100)

The Origin always embodies *harmony* for those who believe in it; reconciling all differences, it lies behind the proliferation of refracted signs in the universe at large. Hence Casaubon represents a combination of "religious elevation" and "learning":

> here was a living Bossuet, whose work would reconcile complete knowledge with devoted piety; he was a modern Augustine who united the glories of doctor and saint.
>
> (ch. 3, p. 47)

Like every Origin, he is a tautology, "a man whose learning almost amounted to a proof of whatever he believed" (ch. 2, p. 45). The same Dorothea who in the famous discussion with her sister Celia over the family jewels, came to regard gems as "fragments of heaven", conceives of herself as a fragmented text who must learn Hebrew, "at least the alphabet and a few roots—in order to arrive at the core of things" (ch. 7, p. 88). Casaubon's logocentric universe is replaced in Dorothea's thought by Casaubon himself who "thinks a whole world of which my thought is but a poor two-penny mirror" (ch. 3, p. 47). Hence, one of the predominant strains of imagery in the early chapters of the novel: those on a quest for Origins want *illumination* which must come from some source outside themselves. If the acolyte inhabits the naves of cognitive shadows and reflections, the Origin must be illuminated Unity. The artificial distinction manifests itself in a psychological chiaroscuro. Dorothea is often seen in relief against some background that looms large and which places her, from one point of view at least, in the shadows of an historical epic frieze. It is not merely that the novel's first sentence introduces us to a woman "whose beauty seems to be thrown into relief by poor dress", but also that the gloom of Lowick "had no bloom that could be thrown into relief by that background" (ch. 9, p. 99). The realm of relief or fresco is part of the world of assumed antithesis which recognizes a distinction between foreground and background, both historical and aesthetic. Perhaps its most ironic commentator is Naumann, the Nazarene painter whom the Casaubons meet in Rome. Clad in her Quakerish grey drapery with long cloak and ungloved hand, Dorothea is in the attitude of some historical bas-relief, awaiting illumination. Her presence in the museum creates a juxtaposition which appeals to those who wish to use the "here" only as a vehicle for gaining access to the "there" of historical antecedent:

> There lies antique beauty, not corpse-like even in death, but arrested in the complete contentment of its sensuous perfetion: and here stands beauty in its breathing life, with the consciousness of Christian centuries in its bosom.
>
> (ch. 19, p. 220)

The Naumanns of the world of course see the contrasts for what they are—opportunities for caricatures, seized when he uses Casaubon's head as the model for St. Thomas Aquinas. Whereas so many of the other characters search for an historical model that lies back of and behind the corrupted "texts",

Naumann arbitrarily uses the "living" Casaubon as a model for he historical St. Thomas, creating a mock-relief in the process of substitution. Conversely, moments of real moral illumination in the novel are invariably the consequence of some deadening in historical contrast. Following her return from the honeymoon in Rome, "each remembered thing in the room was disenchanted, was deadened as an unlit transparency" (ch. 28, p. 308). Chiaroscuro tends to diminish in *Middlemarch* at those moments when an individual comes to recognize that "sources" do not always reveal connection, but are organizational fictions. At the outset, every dwelling in *Middlemarch* seems to ooze with a contrast between the shallowed dimensionality of present objects and some deeper set background, represented best perhaps in Farebrother's parsonage where the objects "standing in relief against the dark wainscot" present a unique physiognomy (ch. 17, p. 198).[6] The spatial algebra of historical consciousness—background is to foreground as Origin is to descent, providing illumination, enchantment and obsession as the common denominator—is violated upon the discovery that the Origin can also be an imaginative corruption. It is Ladislaw, as we would expect, who first thinks to himself, in one of the novel's great puns: "She must have made some original romance for herself in this marriage" (ch. 21, p. 241).

Lydgate too compensates for his own obscure Origins by an obsession with locating some Ur-tissue that might explain the various systemic functions which seem to be independent:

> . . . it was open to another mind to say, have not these structures some *common basis* from which they have all started, as your sarsnet, gauze, net, satin and velvet from the raw cocoon? Here would be another light, as of oxy-hydrogen, showing the very grain of things, and revising all former explanations. Of this *sequence* to Bichat's work . . . Lydgate was enamoured.
>
> (ch. 15, pp. 177-78).

A "common basis" which lies behind some "sequence" implies the necessity of locating some missing link, "new connections and hitherto hidden facts of structure which must be taken into account in considering the symptoms of maladies and the action of medicaments" (ch. 15, p. 177). Lydgate's idol, the Frenchman Bichat, demarcated one of the nineteenth century's most famous medical cul-de-sacs by positing a "primary tissue", a sort of cellular phlogiston, from which various organs were descended. As Casaubon's researches lead to the construction of compartmentalized boxes of notes, beginning with the first letter of the alphabet and as George Eliot herself had commenced a novel with the first two letters of the alphabet in the process of creating an emotional Adamic everyman, so Lydgate's career begins at the beginning. He takes from its shelf the first volume of an encyclopedia and becomes enamoured with the entries under "Anatomy". The portals which opened upon Dorothea's marriage—"everything he had said seemed like a specimen from a mine, or the inscription on the door of a museum" (ch. 3, p. 55)—are translated into Lydgate's *valvae*, the portals of the human heart, which first attract his attention.

The remainder of his life becomes devoted to "filling the vast spaces" (ch. 15, p. 173) which lie between himself and the great originators, the science of first things. Perhaps the most poignant feature of Lydgate's plight is his attempt to break away from an Origins-dominated world view. He becomes early smitten with an interest in "structure", investigating the nervous system with the aid of galvanic experiments. But what neither he nor Casaubon nor Dorothea can ever do is to acknowledge the possibility of either a divided source or conflicting motives. Discontinuity of development is simply not broached as a possibility, and it is for precisely this reason that Lydgate is so disillusioned by the Madame Laure episode. Her foot really slipped, but she "meant to do it" (ch. 15, p. 182) suggests a conflict between motive and action rather than some commonly shared source. Again, with Lydgate, there is the pull of postponement; like Casaubon's delayed "beginning", Lydgate sees marriage as impetuous if not removed to "some distant period". It is almost as if some conservation of absence were at work here—as if the desire to fill some gap which separates the discoverer from an Origin shifts that gap to the end of the sequence, delaying Endings. The isolation in some "middle" creates a self-induced wager:

> He was at a starting-point which makes many a man's career a fine subject for betting if there were any gentlemen given to that amusement . . .
>
> (ch. 15, p. 178)

The physical embodiment of that "long shot" is Fred Vincy, for his life can begin only when he is "made" by Featherstone's will. And it is that absent bequest—the non-materialized Origin —which prompts the speculation that leads to his indebtedness. In one sense he hypostasizes an unknown Origin as collateral, a displacement common in the social dynamics of *Middlemarch*. And when he is forced to deny such speculation, old Featherstone asks him to contradict the story by bringing proof in the form of documents which become a substitute for authority:

> "But I contradict it again. The story is a silly lie."
> "Nonsense! you must bring dockiments. It comes from authority."
>
> (ch. 12, p. 137)

Like all the other people who regard authority, origins, and text synonymously, Fred Vincy is asked to collect proof in the form of a written statement. His "dockiments" would presumably join Mr Brooke's pre-campaign trail ammunition, "his documents on machine-breaking and rick-burning" (ch. 3, p. 48) piled in a heap in a study which forms an "authoritative" base for later claims:

> "Yes," said Mr. Brooke, with an easy smile, "but I have documents. I began a long while ago to collect documents. They want arranging, but when a question has struck me, I have written to somebody and got an answer. I have documents at my back. But now, how do you arrange your documents?"
> "In pigeon-holes partly," said Mr. Casaubon, with rather a startled air of effort.
>
> (ch. 2, pp. 41-2)

One of the ways of measuring the change that comes over the Middlemarch community during the course of the novel is the shift in the symbolic status of documents. Early in the novel documents are regarded as sources of authority, the means by which some proof is accumulated or evidence is acquired. Documents are always "fragments" of some larger tapestry and hence always point beyond themselves. They tend to have synecdochic value insofar as the various scraps of paper represent, if correctly arranged and sifted, some larger truth. It is in such a light that Casaubon arranges his notes in compartments and that Fred Vincy is requested to furnish proof that he has not speculated, the irony lying of course in the fact that a piece of paper is to be used to ascertain a *negative* involvement. What he is really being asked to do is to document a lack of proof, the same task at which Casaubon has been labouring for years. And Casaubon's will possesses the same symmetry, really; it is not a bequest but a negative injunction, providing *no* inheritance upon the fulfilment of certain conditions. The codicil is another "authority" suggesting Casaubon's lack of authority! Stated in another way, the documents become, quite arbitrarily, part of the burden of guilt disguised as bequests. Casaubon's will has a fictional, creative base, since it *creates* suspicion rather than authorizes distribution. Perhaps the best example of all in the novel is old Featherstone's will, upon which Fred Vincy has staked so much. The diminishment of this particular "beginning" for Fred is surely signalled by the existence of one will behind another. His point of Origin is part of a sequence of infinite regress, and not some commencement of a delayed life. Even were Mary Garth to obey Featherstone's final request, she still would not know which will had priority, for the two wills cancel each other. She has no power to act, and he has no real power to authorize. In the beginning is a binary set that is arbitrarily established and not a communally shared Origin from which benefits flow, the "homogenous origin of all the tissues" (ch. 45, p. 495) which Lydgate has posited.

Gradually, those who draw up documents in *Middlemarch* became conscious of their ultimate arbitrariness. After Casaubon's death Dorothea occupies herself with maps and papers relating to Lowick, the pragmatic accoutrements by which we set out affairs in order:

> One morning, about eleven, Dorothea was seated in her boudoir with a map of the land attached to the manor and other papers before her, which were to help her in making an *exact statement for herself* of her income and affairs.
>
> (ch. 54, p. 584, italics mine)

This event takes place immediately after she has sealed and put in a drawer forever one of the last instructional documents of her late husband, a "Synoptical Tabulation for the use of Mrs. Casaubon", one of the cornerstones of Casaubon's imaginary scholarly edifice. Both documents are tabulations, but Dorothea is now willing to acknowledge, at least passively, that all inventories have the self and not the world as the unstated recipient. It is part of a shift in the status of texts, part of the change from envisioning the document as *fragment* to seeing it instead as part of an arbitrary *collection* whose object is the self.

Fragments have a phenomenology that implies descent from some prior status of wholeness, and in *Middlemarch* they tend to accumulate about those people whose mission it is to prove that the many stem from some One. Fragments are adjuncts to the telos of reform and have an historical component precisely to the extent that some cataclysm in time separates *them* from *it*. In Levi-Strauss' nomenclature the fragment might be imagined to be nature striving to be culture.[7] The danger which threatens those obsessed with the document-as-fragment lies in the fact that it is too often made to do more than its nature will allow:

> "That is fine, Ladislaw: that is the way to put it. Write that down, now. We must begin to get documents about the feeling of the country, as well as the machine-breaking and general distress."
>
> "As to documents," said Will, a two-inch card will hold plenty. A few rows of figures are enough to deduce misery from. . ."
>
> (ch. 46, p. 500)

The aim here is to deduce a common source in human emotion for the "feelings" which are somehow represented in figures. Brooke is enlisting the restless Ladislaw in yet another of those quests for homogeneity. What is at stake of course is a gross misunderstanding of the nature of the deductive process. There is no single source for either human authority or human misery, any more than Rome, that city of fragments, as Dorothea discovers on her honeymoon, illuminates historical consciousness. It is rather more rightly understood as the "interpreter of the world" (ch. 20, p. 225) which suggests the possibility of other interpretations. Everyone's language is unique unto himself. The decline of any conviction in a "source" is manifested as the democratization of the vernacular:

> "Are you beginning to dislike slang, then?" said Rosamond, with mild gravity.

"Only the wrong sort. All choice of words is slang. It marks a class."

(ch. 11, p. 126)

When Fred Vincy recognizes that he can no longer depend upon Feathstone's will, but must instead learn how to keep the clerk's memoranda at Caleb Garth's warehouse, he must literally learn how to write anew: not the scholarly manuscript of the would-be cleric—"easy to interpret when you *know beforehand* what the writer means" (ch. 56, p. 611)—but the transactional style that depends less upon an understanding of origin or intention:

"Now, Fred," said Caleb, "you will have some desk-work. I have always done a good deal of writing myself, and I can't do without help, and as I want you to understand the accounts and get the values into your head, I mean to do without another clerk. So you must buckle to. How are you at writing and arithmetic?"

(ch. 56, p. 610)

He is among those who must keep records, not in order to construct a proof, but to transmit arbitrary information whose independent components have a more or less equal status. Fred's work comes to assume the characteristics of Mary's hobby, "copying the labels from a heap of shallow cabinet drawers in a minute handwriting" (ch. 57, p. 622) or Dorothea's compulsive desire to write out "her memoranda" to the housekeeper whenever Will drops in (ch. 62, pp. 682-83). Like Will's own portfolio, all of these documents are not fragments at all, but arbitrary collections without any potential for internal development and lacking a clearly defined beginning or ending other than the arbitrary. These are the "circumstances" toward which texts accrue in *Middlemarch*. Lydgate's list of household furnishings drawn up for his creditors and Bulstrode's "pocket-book to review various memoranda there as to the arrangements he had projected and partly carried out in the prospect of quitting Middlemarch" (ch. 70, p. 764) are contingency texts, preparations for possibilities rather than steps in a proof. Like Rosamond's invitation lists, these collections of documents, bills, memoranda, and lists have value only as exchange. They facilitate social transaction, but have no worth outside their denotative systems. Such are

135

"service papers" which authenticate social intercourse; they do not form a part of what George Eliot calls in one place "geognosis".

The character in the novel who first recognizes this distinction is Farebrother whose insect collection, unlike Casaubon's pigeon-holes, has only a private value within a system of potential exchange. His "old texts" (ch. 17, p. 202) include items about a variety "of Aphis brassicae", or a learned treatise on the "entomology of the Pentateuch" (ch. 17, p. 202) which has fictional status only:

> "I have some sea-mice—fine specimens—in spirits. And I will throw in Robert Brown's new thing—*Microscopic Observations on the Pollen of Plants*—if you don't happen to have it already."
>
> "Why, seeing how you long for the monster, I might ask a higher price. Suppose I ask you to look through my drawers and agree with me about all my new species?"
>
> (ch. 17, p. 204)

Farebrother's collection is almost a parody of the research into Origins that characterizes the would-be discoverers in *Middlemarch*. The curator of specimens rather than fragments, he alone recognizes that his fascination with what he calls "natural history" is private insofar as it is likely to reveal much more about himself than about any lineage in the animal kingdom. His is simply an insect collection in which one specimen is the equivalent of any other, except during exchange. They can be arranged into an almost infinite number of communities, including an imaginary parliament. Unlike the other clerics and exemplars of piety in the novel, he lacks a text, always electing to deliver his sermons "without a book" (ch. 18, p. 208). Rather than looking for the general law which is supposed to lie behind random events in the universe, Farebrother alone is aware that the individual imposes himself upon any formulation in an activity akin to translation. Everyman his own anthropomorphist is a sentiment surely relevant to the translator of Feuerbach. Farebrother it is who always reminds us of the dangers which stem from mistaking the convenience of an interpretation for the status of an Original that demands obligations; contrasting himself with Bulstrode, Farebrother reminds Lydgate: "I don't *translate* my own convenience into other people's duties" (ch. 17, p. 206, italics mine). The problem in *Middlemarch* is that systems of exchange and substitution which are essentially horizontal are continually making claims which presume vertical priorities in such a way that the discontinuous is never acknowledged.

Farebrother is clearly a man of "endings", for the Vicar loves to play at cards with the hopes of winning those small sums that make life easier:

> The vicar was a first-rate billiard-player, and, though he did not frequent the Green Dragon, there were reports that he had sometimes been there in the daytime and had won money.
>
> (ch. 18, p. 209)

Although his friends regard Farebrother's casual card games and billiard-playing as "ignoble", the Vicar is clearly distinguished by his love of games as opposed to myths.[8] The money "had never been a motive to him" (ch. 18, p. 209), but rather the physical translation of winning or losing. His approach to gambling, because it is so motiveless, is in direct contrast to those in the community who are always attempting to secure the metaphoric windfall that will make their postponements worthwhile. Their motivation is perhaps best seen, in terms of George Eliot's crisis of the antecedent, as the urge to recovery. and such urges participate in the structural pattern of the labyrinth.[9]

As the imagined Origin retreats into the distance, the researchers in *Middlemarch*, in contrast to Ladislaw or Farebrother, recognize that they have paid an enormous price. Neither Casaubon, nor Lydgate, nor Dorothea see any tangible return on their investment. Every potential fulfilment becomes part of a vague future; such is the maryrdom of the ardent. The sacrifice consists of neutralizing the present in favour of a gamble upon the future benefits, and when that reward becomes illusory, life assumes the dynamics of an enormous risk. One consequence of this risk is a kind of speculation which creates its own centre out of nothingness. Fred's speculation upon the horse which he does not own; Casaubon's will, a mode of borrowing time posthumously; Lydate's borrowings to purchase the household goods for his marriage; and Bulstrode's too easy acquiescence to Raffles' threat of blackmail, in effect giving the banker a rented past are all desperate gambles by which the gambler attempts either to blot out the past (erasing the gap which separates him from Origins) or, conversely, to bring the condition of windfall from the future to the present. In either case, from a structural point of view, gambling is part of the dynamics of an "expanded middle".

All of this activity comes under the general rubric of speculation, part of the new mercantilism that intrudes upon an older, more traditional historical consciousness in the novel. But the implications of this gambling in which all of those engaged in the quest for Origins find themselves involved, suggests something larger. It is not merely that men named Rigg and Raffles come to have such an important bearing on the action of the novel. But rather that increasing ontological risk would appear to be a corollary to the decline of traditional authority. What Fred Vincy does, in effect, is to make Fate his authority rather than Featherstone by creating an infinite sequence of dependencies, with one horse becoming collateral for another. Such a world resembles that of Lydgate where he uses that which he does not own—a successful practice—as the basis for borrowing against the future. Casaubon does the same, negatively, in the codicil to his will: he speculates by putting his money on Dorothea's future at the moment when he has no future! The structure of the risk is worthy of note, because it tends to shift the pattern of infinite regress, which had been imagined to be in the past by those who quest for Origins, into future time.

Additionally, the act of gambling tends to neutralize those objects which provide the basis for the speculation. To put up "stakes" is one way of saying that one does not own the object, but is instead willing to play for it. Edmund Bergler suggests that gambling is a highly symbolic activity where the items wagered are less significant *per se* than they are as part of a larger system with its own language that is increasingly private.[10] The compulsive nature of the enterprise makes it a perfect metaphor for a world without a clearly defined beginning or ending. The gambler can get in or out at will, creating the most arbitrary termini, as Lydgate discovers when, in debt, he visits the Green Dragon:

He had looked on at a great deal of gambling in Paris, watching it as if it had been a disease. He was no more tempted by such winning than he was by drink. He had said to himself that the only winning he cared for must be attained by a conscious process of high, difficult combination tending towards a benificent result. The power he longed for could not be represented by agitated fingers . . .

But just as he had tried opium, so his thought now began to turn upon gambling—not with appetite for its excitement, but with a sort of wistful inward gaze after that easy way of getting money, which implied no asking and brought no responsibility.

(ch. 66, pp. 720-21)

How the individual wins in this world has undergone a marked change. Because that which is risked is not owned at all, the gambler comes to imagine himself as triangulated, part of a "third party" dynamic in which he is merely an agent of Fate or Luck. Hence not merely the sum wagered, but the participant is de-objectified, creating a kind of self-delusion that he is not gambling at all. Gambling is·a metaphor that George Eliot seems to have been fond of, for she places Gwendolen Harleth at a continental gaming table at the commencement of *Daniel Deronda*. It would seem to be part of the attempt to put an arbitrary value and often an arbitrary utility upon those objects and those people who have lost sight of Origins, whether it be Bulstrode's gambling "loan" to Lydgate upon administering Raffles' death, or Trumbull's acitivity at another raffle, where not merely value, but the identification of the object is a function of exchange:

"Now, ladies," said Mr. Trumbull, taking up one of the articles, "this tray contains a very recherchy lot—a *collection* of trifles for the drawing-room table—and trifles make the sum of human things—nothing more important than trifles—(yes, Mr. Ladislaw, yes, by-and-by)—but pass the tray round, Joseph— these bijoux must be examined, ladies. This I have in my hand is an ingenious contrivance—a sort of practical rebus I may call it: here, you see, it looks like an elegant heart-shaped box, portable— for the pocket; there, again, it becomes like a splendid double flower—an ornament for the table; and now"—Mr. Trumbull allowed the flower to fall alarmingly into strings of heart-shaped leaves—"a book of riddles! No less than five-hundred printed in beautiful red . . ."

(ch. 60, p. 653, italics mine)

The amount bid may not reflect the value of the object at all, but rather serves to create it, at least for the buyer.

Part of Trumbull's pitch consists of an attempt to convince his audience that a particular *objet d'art* inherits some secret of the old masters now lost forever—another way of saying that it is a fragment—or to otherwise lend history to the piece by positing a fictional past that will be revealed in the future:

> Suppose it should be discovered hereafter that a gem of art has been amongst us in this town, and nobody in Middlemarch awake to it.

(ch. 60, p. 656)

In urging Middlemarchers to bet on it, Trumbull is doing much the same as George Eliot's narrator did with regard to Lydgate: "He was at a starting-point which makes many a man's career a fine subject for betting . . ." (ch. 15, p. 178). The one upon whom we gamble tends to become a gambler in George Eliot when the starting-point is threatened or doubted. His career or the career of the object becomes vulnerable to numerous translations upon the recognition of discontinuity. A "text" of riddles that is itself a riddle is a sure emblem of that condition of sourcelessness.

The linguistic condition corresponding to this fluidity of enterprise would be gossip, that attempt by diverse mouths to approach an original truth which seems to recede into the distance. Although Casaubon had early in *Middlemarch* cautioned Dorothea against the "mirage of baseless opinion" (ch. 20, p. 233) as an excuse for prolonged research, the course of the novel makes abundantly clear that floating opinions—gossip—has a determining power that is remarkably efficient:

> News is often dispersed as thoughtlessly and effectively as that pollen which the bees carry off (having no idea how powdery they are) when they are buzzing in search of their particular nectar.

(ch. 59, p. 645)

In *Middlemarch* gossip always precedes the revelation of facts and is often a reasonable facsimile to such an extent that it has

140

the appearance of determining the facts. It is commentary and
conjecture most often disguising itself as an account of Origins:

> The statement was passed on until it had quite lost the stamp of
> inference, and was taken as information coming straight from
> Garth, so that even a diligent historian might have concluded
> Caleb to be the chief publisher of Bulstrode's misdemeanors.
>
> (ch. 71, p. 772)

It is surely part of that "power of generalising which gives men
so much the superiority in mistake over the dumb animals" (ch.
58, p. 638). The last quarter of the novel is almost entirely spent
in unravelling the relationship between gossip and the scandal
that envelopes first Bulstrode and then Lydgate as a consequence of Raffles' mysterious death. It is not the presence of an
Origin, but its very opposite, the absence of material Origin,
that promotes the linguistic "filler" that is gossip: "In this case
there was no material object to feed upon, but the eye of reason
saw a probability of mental sustenance in the shape of gossip"
(ch. 71, p. 769).

In this sense gossip represents a fundamental departure from
a consciousness fascinated with historical tributaries or within
the confines of the pigeon-holes, gossip is a notoriously elastic
meta-language which confuses creation and translation, in the
process arbitrarily locating its own centre. Rosamund is
shocked to realize that she has "married a man who had
become the centre of infamous suspicions" (ch. 75, p. 813).
Additionally, gossip would seem to achieve far more than the
Reform Bill in democratizing the increasingly mobile population of Middlemarch. Since any individual is free to make his
own additions or deletions from a "received" story without
incurring the fear of a single authorial responsibility, the elite
like Bulstrode can be levelled anonymously. In short, gossip is a
marvellous paradox: it is an authorless language which creates
its own public authority for the very reason that it can never be
more than a fragment. As such, its virulence serves as an
oblique commentary upon the work of all the *originators* in
Middlemarch, for the very form of the mode is tantamount to an
acknowledgement of its status as a corrupted text:

> Everbody liked better to conjecture how the thing was, than to
> know it; for conjecture soon became more confident than

knowledge, and had a more liberal allowance for the incompatible.

(ch. 71, p. 775)

Gossip can never have an archaeology, because it is an ever-growing consciousness, obsessively displacing absence. It has a life of its own, devoid of determinable beginning or ending. This language which assumes the status of a mass epic in *Middlemarch* is centreless in such a way that it resembles, not just a little, the Raffles who so suddenly appears out of the past. When asked to go to his home, the ill man replies that he cannot because he has no fixed location to call home. Like Raffles and the gamblers, the life of the gossip is the life of rootless "speculation", and hence without ending.

The transformation of a world permeated by what Comte called "the vain quest after absolutes"[11] into the antecedentless realm of systemic adaptation, the collapse of linear succession into the tangled skein of "circumstance", the expanded middle, leaves an impact upon consciousness and community. There arises the confrontation of a plurality of selves, more or less discontinuous, with a field of problems to be dealt with on an *ad hoc* basis. Perhaps this helps to account for the shift in narrative dimension within George Eliot's novel. The first four books, so characterized by the epical convention of high relief, gives way to the flattened plane that so many critics have noted—that shallowing of the third dimension, background, which transforms a frieze into a tapestry or a spider web. This marks a displacement, really, from the spaces shaped by a conviction in some uniqueness which is imagined to lie behind any *progressus* into a belief that any problem is one of translation, interpretation, or adaptation. And this latter activity involves the fluidity of fitting and trimming rather than the single-mindedness of questing or terminating. Perhaps Farebrother's comments are the most apropos, since his metaphor combines the shallowed possibilities of determination from any fixed point, but compensates by positing the possibility of some triumph of the therapeutic. Redemption suddenly does not require an Origin:[12]

"But, my dear Mrs. Casaubon," said Mr. Farebrother, smiling greatly at her ardour, "character is not cut in marble—it is not something solid and unalterable. It is something living and changing and may become diseased as our bodies do."

(ch. 72, p. 791)

This flatness gives an increasingly neutral aspect to character as well as moral prospect (vision). Rosamond Vincy behaves with a chill neutrality toward Lydgate, a phrase repeated several times. And when Will Ladislaw comes to collect his portfolio, for Dorothea "it was as if a crowd of indifferent objects had thrust them asunder" (ch. 62, p. 684). Everyday details produce the ennui that becomes part of the pathos of *Middlemarch*; the deeply etched channels that formerly led to some reservoir of truth or knowledge have been altered for Dorothea

... in the long valley of her life, which looked so flat and empty of way-marks, guidance would come as she walked along the road, and saw her fellow-passengers by the way.

(ch. 77, p. 830)

When life is no longer a natural sequence of events or an understood succession of descent, but rather an interpreted series, objects as well as people experience not only spatial and temporal discontinuity—the restlessness of all the commuters in the novel—but an internal schism. Lydgate perceives not one, but two selves, "that he was getting unlike his former self" (ch. 70, p. 766) at the same time that Bulstrode recognizes that a recovered Raffles would mean the re-existence of an old Bulstrode which he cannot face. The revelation of Ladislaw's "true" origin leads Mr Hawley to endow him with the physiology of a grafted hybrid, hopelessly divided:

A high-spirited young lady and a musical Polish patriot made a likely enough stock for him to spring from, but I should never have suspected a grafting of a Jew Pawnbroker. However, there is *no knowing what a mixture will turn out beforehand.*

(ch. 71, p. 773, italics mine)

This structural mirroring is George Eliot's way of suggesting that the deflection from one's given Origin produces a kind of schizoid split in personality. Early in the novel Casaubon had refused to acknowledge discontinuity, the likeness-in-difference that had separated his profile from that of Aquinas. Dorothea had similarly initially identified Will Ladislaw as a descendant from the source, the miniature that graced the walls at Lowick. Only later when, fearing that she may never see Will again, she offers to return the picture of his ancestor—only then, upon his refusal, is the historical internalized:

> "No; I don't mind about it. It is not very consoling to have one's own likeness. It would be more consoling if others wanted to have it."
>
> "I thought you would like to cherish her memory—I thought—" Dorothea broke off in an instant, her imagination suddenly warning her away from Aunt Julia's history—"you would surely like to have the miniature as a family memorial."
>
> "Why should I have that, when I have nothing else! A man with only a portmanteau for his stowage must keep his memorials in his head."
>
> (ch. 54, p. 588)

The "two-penny mirror's" reflection of some higher truth represents a misunderstanding of human existence. Dorothea must come to accept Will for what he is rather than seek to memorialize his Origin. Discontinuity is real for Will, breachable to Dorothea. Whereas she sees historical lineage, he sees only the pictorial reflection symbolizing a discontinuity that makes him an *isolato*. The emblematic episode which illustrates the necessity to acknowledge the fragmentation at the core of things occurs on the hustings during Brooke's abortive campaign. When he confronts his own echo (in the form of an effigy hung by the opposition camp) alternately expanding and contracting his speech, much in the manner of gossip, he loses the sense of a unique self and with it, the politician's motivation.

Hence, the latter two books of *Middlemarch* present the reader with a changed moral universe, partially in consequence of this alteration in the status of the Origin. For it is not merely that Lydgate's culpability remains forever indeterminate, but that even Bulstrode's role in Raffles' death is the role of the circuitous, unwilling criminal who transgresses through surrogates. His crime is one of omission rather than commission, since he simply fails to give all the details of the treatment to the attending housekeeper. Evidence is no longer to be taken as an accumulation of signs which lead to some act in the past, as it had been for Casaubon's reading of mythic traces, but rather that the evidence may well be an absence. The disappearance of the logocentric universe means, to pun upon the increasing entanglements of "circumstances", that blame is largely *circumstantial*. It represents a shift from a world illuminated by the *a priori* to a world where the determinations and judgements are always part of the greying of the *de facto*, "a pale shade of bribery which is sometimes called prosperity" (ch. 76, pp. 825-26). In one sense such a realm is one of infinite potential: it is "possible that Bulstrode was innocent of criminal intention"; "possible that he had nothing to do with [the housekeeper's] disobedience" (ch. 76); possible that Bulstrode's *de facto* cheque was not intended as a bribe. Potentiality seems to expand in direct ratio to the diminishment of externally identifiable responsibility—for anything. Casaubon had felt entirely responsible for his ward, Will Ladislaw; his is the responsibility of a relationship "not thereby annulled in [its] character of determining antecedents" (ch. 37, p. 406), even after Will has visited Dorothea in his own absence. But, by the end of *Middlemarch*, beyond the crisis of the determining antecedent, direct responsibility or motive is difficult to locate and identify. And one index of this disappearance of individual motive, causality, and responsibility is the proliferation of agents, people whose sole function is that of filling the void between discontinuous groups, thereby softening authority. These folk, like the housekeeper who tends Raffles in his last illness or Bulstrode's patient wife who is enlisted (as a surrogate for Bulstrode) to give her nephew the laundered money that is his by right, exist, like the Dorothea on errand to Rosamond Vincy, as go-betweens. They create the possibility of deniability in those whom they represent, part of the transactional, therapeutic activity that deflects intentionality from a single identifiable source.

All of this may be merely an extension of that shift by which private responsibility became enlarged and flattened during the Victorian period, becoming part of the infamous General Will, the abstraction of presumed consensus. By the novel's end, the great plans for the hospital which was to be financed by private subscription are being assumed by the municipal authority and now include a projected cemetery, a preparation for contingencies (endings) rather than the research into beginnings to which Lydgate had early pledged himself. And the diseases of the last chapters—the threat of cholera from Danzig or the gout in whose attendance Lydgate culminates his sad career—are illnesses whose origins are vague by virtue of being either exotic or unknown. One is an illness of the very poor, the other, of the very rich. And Will Ladislaw, who had previously renounced any interest in the "sources of the Nile", becomes intrigued, as a penultimate scheme prior to standing for Parliament, in colonization, a tacit admission of public involvement in discontinuity—the "likeness-in-difference" of the would-be colonial administrator. It is an ironic comment upon Dorothea's realization that reform is made difficult when "everything seems like going on a mission to people whose language I don't know" (ch. 3, p. 51). The notion of some essential or at least historically primary language like Hebrew or Greek, gives way progressively in *Middlemarch* · to a proliferation of discontinuous, often unique, languages that must be understood on their own terms: gossip; the interchangeable adjectives of the auctioneer; the redundantly legalistic language of wills; the babbling rhetoric of poor Brooke on the campaign trail; Hawley's "awful language"; and finally, the metonymic language of the child or the childish. None are corrupt because none are pure.[13]

George Eliot's novel itself participates in the same displacement from Origins which her characters undergo. In the supplementary chapter beyond the ending, appropriately entitled "Finale", her narrator assents to the entirely arbitrary distinctions between the limits that originate and those that terminate: "Every limit is a beginning as well as an ending" ("Finale", p. 890). In so recognizing the network of conditional relationships as opposed to the narrow lineage of historically ordered descent, she echoes the effusive Mrs Cadwallader who, in explaining the woes of the clergyman's wife, listened to her husband's sermons backwards—first the ending, then the middle, and finally, the beginning, because she "couldn't have the end without them" (ch. 34, p. 359). Origins are only pragmatic, as Will Ladislaw realizes early on. In his debate with Lydgate, the doctor had insisted that Ladislaw's writings for the *Pioneer* constituted a betrayal, because they lead people to believe that society can be healed by the political process. Ladislaw's "text", as he calls it, has as its objective only the balancing of claims:

> That's very fine, my dear fellow. But your cure must begin somewhere, and put it that a thousand things which debase a population can never be reformed without this particular reform to begin with . . .
>
> (ch. 46, p. 506)

Ladislaw is here distinguishing, like George Eliot in the opening sentence of the "Finale", between an Origin and a beginning, between some whole sacred source, and an arbitrary limit whose function is only denotative.

The growing good of the world comes to be dependent not upon those determining antecedents, which turn out to be functional rather than real, but on "unhistoric acts" and "unvisited tombs". The attempt to define Lydgate's "fair unknown", the "primitive tissue", is transformed into an extention of the therapeutic, the business of obligatory servicing. Fred Vincy produces a sort of Victorian do-it-yourself book on the *Cultivation of Green Crops and the Economy of Cattle-Feeding* while his wife *translates* and *adapts* one of the ancients, Plutarch, into a "little book for boys", not exactly Casaubon's *magnum opus*, but a document of sorts. And the quest for some single, uncorrupted author(ity) at the heart of the matter seems superfluous to Middlemarchers who cannot decide whether the author is Fred or Mary:

> In this way it was made clear that Middlemarch had never been deceived, and there was no need to praise anybody for writing a book, since it was always done by somebody else.
>
> ("Finale", p. 891)

Motivation, responsibility for good or evil, is relativized by the absence at the Origin, And that absence creates, in place of the attempt to clarify that which came before, a systemically ordered mode of exchange. Will and Dorothea are "bound to each other by a love stronger than any impulses which could have marred it" and Will is returned to Parliament by a "constituency who paid his expenses" (Finale", p. 894), suggesting that the business of life involves emotional and political balancing acts rather than reform—an emphasis upon

147

the "bottom line" mentality of the business statement rather than the martyred quest for some antecedent unity. The conclusion of the novel is filled with images of people in motion: Will commutes from London; the two sisters visit one another's children with increasing frequency; and the community scurries about its business. All, by the end of the novel, are commuters, participants in a decentred universe, where, as George Eliot would have it in her "Prelude", people are *"dispersed* among hindrances, instead of *centering* in some long-recognizable deed". It is a world no longer characterized by pigeon-holes of containment or "plans" for cottages, but rather by socially regulated locomotion.

In George Eliot's "Finale", which matches other conclusions in Middlemarch in its arbitrary, flat, guide-book tone,[14] gambling has been institutionalized in Lydgate's heavy life insurance policy which, somewhat fortuitously, "makes" Rosamond. Gossip no longer indicts or motivates, but indulges itself in the leisure of *de facto* negative prescriptions: "she ought not to have married Will Ladislaw" ("Finale", p. 894). The passive voice dominates our Endings, detached as they are from the grounding of a definable sacred. For the point, made best by Farebrother, is that the sacred is whatever we will it to be: "he had just set up a pair of beautiful goats to be pets of the village *in general,* and to walk at large as sacred animals" (ch. 80, p. 843, italics mine). Whether it be umbrella rings or goats for children, objects have a potentiality no longer determined by antecedents. The evidence suggests that the sacred is not to be defined by a process analogous to self-consciousness in its devotion to recovery, but rather that its outlet is transitive. One of the most symbolic scenes in the novel occurs when Celia refuses to mourn the deceased Casaubon, directing her thoughts toward a different "orientalist", her child.

> ". . . We should not grieve, should we, baby?" said Celia confidentially to that unconscious centre and poise of the world, who had the most remarkable fists all complete even to his nails, and hair enough, really when you took his cap off, to make—you didn't know what:—in short, he was Bouddha in a Western form.
> (ch. 50, p. 533)

In a world where Casaubon's "remote source of knowledge",

Lydgate's "primary tissue", and Bulstrode's "sacred accountability", to borrow their respective nomenclature of Origins, no longer have primacy, the centre is not self-consciousness, but the unconscious and the unhistoric—the child. And the children who emerge as the foci of their parents' communities in the twilight of *Middlemarch*, like George Eliot's own narrative "Finale" itself, create their own arbitrarily fictional, indeterminate Endings—the coda to our Origin-bound, egoistic epics.

NOTES

In this essay all citations from *Middlemarch* are taken from the Penguin Edition, edited by the late W.J. Harvey (Harmondsworth, 1965).

I wish to acknowledge the influence of Edward Said, *Beginnings* (New York, 1974). Although his "origin" differs from mine, there are occasionally similar manifestations upon consciousness. I also wish to acknowledge the helpful conversation and gentle corrections of my colleague, Dr Arthur Lindley.

1 For a discussion of the significance of Naumann's appearance in *Middlemarch*, see Hugh Witemeyer, "George Eliot, Naumann, and the Nazarenes", *VS* 18 (1974), 145-58. Witemeyer correctly concludes that the Nazarenes represent yet another of those attempts at recovery and restoration, in this case the retrieval of medieval Christian iconography. Like Casaubon's retrograde research, the Nazarenes represent a misplaced historicism. Additionally, in terms of my own argument, the presence of the group of painters in Rome is part of George Eliot's epic dimensionality, with their emphasis upon large canvases of frieze-like illumination and perspective.

2 J. Hillis Miller, *The Form of Victorian Fiction* (Notre Dame and London, 1968), pp. 29-50.

3 Reva Stump, *Movement and Vision in George Eliot's Novels* (Seattle, 1959).

4 See Said, pp. 197-220 for an excellent discussion of the way in which a "text" comes to have a life of its own, with the prestige of necessary preservation. A preserved or reconstructed "text" offers an obstruction to on-going research, often creating its own gaps and postponements as part of a displacing function.

5 W. J. Harvey, "The Intellectual Background of the Novel" in *Middlemarch; Critical Approaches to the Novel*, edited by Barbara Hardy (London, 1967), pp. 34-5. See also the excellent essay by Janet Burstein, "Victorian Mythography and the Progress of the Intellect", *VS* 18 (1975), pp. 309-24.

6 This shift in spatial perspective in the novel involves a gradual diminishment of contrast metaphorized as a sort of levelling, not only

between omniscient and participatory narrators or between a crepe-clad Dorothea and a Dorothea no longer in mourning, but between a long view of events and a view more discontinuous because it is necessarily limited. The numerous miniatures on the walls at Lowick or Fred Vincy's "aerial perspective" on his future prior to the probating of Featherstone's will, surely belong to this epical sweep by which so many characters see the world prior to the crisis of history.

7 Claude Levi-Strauss, *The Savage Mind* (Chicago, 1962), pp. 217-44.

8 *Ibid.*, p. 32. Farebrother's enjoyment of games in Middlemarch places him in direct opposition to the various forms of mythography. For Levi-Strauss, games have a *disjunctive* effect, since they end in the establishment of a sense of difference (winners and losers) between teams or players, whereas myths *conjoin* by bringing together previously discontinuous members, say, initiates and uninitiates.

9 J. Hillis Miller, "Narrative and History", *ELH*, 41 (1974), pp. 455-73. For Miller, the image of the tapestry functions in the same way as my labyrinth insofar as both structures enable the participant to create his own "centre".

10 Edmund Bergler, *The Psychology of Gambling* (New York, 1970 edition), p. 15-32. So far as I am aware, the only scholar to mention gambling in the context of George Eliot's novels is Calvin Bedient, *Architects of the Self: George Eliot, D.H. Lawrence, and E.M. Forster* (Berkeley, 1972), p. 64, who uses the word to talk of an aspect of Eliot's approach to character development and then curiously drops the idea.

11 The "vain quest after absolutes" of which the notion of an Origin was Comte's favourite was to be replaced in the positivist era by a study of the laws of phenomena of which "their invariable relations of succession and resemblance" were to attract the generalists' attention. See the "Introduction" to *August Comte and Positivism*, edited by Gertrud Lenzer (New York, 1975), xxxv.

12 For Philip Rieff in *The Triumph of the Therapeutic* (London, 1966) this ability to maintain a kind of neutrality among various choices is possible only when the notion of a single source for all difficulties abates. Myths become meliorative independently of the impulse toward restoration.

13 Although space does not allow a full discussion of the meanings which accrue to language in the course of *Middlemarch*, one of the things which prevents Ladislaw from being dominated by some mythic antecedent is the ease with which he converts (translates) aesthetic theories to discontinuous languages. It is not merely that "art is an old language" (ch. 21, p. 238), as he tells Dorothea, but that it is also a vague language, having a metaphoric quality which gives it more potential than does line (ch. 19, p. 222). Such is part of the generalising power, the "wideness" of which Naumann complains. For George Eliot's somewhat parallel views see "The Natural History of German Life" (1856), in *Essays of George Eliot*, edited by Thomas Pinney (New York, 1963), p. 288.

14 Actually, the "Finale" narratively constitutes a second Ending, paralleling the two Origins—chronological and fictional—which results

from the displacement in time of the "beginning" of *Middlemarch*. The "revision" in the lives of the main characters has its echo in a kind of structural and narrative revision that is the "Finale". Perhaps no scholar of the Victorian period understands the metaphysics of multiple (i.e. arbitrary) Origins and Endings better than John Fowles who has recently revised the Ending of *The French Lieutenant's Woman*.

8

The Hero as Dilettante: *Middlemarch* and *Nostromo*

by GEORGE LEVINE

The distance between George Eliot's *Middlemarch* and Joseph Conrad's *Nostromo* is by no means an absolute. They are recognizably part of a continuous literary tradition and echo each other in startling ways. Seen together, they can suggest how the conventions of Victorian realism and of the moral aesthetic were transformed into the materials of modernism. The most ambitious enterprises of their creators, separated by thirty-two years, they are both encyclopaedic imaginative articulations of a late-century vision in which the vacuum created by a dying religion was being filled by a mythology of science. They represent different responses to a scepticism that, beginning as a condition for tough-minded empirical pursuit of scientific truth, was moving toward subversion of the idea of "truth" itself. Science was becoming solipsism; truth, a property of language not nature, was disappearing, like God, into a monstrous and impenetrable silence.

The case for seeing these books as not comparable is made most lucidly by Edward Said. (Although his reference is actually to *War and Peace*, his arguments are surely meant for books like *Middlemarch*, also.) His three main reasons are, first, "*Nostromo* aspires to no authority on matters of history and sociology"; second, it does not "create a normative world that resembles our own"; and third, it is "assuredly not the product of a great established literature."[1] But "authority" is as important and (almost) as problematic in *Middlemarch* as it is in *Nostromo*. Unless we take the book as a completed assertion rather than as

152

a process, and disregard the tortuous narrative, it is inaccurate to claim that *Nostromo* does not "aspire" to authority, to locate a decisive voice. No doubt the aspiration fails, but the experience of it is central to the book.

Middlemarch, moreover, under the scrutiny to which modernist critics subject it,[2] begins to look unstable and "unauthoritative". Like *Nostromo* it is preoccupied with locating a vantage point that will make its complex of relationships coherent. Relationships turn out to be extremely difficult to define precisely without something like the artificial conditions of scientific experiment, with microscopes, shifts of perspective, controls. But scientific control is both elusive and artificial, and for the text to achieve authority it must leap beyond the calculable and controllable.

The distinction between the two texts is further blurred by the idea of the "normative". Although the very title of *Middlemarch* suggests a world that "resembles our own", the book encompasses an extreme, almost Dantean, imagination of the world, as the surface of realism is informed by a mythic energy. Midway in our life's journey, we descend into a kind of hell; the "normative" world turns out to be filled with vampiric relations, Faustian overreachers, voices from beyond the grave.[3] The conventions that govern the geographically remote world of Costaguana are those of folk tales or romantic adventures, but the novel reasserts the normative in the midst of extremes: it builds like *Middlemarch*, a recognizable community within which dwell capitalists, industrialists, petty officials, hostelers, dockworkers, journalists, traders, and peasants. And if we expect extremes under *Nostromo*'s tropical sun, it comes as a shock, thinking back on *Middlemarch*, how much violence, psychological and physical, is incorporated in that little world: murders, riots, blackmail and briberies, political rhetoric, deaths. Moreover, at a moral centre of both books there is an inescapable analogy between Charles Gould, making his silver bear the burden of the ideal as he succumbs to its material power, and Nicholas Bulstrode, justifying his wealth by Providence, and killing to preserve it.

There are enough such possible parallels to suggest a similarity in the raw materials of these two novels. Both are large historical fictions that attempt to create entire societies and—in the established tradition of Walter Scott that their authors knew well—to read the fates of characters in the context of larger social and national movements from which they cannot withdraw. Both are preoccupied not only with Said's "authority" in personal, political, and literary senses, but with the relation among "feeling", idea, and action, with the way scepticism impedes action but is a condition of intelligent action. As multiple perspectives layer and qualify each experience, history—even in *Middlemarch*[4]—seems strangely unprogressive and nonchronological. In *Middlemarch*, the universe becomes a "tempting range of relevancies",[5] full of connections too subtle for ordinary consciousness. As her husband, G. H. Lewes, was writing at roughly the same time: "Every Real is the complex of so many relations, a conjunction of so many sensations, that to know one Real thoroughly could only be possible through an institution embracing the universe."[6] A struggle for such an intuition seems to mark the achronology of *Nostromo*, where true connections remain yet more obscure.

I am not discussing similarity in order to argue identity. Nor am I claiming any direct influence (though it would be surprising if Conrad had not read *Middlemarch*).[7] Literary history is a complex of continuities and discontinuities, rarely more so than in the implicit history that connects and disconnects these two novels. The facile compartmentalization of "modern" and "old-fashioned" cannot suffice. Recent emphasis in criticism on originality, newness, or belatedness, has its uses, and it is particularly useful to imagine, as Said's analysis requires, the absoluteness of all beginnings: "with regard to what precedes it, a beginning represents . . . a discontinuity" (Said, p. 35). But discontinuity is only comprehensible in terms of some posited continuity.

Middlemarch, for example, represents a continuity: it marks, as Henry James put it, "a limit to the development of the old-fashioned novel".[8] But it is also a beginning, particularly of the self-conscious attempt to imagine a secular-scientific community in a world cut off from traditional continuities implied by earlier fictions. Conversely, *Nostromo* is impelled by an explanatory energy to overcome the discontinuities of its style. Why, otherwise, are there so many attempts to make clear when each event took place (e.g., "rather more than a year later"; "a year and a half later."[9])? Why do we return to various actions to fill out our sense of what actually happened, as with the wonderful chapter describing Decoud's suicide, an event about which the primary fact is its absolute solitude? Who but a desperately explaining narrator could know or let us know about it? One aspect of *Nostromo*'s narrative is a desperate effort to make itself continuous with the tradition to which *Middlemarch* is so closely allied, and from which it also separates itself.

1

The point where the problem of discontinuity and relationship and validation of authority most sharply focus is in the intersection of the narratives dealing with Will Ladislaw and Martin Decoud. The perspective of analogy once suggest-ed, the *dramatis personae* of both novels begin to blend into each other, as though Conrad had taken George Eliot's raw material and given Mr Brooke—or his intellectual counterpart, Captain Mitchell—the responsibility of the narration. Charles Gould, a Bulstrodian idealizer of wealth in one aspect, becomes, in his relation to Emilia, a Casaubon in relation to Dorothea: monomaniacal, cold, tended to by a self-sacrificing wife who accepts his psychological betrayal of her. Emilia certainly occupies a Dorothea-like position in the novel, but Dorothea's qualities are manifest also in Antonia Avellanos, whose ineffectual father—like Dorothea's inadequately avuncular Mr Brooke—[10] takes direction of a political news-paper.

As a preliminary example of how such analogies might illuminate each other, we can take the case of Charles Gould. His idea of making the mine a means to a generous and humane order in Costaguana, incorporates with all their moral and intellectual ambiguities, the large idealisms of Lydgate and Casaubon, whose ambitions have always been seen to reflect each other. But the Gould enterprise suddenly juxtaposes these with Bulstrode's; we see that like him, the others are imposing ideal structures on resistant materials. How far is the ideal consonant with the facts of experience? Adequate explanation for all three becomes a means to power. And as with Gould, all three fail because of inadequate relations with women, whose explanations imply another relation to power. (All of these narrations point to the larger problem of fiction's explanatory powers, and the possibility of the consolation of meaning for the loss of a beneficent God.)

In achieving a larger-than-life national ambition, Gould makes manifest the very large implications of the ironically treated protagonists of *Middlemarch*. Charles Gould is given the "medium" of which Dorothea Brooke is, among the provinces, deprived, and in it is allowed the scope of "an epic life" (*M*, p. 3). Yet his reform of a nation, within the scope of epic or romance traditions, is not free of bitter ironies. Here, too, sustaining an ideal enterprise against the compromising demands of circumstance is virtually impossible. Although *Nostromo* sets the problem against a nature "placid" and ruggedly indestructible, Gould is impeded as much by the conditions of a restricting society as is Lydgate or Bulstrode.

The problem of compromise in an ideal pursuit will return in Ladislaw's narrative, but here we can note that the constructed, civilized selves of Lydgate and Casaubon are based in biological (i.e., "natural") drives and limitations that turn out to be more significant than their drives to order. The natural, too, imposes itself on Gould—overtly in the mountainside he penetrates with more passion than he can spare for Emilia (note, too, how all the marriages remain childless). These characters all imagine that they possess the intelligence to make an idea operate on society or in nature. They suffer from the fantasy of control and are ultimately dominated by materials beyond any "idea". The knowledge required for a full mediation between external facts and man's capacity to impose (or discover) order must belong to other sorts of ambition.

Conrad and George Eliot explore the possibilities of such knowledge in the characters of the less heroic Decoud and Ladislaw. I want to examine their relation to this problem with the same sort of achronological playing back and forth between texts as I have used with Charles Gould and his analogues. Clearly without the concentrated ambitions of these other characters, Decoud and Ladislaw come much closer to representing the diffuseness and complexities of the texts they inhabit. They are aliens in their worlds who, by some perverse workings of a medium resistant to ideals, achieve what can be achieved.

Both Ladislaw and Decoud are described as dilettantes, and they are also, in Matthew Arnold's sense of the word, too, "aliens". Like the young Arnold, who played the role of dilettante-dandy and surprised even his family with the seriousness of his poetry, they allow playfulness and cynicism to keep them disengaged from the demands of social and political life. In both cases, the triviality of their lives overlays a gravity they must ultimately face. Decoud's sense of friendship, for instance, means to him " the frank unreserve, as before another human being, of thought and sensations; all the objectless and necessary sincerity of one's innermost life trying to react upon the profound sympathies of another existence"(*N*, p. 191). Ladislaw is slighter than Decoud, and as Henry James says, there is evidence of too great an indulgence and predisposition toward him on George Eliot's part so that, while she does indeed treat his lightness ironically, "the impression once given that he is a *dilettante* is never properly removed." But James too recognizes that in George Eliot's conception, Ladislaw is meant to show "a large capacity for gravity" (James, p. 263).

Whatever seriousness may be discovered, however, the point of their entrances into their novels is their diffuseness and disengagement. Both of elaborately mixed blood, they find themselves drawn into political journalism by accident. Decoud "had studied law, had dabbled in literature, had hoped now and then in moments of exaltation to become a poet." To "pass the time", he had "condescended to write articles on European affairs for the *Semenario*" (*N*, p. 134). Ladislaw is as aimless, with a fine "sense of the ludicrous". Just back from Heidelberg, he now, as Mr Casaubon accurately and contemptuously describes him, "wants to go abroad again without any special object, save the vague purpose of what he calls culture, preparation for he knows not what. He declines to choose a profession" (p. 59).

Conrad's rhetoric about Decoud is hostile; George Eliot's about Ladislaw is only affectionately diminishing. "As a matter of fact," says Conrad, Decoud was an "idle boulevardier", and his "cosmopolitanism" was "in reality a mere barren indifferentism posing as intellectual superiority" (N, p.134). George Eliot, like her Dorothea, is more indulgent than Conrad; but as narrator she is far more negative than Dorothea. Dorothea says of Will before she really knows him that people such as he "may seem idle and weak because they are growing. We should be very patient with each other" (M, p. 61). "Will", remarks the narrator with an irony not far from Casaubon's, "had declined to fix on any more precise destination than the entire area of Europe. Genius, he held, is necessarily intolerant of fetters" (M, p. 61). Described as someone who had experimented with everything from opium to lobster, Will is sharply placid: "Nothing greatly original had resulted from these measures." And with an irony usually reserved in George Eliot for the egotists who will destroy themselves or others, she notes that he had "a generous reliance on the intentions of the universe with regard to himself. He held that reliance to be a mark of genius" (M, p. 61).

Although Ladislaw's cynicism is often a youthful failure of self-understanding, while Decoud's is a conscious construction, both characters fit Hillis Miller's description of the victim of what Arnold called "the modern spirit": "forced to conduct oneself according to inherited institutions, beliefs, laws, and customs which no longer seem at all appropriate to actual conditions, [in] doubt of the possibility of ever finding the proper form of life."[11] Refusing to take life seriously, Decoud and Ladislaw manouevre into a better position to understand the irrationality of life's demands and the possibilities of a satisfying way of being. To achieve this understanding is the condition for any meaningful action; such understanding requires a complex sensibility. Ladislaw, of course, is regularly described as Shelleyan (with its implications both of rebelliousness and sensibility), and Decoud lives and dies "faithful to the end to the truth of his own sensations" (N, p. 194).

In Victorian science, the more complex and various the organism, the "higher" and the more implicated it is with other organisms. For George Eliot, as for Lewes, the self only exists when the biological organism is part of a social organism.[12] Thus Decoud and Ladislaw cannot remain disengaged, and eventually pay the price of life. The very complexity of their sensibilities guarantees engagement; and the way they are enticed into life constitutes the central paradox of their positions in the novels. The similarities in the narratives describing this progress is striking. Decoud is invited by Don Jose Avellanos to "take the direction of a newspaper that would 'voice the aspirations of the province'" (*N*, p. 139). Decoud comes to Costaguana, but, as his sister says, only because "you want to see Antonia" (*N*, p. 137); for the sake of remaining he writes trashy political rhetoric in a journal called *Porvenir* (The Future). Ladislaw is invited by Mr Brooke because "the political horizon was expanding" and Ladislaw had the power "to put ideas into form", and the journal he has purchased might "clear the pathway for a new candidate" (*M*, p. 215). "Why not?" Will asks himself, "and he studied the political situation with as ardent an interest as he had ever given to metres or medievalism" (*M*, p. 337). Ladislaw remains in Middlemarch to be near Dorothea. He writes trashy political rhetoric (Brooke calls him another "Burke") in a journal called the *Pioneer*. Both characters find themselves, then, in a losing political cause; yet we are meant to believe that Ladislaw goes on to serious politics, and that Decoud becomes a founder of the nation of Sulaco.

Sexual energies really create their vocations. This sort of narrative, apparently as traditional as Don Quixote's quest for Dulcinea, is assimilated here into the tradition of evolutionary thought. Life draws Decoud to Antonia as it had drawn Lydgate to Rosamond. Moreover, Decoud carefully distinguishes, in what he calls his "sane Materialism", between the "friendship" he can feel for his sister, and the sexual attraction he has to Antonia (*N*, p. 191). Seeing his situation with a cynical-scientific detachment, he thinks of his preoccupation with Antonia as "a ridiculous fatality" (*N*, p. 137).

In that their most meaningful actions are accidents of sexual relations, neither of these strange semi-heroes seems to live by an authentic principle of moral life, or with a coherent imagination of experience. For both, the private and public seem gratuitously related, and the authority for the connection rests with a woman whose intensity of engagement mocks the facile scribbling of the men. Antonia is solemnly committed to the nation implicitly mocked in Decoud's excessive support for its "reform" government. Dorothea is humanitarian rather than politician and doesn't believe in political reform before one has done one's best to make life better for those to whom one is immediately responsible.

The couples thus enact a clash between intelligence and feeling that both texts attempt to reconcile, and this clash is intrinsic to the world that the myths of contemporary science was opening to them. The men are, in the texts, "completed" by women whose intensity of feeling requires action. In George Eliot's world, "Feeling is a sort of Knowledge."[13] In Lewes's more systematic epistemology, feeling *is* knowledge—the source of all that can be known. But Antonia and Dorothea not only evoke feeling, they imagine the feeling of others and thus cannot be satisfied without relieving pain. Dorothea's obsession with this becomes something of an affectionate joke. But Ladislaw is infected by feeling and transforms himself from dilettante to politician, "an ardent public man". Yet the intelligence that holds the men aloof at the start returns in the voice of the narrator herself, whose "masculine" intelligence reminds us that Ladislaw's cause, Reform, had, forty years later, made little difference in the quality of life in the land.

The narrator's irony in *Middlemarch* is Antonia's story in *Nostromo*. Like Dorothea, she cannot bear to "abandon" her countrymen, "groaning under oppression" (*N*, p. 418). Having seduced Decoud into morality and feeling ("I have erected my passions into duties," he thinks [*N*, p. 409]), she becomes his antagonist after his death. To help those Costaguanans suffering under oppression, she proposes the reunification of Sulaco with Costaguana: "I am convinced that this was from the first poor Martin's intention" (*N*, p. 418). Under the pressure of feeling, she transforms Decoud's text. As he was forced to engagement in life, so—with the sanction of Antonia's feeling—Sulaco, the artificially detached, will be re-engaged in the country from which Decoud had separated it.

But the ironies in these women's relation to the men they complete do not work toward satire; rather, they enact what has been called the "cosmic joke"[14]—the ironic disparity between humans and the world they inhabit. The disaster that issues from Decoud's relation to Antonia implies the impossibility of validating ideas through action, of moving coherently from observation to action, from thought to feeling. Yet the movement redeems Decoud—for a moment at least—from the intensely hostile rhetoric of the narrator. We learn that Decoud adopts as a disguise of genuine feeling what was, until his return to Antonia, his true being. In Costaguana, Decoud "can no longer dismiss their tragic comedy with the expression, 'Quelle farce!'" (*N*, p. 153): "He was surprised at his own sensitiveness." At last, to defend himself from the pain to which his "infatuation" for Antonia was exposing him, "He soothed himself by saying he was not a patriot, but a lover" (*N*, p. 153). Decoud will later think that the word "patriot" "had no sense for cultured minds, to whom the narrowness of every belief is odious" (*N*, p. 162). While the narrative seems to endorse Decoud's attitude toward politics and belief because it is confirmed by events, he finally acts as though he were a patriot (is outraged by the weakness of the council determining to surrender to Montero), and he is taken for one by Sulacan society.

2

The complication here is analogous to the insight of George Eliot that the more sensitive is always defeated by the less; and this suggests that we need to consider more extensively the nature of the "sensitiveness" that comes upon Decoud as a surprise. The sensitive literally sense most and will therefore be most apt to see the complexities that might impede action. To adopt a "theory", an idea, a "maxim", is to impose an ideal structure that must radically distort reality. But at the same time every idea must be corrupted and "lose its 'virtue' the moment it descends from its solitary throne to work its will among the people."[15]

Belief is indispensable to human existence. Here we are in the presence of the central Conradian paradox that makes him so available to modernist reading, that one cannot live without illusions as one cannot live with them. George Eliot's world comes close to anticipating this paradox, for the narrator's wisdom extends beyond the deliberately limited vision of her most ideal characters. It is perhaps because the narrator knows too much that George Eliot sets her fictions back at least a generation, to a time when it remains possible not to know, when one might be "sensitive" and not impeded.

Ladislaw, in any case, is too alert to believe that an absolute can be embodied in action. He, like Decoud, argues against a "theory of political purity" (*N*, p. 158). Like Decoud, he argues for action knowing the inadequacy of the act: are we "to try for nothing till we find immaculate men to work with?" (*M*, p. 341). Here, Ladislaw battles against one of Middlemarch's idealists, Lydgate, one who is entrapped in the "small solicitation of circumstance" and driven from his idea. But Ladislaw, like the realist novelist, asserts the complicating energies of a "mixed" reality as he attempts to change it, through language, which is the medium of the ideal.

As Decoud and Ladislaw are enmeshed in compromise and the ideal at the same time, they are allied most closely with their creators. Ian Watt has pointed out that Decoud's motive in writing to his sister before he embarks with Nostromo on the lighter is "one of the two main personal motives behind Conrad's writing in general": "a desire to leave a correct impression of the feelings, like a light by which the action may be seen when personality is gone, gone where no light of investigation can ever reach the truth which every death takes out of the world."[16] Decoud is one of the most obviously autobiographical figures in all of Conrad, more clearly so because of the extreme distance from which the narrator tries to see him. As Gustav Morf suggests, Decoud is "nothing less than the exact picture of what Conrad thought would happen to him if he returned to his native country."[17] This can be taken as another way of saying that Decoud tests the novelist's sense of what happens when the novelist, instead of writing about experience, lives it. Decoud commits suicide.

The autobiographical aspect of Decoud is underlined in a letter of Conrad's:

> If one looks at life in its true aspect then everything loses much of its unpleasant importance and the atmosphere becomes cleared of what are only unimportant mists that drift past in imposing shapes. When once the truth is grasped that one's own personality is only a ridiculous masquerade of something hopelessly unknown the attainment of serenity is not very far off.[18]

Royal Roussel says that this attitude underlies "the ironical stance of Decoud in *Nostromo*".[19] But this detachment is also condemned by the fiction, and it implies the other side of Conrad: the very Victorian passion for "solidarity", as he calls it in the Preface to *The Nigger of the "Narcissus"*.[20] Decoud's death results from too great a fidelity in his own sensations, from absence of faith during sensuous deprivation, and from solitude; his life acquires meaning only through "language", friendship, the expression of feelings to another—through the novelist's art.

Conrad's engagement with Decoud is paralleled by George Eliot's with Ladislaw. "The author," says Henry James wickedly, "is evidently very fond of him" (James, p. 262). Speculation has variously turned him into G. H. Lewes and, more recently, Johnny Cross.[21] But the major point is that he carries a heavier burden of authority than his lightweight dilettanteism would seem to justify. He represents an aspect of George Eliot that appears no more often in her actual letters than the spokesman for solidarity appears in Conrad's. Ladislaw has precisely the qualities necessary for the novelist, except that he too is drawn into experience.

His sensitivity, however ironically treated, becomes the precondition for genuine art or genuine action. In a famous passage, in which he responds to Dorothea's question, will you "be a poet?" his answer is accurate in a way the rest of the text endorses:

> That depends. To be a poet is to have a soul so quick to discern that no shade of quality escapes it, and so quick to feel, that discernment is but a hand playing with finely-ordered variety on the chords of emotion—a soul in which knowledge passes instantaneously into feeling, and feeling flashes back as a new organ of knowledge.
>
> (*M*, p. 166)

"But you leave out the poems," Dorothea replies, apparently undercutting Will's Paterian intensity. But not really. The implicit criticism of Ladislaw here is similar to that of Decoud: his ideas do not issue in action. But neither do the ideas of the novelist, except in the action of writing. And the quickness of discernment to which Ladislaw aspires might make action based on feeling compatible with intelligence—as it does with Dorothea in her relations to Rosamond and Lydgate. Through Will and Dorothea, *Middlemarch* as a text aspires toward the possibility of this sort of continuity, despite the likelihood that it will be trapped in the dualism of aesthetic versus moral that leads, in Conrad's world, from feeling into despair.

There is other evidence of the narrator's endorsement of elements in Ladislaw that might seem frivolously light. A few pages earlier, the narrator had told us how much easier it was for Dorothea to dream of devotion to Casaubon than "to conceive with that distinctness which is no longer reflection but feeling—an idea wrought back to the directness of sense, like the solidity of objects—that he had an equivalent centre of self, whence the lights and shadows must always fall with a certain difference."[22]Moreover, this power to shift perspectives is one of the qualities that accompanies Will's lightness: "Will, too, was made of very impressible stuff. The bow of a violin drawn near him cleverly, would at one stroke change the aspect of the world for him, and his point of view shifted as easily as his mood" (*M*, p. 284).

Will here foreshadows the more solemn Daniel Deronda whose almost Christlike selflessness threatens to issue into Decoudian aimlessness. Deronda's sensibility is almost paralytic: "His imagination had so wrought itself to the habit of seeing things as they probably appeared to others, that a strong partisanship, unless it were against an immediate oppression, had become an insincerity for him."[23] As for Decoud, a strong "belief" is invalidated by the nuanced particularities sensed by a poet's, or novelist's, imagination.

The distance between George Eliot's moralism and Pater's aestheticism shrinks to nothing here, where we find the borderland among Victorian empiricist epistemology, ethical theory, art, and social action. Deronda, Ladislaw, and Philip Wakem, of *The Mill on the Floss*, belong in a tradition that has its most notorious representatives among Pater's sensitive protagonists, Arnold's aliens, and James's artists. Philip Wakem, the crippled aesthete of the midland flats, represents the problem most touchingly; alienated from work and society by his hump back, too sensitive for the midland world, he explains to Maggie why he is not a painter:

I think of too many things—sow all sorts of seeds, and get no great
harvest from any one of them. I'm cursed with susceptibility in
every direction, and effective faculty in none. ["You leave out the
poems, " says Dorothea to Will, cursed not by his back but by his
unEnglishness.] I care for classic literature, and mediaeval
literature, and modern literature. I flutter all ways, and fly in
none.[24]

This incapacity to live, it becomes increasingly clear, is the
enabling condition of the writer, and it is no accident that the
sensibility of the narrator of *The Mill on the Floss* is closer to
Philip's than to any others. (Consider, for example, the opening
vision from the arm chair, and the closing perspective.[25]) The
artist's one possible action is the articulation of sensibility,
withdrawn from engagement in large human action. Philip is
forgiven because he is crippled, and because his sensibility
expands into active compassion, a true moral rather than
merely literary solidarity.

Ladislaw's position is more complex, and the burden of
moral responsibility George Eliot placed on him seems
incongruous with the way he is allowed to be in the *Middlemarch*
world. The problem he is invented to resolve or mediate is a
risky one, threatening to push the writer into a crippling
aestheticism or a despair of moral action. On the tightrope,
Ladislaw is saved by apparent triviality. Eugene Hallahan's
summary of Ladislaw's intended role in *Middlemarch* can help
explain this: "he manages to avoid the consequences of . . .
visionary excess by embodying a medley of admirable traits
such as are found scattered in other characters."[26] He avoids
"one-sidedness", and unlike Mr Brooke, who has "gone into"
everything, Ladislaw is capable of "combining a wordly
smattering of various bits of knowledge with a constructive
power for envisioning a primary unifying involvement in a
single field of activity" (Hallahan, p. 157). Perhaps.

But Will's relation to the enterprise of Lydgate and
Casaubon, is like Philip's to the obsessed activities of Mr
Tulliver and of Tom, and like Decoud's to Gould's idealizing of
the mine. Both Ladislaw and Decoud are embodiments in the
text of an ironic vision of human attempts to impose a single
mythic structure on the complexities of experience. Hillis Miller
suggests that Will is "the spokesman" for George Eliot's

"demolition" of the theory that history is purposive and progressive.[27] Both Will and Decoud can be seen as exponents of a Darwinian theory of life and history, a theory stripped—as it is in Pater's early essay on Coleridge[28]—of unifying metaphysical additions. The world evolves; "progress" is an ideal imposition on a neutral evolution. The primary "scientific" difference is that although Will accepts comfortably the incongruity between the human ideal and the lived actuality, he inhabits a world in which there is a crude correspondence between the laws of cause and effect and morality. Will believes that purposive reform is possible, and he becomes a reform politician.

It would be a mistake to dismiss as an irrelevant sentimentalism, the narrator's talk, at the end, of "the growing good of the world'. The wise (and almost cynical) narrator knows that political reform (as opposed to Antonia-like revolution) is deceptive; history does not follow the purposive intellectual grooves of its most alert people, but changes develop organically and biologically, through the incremental inheritance of the qualities developed in the characters of such "diffusively" good people as Dorothea, and through her on her husband, her children, and the people upon whose lives hers has impinged. Such qualities are literally inherited.[29]

The moral implications of such a "biology" have disappeared from Decoud's world. For him, and for Conrad, the material cosmos is utterly incompatible with human development, in which consciousness is not a biological fact to evolve progressively, but a mechanical aberration in matter. The "science" of this is articulated in T. H. Huxley's "Evolution and Ethics" (clearly connected to Conrad's *Heart of Darkness*). To Huxley, the "cosmic process" is at odds with ethical development; force triumphs over sensibility; thought is a "malady"; and pain attains its highest level in man.[30]

Science and ethics, pointing toward the value of detachment, join another tradition of disengagement, nicely articulated by John Morley in a review of Pater's *Renaissance:*

> The speculative distractions of the epoch are noisy and multitudinous, and the first effort of the serious spirit must be to disengage itself from the futile hubbub which is sedulously

maintained by the bodies of rival partisans in philosophy and philosophical theology. The effort after detachment naturally takes the form of criticism of the past, the only way in which a man can take part in the discussion and propagation of ideas, while yet standing in some sort aloof from the agitation of the present.[31]

The connection of Pater to Arnold implicit here suggests a similar relation in this tradition of Conrad to George Eliot. Pater's withdrawal extends beyond Arnold's quest for culture because, in Pater, the possibility of objective understanding has been replaced by the ultimate logic of empiricism: since all experience is "sensation", the best we can do is remain faithful, Decoud-like, to the truth of one's own sensations. What one analyses is not the object as it really is in itself, but the conditions of the "impression".[32]

Arnold's moral ideal is aestheticized into a temperamental ideal, for the greatest sensibility is susceptible to the finest "shade of quality", as Ladislaw had put it. This is all scrupulously "scientific", in truth, one of the mythic forms of the new science. The pervasiveness of the scientific underpinning of the new aestheticism is manifest, as well, in a passage from one of Henry James's critical essays:

> Experience is never limited, and it is never complete; it is an immense sensibility, a kind of huge spider-web of the finest silken threads suspended in the chamber of consciousness, and catching every air-borne particle in its tissue. It is the very atmosphere of the mind; and when the mind is imaginative— much more when it happens to be that of a man of genius—it takes to itself the faintest hints of life, it converts the very pulses of the air into revelations.[33]

Recognizably Paterian, with echoes of Ruskin in the first two clauses, and our old friend, the metaphor of the web, in the third clause, it also draws directly on what any interested layperson would have been absorbing from science at the time. The Paterian emphasis on experience—"not the fruit of experience, but experience itself is the end"[34]—is an outgrowth of empiricist epistemology. But empiricism was teaching also that one could never perceive everything, even of what seems to be given before you,[35] and that all experience, like all matter, is in constant motion. Our sensations then work like Pasteur's experiment, in which he discovered that air was full of floating solid particles,[36] retrieving some of the infinitesimal matter for our experience. The "pulse" of the air is literal scientific fact, the appalling truth that Conrad discovered when being shown an x-ray machine, that all life was the wavelike movement of matter so fine and attenuated as to be invisible.[37] The true scientist, like the true artist, experiences the subtlest motions of matter, and imagines and hypothesizes worlds on the basis of the minutest suggestions.

Here is a conflux of the various elements of the tradition to which Ladislaw and Decoud belong: science, matter, a theory of knowledge, sensibility and experience. The condition of the fullest understanding is withdrawal from the hubbub; the effect of the refined sensibility that might achieve full understanding turns out not to be—as Arnold dreamed—a transformation of culture, but, as Conrad saw it, the writing of books. To be sensitive is to be crippled.

3

I have been trying to suggest that the striking but apparently accidental similarities between Ladislaw and Decoud actually reflect certain profound and historically important similarities in the world views of George Eliot and Conrad. In his public stances, and even in the voice of Marlow, Conrad draws on the Victorian Carlylian tradition of hard work and rigorous self-discipline: unselfconscious work is a sign of health; the pursuit of happiness is chimerical. "Work while it is called Today," Carlyle endlessly quotes, "for the Night cometh wherein no man can work."[38] George Eliot also agreed with Carlyle that the decrease of desire and personal ambition is a condition for the richest life in a world where pain is the norm and the self is insignificant.[39] For her, too, as we hear it from Adam Bede and Felix Holt and Caleb Garth, work is the condition of moral salvation. Yet in Ladislaw and Decoud, both writers imagined characters who belonged to an alternative, anti-Carlylian tradition, built by Pater our of Arnold's Hellenism.

The differences between these characters, and the way they are managed by their narrators, signifies important changes in the tradition. They manoeuvre through a world of more or less obsessed idealists very differently, although for both, integrity depends on alienation, and alienation leads to expulsion. Decoud's story points finally to what Ladislaw's story attempts to avert: the writer's expulsion from the community in the very act of faith to those sensations that might allow some secret solidarity—some Wordsworthian communion—with others.

Compared to Decoud, Ladislaw is a child. He is allowed a childish exuberance, a rebelliousness, a susceptibility "without any neutral region of indifference in his nature, ready to turn everything that befell him into the collision of passionate drama" (*M*, p. 586). His melodramatizing imagination manifests itself at first only in the flittering dilettanteism we have already noted, but the narrator's indulgence undercuts much of the irony implicit in the narrative. Indeed, the most negative comments come from James Chettam and other members of the community whose shallowness we know. But Decoud's indifferentism comes to us in a bitter rhetoric that not only implies Conrad's hostility to the necessary strategy of withdrawal, but also Decoud's painful disenchantment. Cynicism is invariably the disguise of a frustrated moral idealism. Decoud, the narrator tells us, had "pushed the habit of universal raillery to a point where it blinded him to the genuine impulses of his own nature." (*N*, p. 135). Yet, unlike Ladislaw, Decoud is admired if not liked by most of the people with whom he has to work. In *Middlemarch*, it is the narrator who provides the wisdom that requires us to value Will's excesses of feeling, despite the judgements of the community. In *Nostromo*, neither the character nor the narrators are equal to the complex nature of Decoud. We can note, in his interview with Mrs Gould, the "tremendous excitement under the cloak of studied carelessness", which is followed in a moment by this: "But already there was something of a mockery in Decoud's suppressed excitement" (*N*, p. 183).

Although it is important to recognize the moral intensity of the narrator of *Middlemarch* in the struggle to create a more complex kind of unity out of the shattering of traditional unities, George Eliot's voice is often the voice of disenchantment. It impresses on us the failures of history, the littleness of the self, the pervasiveness of death. Yet she struggles against the wisdom of her own insight to authorize Dorothea's quest (and she is yet another of those ambitious myth-hunting idealizers) for a binding theory. Whereas in *Nostromo*, we are told that Decoud dies because he cannot sustain an illusion, in *Middlemarch* what Decoud would have thought of as illusion carries with it the authority of science. And it is the same science that, in Conrad's world, makes *all* ideas illusion. It is reality read, as Conrad would have been the first to acknowledge, through another "temperament". But, as we can see by looking at the condition of George Eliot's temperament during the writing of *Middlemarch*, even here the difference from Conrad is not great.

The letters at that time are marked with a deep new awareness of death. Her experience of the painful dying and death of Lewes's twenty-six year old son, Thornton, haunts almost every letter for a year. Suddenly she is full of consciousness of death's approach and seems almost to be welcoming it. There is, indeed, a Schopenhauerian quality to these letters — anticipating the unmistakable presence of Schopenhauer in Conrad—a recognition that only the death of desire can bring peace. To Mrs Richard Congreve she wrote, for example:

> My strong egoism has caused me so much melancholy, which is traceable to a fastidious yet hungry ambition, that I am relieved by the comparative quietude of personal cravings which age is bringing.[40]

One of Ladislaw's functions in the novel is to quench this Casaubon-like ambition.

The particularity of Thornton's death was intensified for her by the Franco-Prussian war, a subject that dismayed her and threatened any progressive sense of history. She speaks of Prussian brutality (at the start of the war she had sided with the Prussians) with cynical bitterness as

> the regression of barbarism from that historical tomb where we thought it so picturesquely buried—if indeed we ought not to beg pardon of barbarism, which had no weapons for making eight wounds at once in our body.

> (*GEL*, IV, 135)

She ends the letter on the subject of dying, which "has no melancholy for me, except in the parting and leaving behind which Love makes so hard to contemplate."

Surely such experience impressed forcefully on her the inadequacy of such optimistic progressivist history as is found in Comte's Positivism, or Herbert Spencer's "evolutionary" theory. The "onward tendency of human things", as she talks about it in *The Mill on the Floss*, becomes, with this barbaric "regression", terribly ambivalent. *Middlemarch* is significantly full of comments that imply ironically the failure of moral progress through history. One can detect an almost Decoudian tone, as when the narrator remarks, "As to any provincial history in which the agents are all of high moral rank, that must be of a date long posterior to the first Reform Bill" (*M*, p. 250).

Another element in George Eliot's letters at this time seems to connect her with Decoud. Conrad had talked of his personality as "a ridiculous and aimless masquerade". George Eliot had assimilated humanist postivism with Christian self-denial to see each self as a minute element in the species. In *Middlemarch*, Dorothea must learn this littleness by recognizing the self's impersonal participation in an "involuntary and palpitating" life. But there is also, in letters at this time, a new sense of the insignificance of self that implies something of the developing scientific view of the time. W. K. Clifford had called the self "a cable of feelings".[41] Writing once again about the pervasiveness of death, George Eliot talks of striving for the "impersonal life" through which we may "gain much more independence, than is usually believed, of the small bundle of facts that make our own personality" (*GEL*, IV, 107).

Ultimately Decoud achieves this kind of impersonality, but it turns out to be death, not improvement of the species. Alone on the *Great Isabel*, he is drawn out of the masquerade of personality back into its material and unindividuated source—the sheer matter of the Golfo Placido, which accepts his body "untroubled".

Obviously, in George Eliot's novels we are not ready for such a conclusion; the personal recognitions in *Middlemarch* are transformed into a quest for Dorothea's "binding theory" that "could illuminate principle with the widest knowledge" (*M*, p. 16). While writing *Middlemarch*, she was not only preoccupied with death and the disasters of history, but with the work Lewes was doing, a Lydgatian attempt to bind spirit with matter, to develop a metaphysics of science, a coherent theory of "life and mind". George Eliot could say, in January 1871, "my interest in his studies increases rather than diminishes" (*GEL*, IV, 135).

Decoud and Conrad were to give up on such a binding theory, what Decoud would have called a characteristic of Englishmen, who "cannot act or exist without idealizing every simple feeling, desire, or achievement" (*N*, p. 184). But Conrad does not endorse the refusal to idealize, any more than he endorses idealization. Decoud's death is a consequence of the refusal, and he merges "into the world of cloud and water, of natural forces and forms of nature"; and the narrator tells us, in the Carlylian tradition, that "In our activity alone do we find the sustaining illusion of an independent existence as against the whole scheme of things of which we form a helpless part" (*N*, p. 409). But the critical phrase is "sustaining illusion", which places us and the narrator in an impossible and very modern position. It is not the same thing as the remark of the *Middlemarch* narrator in discussing Will, that "our sense of duty must often wait for some work which shall take the place of dilettanteism and make us feel the quality of our action is not a matter of indifference" (*M*, p. 338). The self is, as in Conrad, affirmed through work; but the affirmation is not an illusion.

Decoud could only survive if he were wrong about the world, or if he chose consciously to *behave* as though he were wrong. Work, Carlyle's salvation, serves in Conrad only to keep us from seeing the truth; the novelist's work—and Decoud's, too, as he talks to Mrs Gould or writes to his sister—is to reveal the truth, a suicidal activity protected from suicide only by the activity of articulation itself. There is no other possibility for a pure materialist empiricism. Decoud's remarkable sensitivity and perceptiveness as a recorder of impressions is the other side of the belief that "ideas" are incompatible with experience. His intellectual audacity, as the narrator calls it, is precisely in his rejection of all traditional ways of making connections. Near his death he sees the world as Dorothea first saw the paintings in Rome, "as a succession of incomprehensible images" (*N*, p. 400). And if Decoud is trapped by his intellectual audacity, the complementary story of Nostromo reminds us that "disenchanted vanity" is "the reward of audacious action" (N, p. 412).

In George Eliot's terms, however, Decoud is not so much a bad man as a bad scientist. Solipsism, the Paterian reading of Victorian empiricist thought, is only necessary if one does not have the scientist's faith in, first, the uniformity of nature, and second, what George Eliot calls "the invariable law of consequence". On the strength of such a faith, one can make great imaginative leaps, reading, as Henry James suggests, "revelations" in the finest particle of experience. Here Conrad's quest for solidarity returns, and here George Eliot gives her faith. Neither her science nor her morality had entered an age of indeterminacy.

Ladislaw, by means of his faith in Dorothea, is allowed the larger faith by which *Middlemarch* implies an ultimate coherence to human experience; Antonia's relation to Decoud differs from Dorothea's to Ladislaw in that — in keeping with a Schopenhauerian misogyny that marks Decoud if not Conrad himself—she becomes an occasion for an "illusion". Dorothea becomes a means to truth beyond the limits of common sense. Her test is a trial of faith in Ladislaw. Worse than the misery of being despised by a lover is "to think ill" of him (M, p. 593). She achieves a refinement of feeling that Lewes called Knowledge: "a vision of relations that are not directly felt."[42] The world of *Middlemarch* is made coherent by a vast sum of what Lewes would call "unapparent relations", the province of the new science that was transforming "reality".

In *Daniel Deronda* this transformed reality transforms realism into something else. These unapparent relations become realities to the mystic hypothesizing of Mordecai, and the world of ordinary common sense itself becomes suspect, and the subject of contempt and cynicism. It happens, too in *Middlemarch*, where coincidences are explained as belonging to the same sorts of causal links that account for more obviously inevitable events. The law of consequence works everywhere: "to Uriel watching the progress of planetary history from the Sun, the one result would be just as much of a coincidence as the other"(M, p. 302). Through an intuition built out of Jamesian experience Dorothea recognizes Lydgate's innocence; and in this, as Michael Mason has shown, the more scientific Farebrother tuns into a bad scientist.[43]Dorothea "disliked this cautious weighing of consequences, instead of an ardent faith in efforts of justice and mercy, which would conquer by their emotional force"(*M*, p. 537). Mere sentimentalism to Decoud. But validated reality to *Middlemarch*.

The ultimate division between the two writers may come down to their perception of the relation between desire and reality. The structure of *Middlemarch*, almost as much as the structure of *Daniel Deronda*, is the structure of educated desire. The various events which are no surprise to Uriel and have their scientific justification in the complexity and minuteness of unapparent relations, offer us a world in which "feeling" and "desire", emerging from a sensibility so fine that it must hold itself tentatively for a long time, provide some sort of rough justice. And they exercise a continuing and refining influence on the slowly evolving course of the world. Dorothea's "justice and mercy", by the testimony of George Eliot's next novel, can be transformed from desire into fact, can be made incarnate.[44]

In *Nostromo*, the structure of desire is the structure of fragmentation and disaster. The idea of justice and mercy is scattered with the pages of Don Jose's *Fifty Years of Misrule* during the Monterist revolt. Decoud's incapacity for faith is justified by the effects of Antonia's. For with her faith is the misperception of unapparent relations. Her longing for justice issues in more injustice. *Nostromo* leaves us at a point George Eliot transcends through the union of Ladislaw and Dorothea: where the idea and the fact co-exist without touching. Decoud becomes a fact in the untroubled waters of the Golfo Placido; Antonia becomes the idea that is the final ironic commentary on Decoud's own ironies. The writer of *Nostromo* seems the only one—and then for only so long as he is writing—to be able to hold the two together. As Conrad said in one of his most moving letters, he remains outside of political action because, "je dois—j'ai besoin,—de garder ma pensée intacte comme dernier hommage de fidelité à une cause qui est perdue."[45]

In the structure of desire, Dorothea must become the focus, for she genuinely completes Ladislaw. The most poignant image of the difference between Conrad and George Eliot comes in a scene whose images and characters echo resonantly with the world of Dorothea. Towards the end of *Nostromo*, the revolution over, the separate state of Sulaco rich and powerful,

Mrs Gould sits in her garden, resembling "a good fairy, weary with a long career of well-doing, touched by the withering suspicion of the uselessness of her labours, the powerlessness of her magic" (*N*, p. 427). Like Dorothea, disenchanted in the Lowick garden, chained to Casaubon's dream of a Key to All Mythologies, Emilia Gould has sought—and failed to find—a coherent faith linked to a coherent action. Charles has deserted her for his idealized mine, and she protects him from his own corruption by the incorruptible silver, in their fruitless marriage, as Dorothea struggles to protect and satisfy Casaubon. But at that moment of disenchantment, it had come into Mrs Gould's mind:

> that for life to be large and full, it must contain the care of the past and of the future in every passing moment of the present. Our daily work must be done to the glory of the dead and for the good of those who come after.
>
> (*N*, p. 427)

The one apparently incorruptible figure in *Nostromo* thinks in the language of George Eliot, whose heroines share this desire exactly. They move to such a vision on a path of pain leading to disenchantment. The shattering of a dream opens a reality that requires recognition of one's implication in a world larger than the self. "If the past is not to bind us, where can duty lie?" Maggie Tulliver cries in her final rejection of Stephen Guest (*MF*, p. 417). Maggie, however, dies before paying the price of the past. Casaubon dies and spares Dorothea the worst. Emilia lives on with the burden.

Knowledge marks Emilia's behaviour. "There was", she thinks, "something inherent in the necessities of successful action which carried with it the moral degradation of the idea" (*N*, p. 427). This echoes with Conrad and Decoud. Whereas Dorothea infects Ladislaw with faith, Decoud has infected Emilia with disbelief, and the disbelief isolates her as much as Decoud. Yet the narrative grants her, in her survival with knowledge and with no novelist's opportunity to protect her idea, a kind of heroism:

> An immense desolation, the dread of her own continued life, descended upon the first lady of Sulaco. With a prophetic vision she saw herself surviving alone the degradation of her young

ideal of life, of love, of work—all alone in the Treasure House of the World.

(*N*, p. 428)

Her marriage is infertile; they are the last of the Goulds.

Dorothea, of course, is fertile, and she ends believing in the work of her husband, although—as we have seen—her very being is an ironic commentary upon it. At the last, we hear of her unhistoric acts (which have become part of the unapparent relations) responsible for the " growing good of the world". The elaborations and complexities and multiplying of perspectives of her novel are affirmed by a binding theory that replaces the dying mythology of Christianity and common sense. The possibility of bringing knowledge and action together, of moving from Ladislaw to Dorothea, of moving from self to other, turns out to be incompatible with the mode of the realistic novel, which dwells, like Decoud, in ironies, and resists ideas and feelings for particularities.

With Emilia Gould we are in the presence of yet another sort of novel. The last we see of her is in " the only moment of bitterness in her life", when she has heard Nostromo's secret and finds Decoud's cynicism confirmed once more. She tells the heartbroken Giselle, weeping over the dead Nostromo, "Console yourself, child. Very soon he would have forgotten you for the treasure" (*N*, p. 459). Emilia, then, is the only character in the novel with full knowledge. She has heard from Decoud of her husband's "sentimentalism" and knows the real motive of Decoud's separatist politics (*N*, p. 183); she knows herself desolate and alone; she knows that the ideal is "degraded" in action; she knows the corruption of the incorruptible Nostromo. Her position is so powerfully imagined because it represents an alternative to Decoud's suicide, yet closer to Conrad's own. Her knowledge, though it produces bitterness at least once, never issues in "barren indifferentism". Unlike Decoud, whose sensitivity is protected by his dilettante-ism, Emilia faces the illusoriness of her life, and yet she thinks as George Eliot thought, after all.

She is in the novelist's position, at the point of the terrible paradox that leaves writing as the only possible action but knowing that writing can affirm ideas only in the recognition

176

that they have no connection with the reality they purport to describe. She is different from the novelist, however, because when Nostromo offers to tell her about the hidden silver, she refuses to hear. Moreover, when Dr Monygham asks what Nostromo had told her, she lies: "He told me nothing." The novelist may not refuse to hear, and may not lie. And Emilia, in order to sustain the ideal in action and fulfil her responsibility to past and present and future, must be corrupted. Like Marlow at the end of *The Heart of Darkness*, she must lie to protect. For the modern novelist this is no option, and the Victorian consonance between the real and the moral is hopelessly smashed.

The progress these two books mark out, then, is progress toward the centrality of the disengaged figure, the writer himself. And the continuities are clear. In *Middlemarch* the world of "common sense" becomes monstrous, one to which the best must refuse unreflecting commitment. Ladislaw is right to stand at its edges and is horrified at the disaster caused by Dorothea's premature faith. In *Nostromo*, not only is the world of "common sense" monstrous, but there is no common sense. Behind the absurdities of greed and desire played out in the revolutionary politics of Costaguana lies a world of unapparent relations yet more monstrous—in its absolute, indifferent unintelligence. The faith of Dorothea pierces through to an ultimate coherence by imposing desire on reality; the wisdom of Emilia detects only the triumph of "material interests". *Nostromo* is a world in which all ideas are corrupted and hence one in which language may have no external reference. Only outside the pulsating world, in the imaginative constructions of fictions, can language thrive. Within it, with Decoud's suicide, the moral-aesthetic tradition becomes two traditions.

NOTES

1 Edward W. Said, *Beginnings: Intention and Method* (New York, 1975), p. 110.

2 J. Hillis Miller, "Narrative and History", *ELH*, XLI (Fall, 1974), 455-73. See also, his "Optic and Semiotic in *Middlemarch*", in *The Worlds of Victorian Fiction*, ed. J. H. Buckley (Cambridge, Mass., 1975), pp. 125-45.

3 See David Carroll's remarkable, "*Middlemarch* and the Externality of Fact", in *This Particular Web*, ed. Ian Adam (Toronto, 1975), pp. 73-90.

Carroll shows how thoroughly vampiric and monstrous the relations in *Middlemarch* are.

4 See Jerome Beaty, "History of Indirection: the Era of Reform in *Middlemarch*", *Victorian Studies*, I(1957), 173-79. Beaty shows how history is woven in as backdrop and direct or ironic commentary on the action.

5 *Middlemarch*, ed. Gordon S. Haight (Boston, 1956), p. 105. Further references will be incorporated in the text, noted as *M*.

6 G. H. Lewes, *Problems of Life and Mind*, 4th edition (London, 1890), I, 342-43.

7 Joseph Conrad, *Letters to William Blackwood and David S. Meldrum*, ed. William Blackburn (Durham, 1958), p. 155. Here Conrad, in one of the two direct references to her I have found in his letters, mis-spells her name as George Elliot (p. 155). But Conrad's familiarity with Victorian literature was great and, if only in deference to the firm of Blackwood, which published her, he calls her one of the "great names".

8 Henry James, Review of *Middlemarch* in *The Galaxy*, (1873). Reprinted in *The House of Fiction*, ed. Leon Edel (London, 1957), p. 267.

9 *Nostromo* (Harmondsworth, 1963), pp. 77, 118. I cite the Penguin edition for convenience. Future references will be in the text, noted with an *N*.

10 U. C. Knoepflmacher, "Middlemarch: An Avuncular View", *Nineteenth Century Fiction*, XXX (June, 1975), 53-81, interestingly discusses the weakness of the uncle figures in *Middlemarch* as an expression of the breakdown of traditional authority; this works as well with *Nostromo*.

11 J. Hillis Miller, *The Disappearance of God* (New York, 1965), p. 11.

12 In Lewes's work the "social organism" is no metaphor but a literal fact. See, for example, *Problems of Life and Mind*, I, 113-14.

13 Thomas Pinney, ed. "More Leaves from George Eliot's Notebook", *The Huntingdon Library Quarterly*, XXIX (August, 1966), 353-76. See, "Feeling is a sort of knowledge", p. 364.

14 See Alexander Welsh, "Realism as a Practical and Cosmic Joke", *Novel*, IX (Fall, 1975), 23-39, for an excellent discussion of the pessimistic late-Victorian world view as manifest in "realistic" fiction.

15 Joseph Conrad, "Autocracy and War", in *Notes on Life and Letters* (New York, 1924), p. 86.

16 Ian Watt, "Conrad's Preface to *The Nigger of the 'Narcissus'*", *Novel* VIII (Winter, 1974), 114; *N*, p. 196.

17 Gustav Morf, *The Polish Heritage of Joseph Conrad* (reprint, New York, 1962), p. 131.

18 *Letters from Joseph Conrad, 1895-1924*, ed. Edward Garnett (Indianapolis, 1928), p. 46.

19 Royal Roussel, *The Metaphysics of Darkness* (Baltimore, 1971), p. 26.

20 Through all his extensive criticism of Conrad, Ian Watt has insisted on this more "affirmative" aspect of Conrad's writing. In addition to the essay on the "Preface", see his "Joseph Conrad: Alienation and Commitment", *The English Mind*, ed. Hugh Sykes Davies and George Watson (Cambridge, 1964), pp. 257-78; and *"Heart of Darkness* and Nineteenth Century Thought", *Partisan Review*, XLV (No. 1, 1978), 108-19.

21 Richard Ellmann, "Dorothea's Husbands", *Golden Codgers* (New York, 1973), pp. 17-38.

22 *M*, p. 157. Lewes defines the Ideal as "what is virtually given, when the process of Inference anticipates and intuites [sic] what *will* be or *would* be Feeling under the immediate stimulus of the object", *Problems*, II, 16-17.

23 *Daniel Deronda* (Harmondsworth, 1967), pp. 412-13.

24 *The Mill on the Floss* (Boston, 1961), p. 350.

25 I am grateful to two former graduate students for their subtle and convincing arguments about the centrality of Philip's vision in *The Mill on the Floss:* Helen Cooper and Stephanie Pinson.

26 Eugene Hallahan, "The Concept of Crisis in *Middlemarch*", *Nineteenth Century Fiction*, XXVIII (No. 4, 1974), 157.

27 Hillis Miller, "Narrative and History", p. 466.

28 Walter Pater, "Coleridge", *Appreciations* (London, 1922): the proximity of much of Pater's thinking here to George Eliot's is striking. "To the modern spirit nothing is, or can be rightly known, except relatively and under conditions. The philosophical conception of the relative has been developed in modern times through the influence of the sciences of observation. Those sciences reveal types of life evanescing into each other by inexpressible refinements of change. Things pass into their opposites by inexpressible refinements of change" (p. 67). Or note this: "Man's physical organism is played upon not only by the physical conditions about it, but by remote laws of inheritance, the vibration of long past acts reaching him in the midst of the new order of things in which he lives" (pp. 67-8). This letter, as we shall see, is directly connected to Dorothea's influence on others and on us.

29 Bernard Paris, *Experiments in Life* (Detroit, 1965) makes the best use thus far of the relation of Lewes's ideas to George Eliot's. He points out that in George Eliot there is such a thing as inherited characteristics in an almost Lamarckian sense. See Lewes's discussion, passim, especially *Problems of Life and Mind*, I, 219.

30 "Evolution and Ethics: Prolegomena", and "Evolution and Ethics", in *Evolution and Ethics and Other Essays* (London, 1911), see especially pp. 50, 54, 81-2.

31 The editor [John Morley], Review of Pater's *Renaissance*, "Mr. Pater's Essays", *Fortnightly Review*, XIII (January-June, 1873), p. 470.

32 *The Renaissance* (London, 1888), p. xi.

33 "The Art of Fiction", pp. 31-2.

34 *The Renaissance*, p. 249.

35 W. K. Clifford, "The Unseen Universe", *Lectures and Essays*, ed. Leslie Stephen and Frederick Pollock (London, 1879), argues that our perceptions are never of the full object we describe. His is a scientific argument that might imply impressionism in art: e.g., "not the whole of a sensation is immediate experience . . . this experience is supplemented by something that is not in it" (I, 260).

36 See T. H. Huxley's discussion of this in "Biogenesis and Abiogenesis", *Disclosures Biological and Geological* (London, 1894).

37 *Letters from Joseph Conrad:* "*all matter* being only that thing of inconceivable tenuity through which the various vibrations of waves (electricity, heat, sound, light etc.) are propagated, thus giving birth to our sensations—then emotions—then thought" (p. 143).

38 The most famous place of the quotation is at the conclusion of "The Everlasting Yea" chapter of *Sartor Resartus*.

39 George Eliot frequently explored the possibility that *not* knowing is healthier than knowing. The most extreme form of this is in "The Lifted Veil", where the capacity to know other's thoughts is a moral and psychological disaster. Certainly, the dangers of heightened sensibility are a continuing concern in her novels.

40 *The Letters of George Eliot* (GEL), ed. Gordon S. Haight (New Haven, 1955), IV, 124.

41 Clifford, *Lectures and Essays*, I, 289.

42 Lewes, *Problems*, II, 23.

43 See Michael Mason, "*Middlemarch* and Science: Problems of Life and Mind", *RES*, XXII (May, 1871), 151-69.

44 "Second-sight is a flag over disputed froud. But it is a matter of knowledge that there are persons whose yearnings, conceptions—nay, travelled conclusions—continually take the form of images which have a foreshadowing power: the deed they would do starts up before them in complete shape, making a coercive type" *(Daniel Deronda*, p. 527).

45 *Joseph Conrad's Letters to R. B. Cunningham Graham*, ed. C. T. Watts (Cambridge, 1969), p. 65.

The above essay will appear in the forthcoming *The Realistic Imagination: Fiction from "Frankenstein" to "Lady Chatterley"* by George Levine, to be published by the University of Chicago Press in 1981 ©George Levine.

9

Fruit and Seed:
The Finale to *Middlemarch*

by SUSAN MEIKLE

On 13 September 1872, George Eliot wrote to Alexander Main, "Middlemarch is done - all except a small Finale, which I prefer reserving a little."[1] She and George Henry Lewes were about to set off on one of the European trips they habitually undertook when she had finished a novel. This time they had *Middlemarch* proofs to correct while they were abroad, and she had the Finale to write. They arrived in Homburg on 22 September, and Lewes records in his diary for 2 October, "Polly finished the Finale to 'Middlemarch', which we sent to Blackwood."[2] Then, with what seems phenomenal speed, there is evidence of the *proofs* of the Finale arriving back in Homburg and being revised and returned to Blackwood by 8 October.[3]

So the manuscript version of the Finale (see pp. 182-83 below) and the alterations to it, which became the Finale of the first edition, were both written within the space of at least a week, and at most a fortnight. There would be little interest in this point if it were not that the events of those weeks may help to account for the particular and striking alterations George Eliot made to the Finale during this time.

Since the renewal of interest in feminism over the past ten years, these alterations have a particular importance, because they appear to point to a moment when George Eliot allowed herself as narrator to make specific charges against society on behalf of women, only to rescind those charges in the revisions of the Finale made in 1874. My contention is, on the contrary, that the charges made are representative of those which are

181

I MANUSCRIPT VERSION	II FIRST EDITION	III 1874 EDITION
1 Certainly those determining acts of her life were not ideally beautiful.	1 Certainly those determining acts of her life were not ideally beautiful.	1 Certainly those determining acts of her life were not ideally beautiful.
2 They were the mixed result of young and noble impulse struggling *with imperfect conditions.*	2 They were the mixed result of young and noble impulse struggling *under tragic conditions.*	2 & 3 They were the mixed result of young and noble impulse struggling *amidst the conditions of an imperfect social state,*
3 Among the *many criticisms which passed on her first marriage nobody remarked that it could not have happened if she had not been born into a society which smiled on propositions* of marriage from a sickly man to a girl less than half his own age, and, in general, encouraged the view that to renounce an advantage to oneself which might be got from the folly of ignorance of others is a sign of mental weakness.	3 Among the *many remarks passed on her mistakes, it was never said in the neighbourhood of Middlemarch that such mistakes could not have happened if the society into which she was born* had not smiled on propositions of marriage from a sickly man to a girl less than half his own age— *on modes of education which make a woman's knowledge another name for motley ignorance— on rules of conduct which are in flat contradiction with its own loudly-asserted beliefs.*	
4 While *this tone of opinion is part of the social medium in which young creatures begin to breathe,* there will be collisions such as those in Dorothea's life, where great feelings will take the aspect of error, and great faith the aspect of illusion.	4 While *this is the social air in which mortals begin to breathe,* there will be collisions such as those in Dorothea's life, where great feelings will take the aspect of error, and great faith the aspect of illusion.	4 in which great feelings will *often* take the aspect of error, and great faith the aspect of illusion.
5 For there is no creature whose inward being is so strong that it is not greatly determined by what lies outside it.	5 For there is no creature whose inward being is so strong that it is not greatly determined by what lies outside it.	5 For there is no creature whose inward being is so strong that it is not greatly determined by what lies outside it.

182

6 *It is not likely that a new Theresa will have the opportunity of reforming* a conventual life, any more than a new Antigone will spend her heroic piety in daring all for the sake of a brother's burial: the medium in which their ardent deeds took shape is for ever gone. But we insignificant people with our daily words and acts are preparing the lives of many Dorotheas, some of which may present a far sadder sacrifice than that of the Dorothea whose story we know.

7 Her finely-touched spirit had still its fine issues, though they were not widely visible. Her full nature, like that river of which Cyrus broke the strength, spent itself in channels which had no great name on the earth.

8 But the effect of her being on those around her was incalculably diffusive: for *the growing life of the world is after all chiefly* dependent on unhistoric acts, and that things are not so ill with you and me as they might have been is *owing to many of those who sleep* in unvisited tombs, *having lived a hidden life nobly.*

183

6 A new Theresa will hardly have the opportunity of reforming a conventual life, any more than a new Antigone will spend her heroic piety in daring all for the sake of a brother's burial: the medium in which their ardent deeds took shape is for ever gone. But we insignificant people with our daily words and acts are preparing the lives of many Dorotheas, some of which may present a far sadder sacrifice than that of the Dorothea whose story we know.

7 Her finely-touched spirit had still its fine issues, though they were not widely visible. Her full nature, like that river of which Cyrus broke the strength, spent itself in channels which had no great name on the earth.

8 But the effect of her being on those around her was incalculably diffusive: for the growing good of the world is partly dependent on unhistoric acts; and that things are not so ill with you and me as they might have been is half owing to the number who lived faithfully a hidden life, and rest in unvisited tombs.

6 *A new Theresa will hardly have the* opportunity of reforming a conventual life, any more than a new Antigone will spend her heroic piety in daring all for the sake of a brother's burial: the medium in which their ardent deeds took shape is for ever gone. But we insignificant people with our daily words and acts are preparing the lives of many Dorotheas, some of which may present a far sadder sacrifice than that of the Dorothea whose story we know.

7 Her finely-touched spirit had still its fine issues, though they were not widely visible. Her full nature, like that river of which Cyrus broke the strength, spent itself in channels which had no great name on the earth.

8 But the effect of her being on those around her was incalculably diffusive: for *the growing good of the world is partly* dependent on unhistoric acts; and that things are not so ill with *you and me as* they might have been is *half owing to the number who lived faithfully* a hidden life, and *rest* in unvisited tombs.

6 A new Theresa will hardly have the opportunity of reforming a conventual life, any more than a new Antigone will spend her heroic piety in daring all for the sake of a brother's burial: the medium in which their ardent deeds took shape is for ever gone. But we insignificant people with our daily words and acts are preparing the lives of many Dorotheas, some of which may present a far sadder sacrifice than that of the Dorothea whose story we know.

7 Her finely-touched spirit had still its fine issues, though they were not widely visible. Her full nature, like that river of which Cyrus broke the strength, spent itself in channels which had no great name on the earth.

8 But the effect of her being on those around her was incalculably diffusive: for the growing good of the world is partly dependent on unhistoric acts; and that things are not so ill with you and me as they might have been is half owing to the number who lived faithfully a hidden life, and rest in unvisited tombs.

implicit in the novel *anyway,* and that events of 1872 and 1874, rather than encouraging a view that George Eliot retreated from addressing the woman question, positively indicate otherwise.

In his essay, "The Text of the Novel: A Study of the Proof", Jerome Beaty provides texts of the ending of the three different versions of the Finale, which are laid out here in parallel. They are, respectively, the manuscript version, the corrected proof of the manuscript version which became the first edition, and the altered version of 1874 which became the version adhered to in the Cabinet Edition of 1876. The general structure of the Finale remains the same in all three versions; the significant changes are to be found in particular words and phrases, which I have underlined, and most especially in the extensive alterations to the third section of the manuscript and first edition and the second section of the 1874 edition.

The first change appears in the second section: the manuscript reads, "struggling *with imperfect* conditions", and the proof is changed to "struggling *under prosaic* conditions". The changed preposition gives comparatively greater force to the power of the conditions affecting the "determining acts" of individual lives, and the change from "imperfect" to "prosaic" subtly shifts the emphasis from a relatively distanced, but not hopeless position—the possibility of perfection is at least contained in imperfection—to a more specific description of those conditions as being by their very nature pervasively humdrum. The effect is to withdraw any suggestion of potential good contained in the first version and to suggest in the revised proof that "ideally beautiful acts" are hardly possible under any circumstances, since "there is no creature whose inward being is so strong that it is not greatly determined by what lies outside it", a thesis that stands unaltered in the centre of all three versions.

The changes between the manuscript and proof copies in the third section are perhaps the most extensive and the most interesting in their implications. In the manuscript, the discussion assumes one single "determining act" in Dorothea's history: her decision to marry Mr Casaubon. In the revised proof for the first edition, the criticism extends more generally to "remarks passed on Dorothea's *mistakes*"; the narrator points beyond Dorothea's single decision to marry Mr Casaubon, but leaves the reader to consider exactly what those other "mistakes" were. In addition, narrative accusations against those people "remarking" on Dorothea's mistakes become more specific in the revised proof, and give the impression of their application beyond the fictional world of Middlemarch to the world of the reader, a position which is made explicit when the narrator later refers to how "we insignificant people" are preparing the lives of future Dorotheas. The sharper focus of narrative judgement is futher emphasized in the change from "*a* society" in the manuscript, to "*the* society into which she was born" in the revised proof. The manuscript suggestion of hypothetical *other* societies which might be more enlightened becomes less important than the crucial relation in any one particular society between its beliefs and practices and their effects on its individual members. And this apparently slight alteration, in turn, points up the more obvious changes to come later in section three, where the narrative focus shifts from the general moral point in the manuscript about "renouncing advantage to oneself", and makes, instead, a specifically feminist accusation that the kind of education offered to women is directly and unavoidably implicated in the "mistakes" they make. In this context, the contrast between the verb "smiled on" and its object, "motley ignorance", has the effect of sarcasm. Motley may be a matter of innocent fun in certain entertaining circumstances, but when applied to "ignorance" it implies the patchy bits of information passed to women as "knowledge", and social responsibility for it amounts to anything from complacent indifference to obvious hypocrisy, which can smugly advocate "rules of conduct which are in flat contradiction with its own loudly asserted beliefs."

The force of accusation in these particular changes to the proof extends also to the fourth section. The important change between versions one and two here is consistent with the new, denunciatory tone apparent in section three. The manuscript reads "while this *tone of opinion is part* of the social medium in which young creatures begin to breathe", and the revised proof reads, "while this is the *social air* which mortals begin to breathe". By substituting "air" for "opinion", the determining power of social attitudes is made absolutely effective rather than partially so. "Opinions" can imply, also, the existence of other, perhaps more congenial, opinions, but in the revised proof that chance is eliminated. And the air metaphor not only underlines the all-pervasive influence of social attitudes, it carries also the sense of vulnerability of those who breathe it and have no escape, should it prove harmful.

The two central and connected ideas which remain unaltered in all three versions and at the centre of the Finale are the unavoidable determining power of dominant social attitudes and practice, and the insistence that "we insignificant people" are responsible for the ways in which individual lives are shaped. Yet despite the fact that this assertion remains unchanged in the manuscript and first edition, its implications are modified considerably by the changes which George Eliot made in the very final statement of the novel. Again discussion is extended beyond Dorothea's particular fictional case to that of the world of the reader. The manuscript version concludes, "for the growing *life* of the world is *after all chiefly* dependent on unhistoric acts, and that things are not so ill with you and me as they might have been *is owing to many of those who sleep* in unvisited tombs, having lived a hidden life nobly." This final section was changed in those few days in Homburg to the revised proof which became the first edition and was retained unaltered in the 1874 edition: "for the growing *good* of the world is *partly* dependent on unhistoric acts; and that things are not so ill with you and me as they might have been is *half owing* to the *number* who lived *faithfully* a hidden life, and rest in unvisited *tombs*." The change from "growing life" to "growing good" seems to be a straightforward refinement of meaning, life in itself not being at stake here, whereas its quality—its "good"—is. The more significant change, however, is that, between writing the manuscript and altering the proofs, George Eliot chose to drop the generally optimistic tone of the words "after all" and "chiefly" and change them to the explicitly qualified "partly". The conviction of, or even desire to believe in, the "good" of the world being affected by the acts of its individual members has been reduced to an almost reluctant acknowledgement of possibility. Similarly, that "*we*" are better off for having shared in the lives of people like Dorothea is, in the final version, no longer positively "owing to the many", but only "*half* owing to the *number* . . . " Not only have the generally possible "many" been reduced to an identifiable number in each case, but the assertion that we owe our well-being almost exclusively to them is replaced by the qualified awareness that such beneficial influence, if it exists, is, after all, strictly limited. This changed emphasis away from the strong influence of individuals on the lives of others reveals a problem created by the novel which the more optimistic tone of the manuscript version does not admit, but which the alterations in the proof seem to move towards acknowledging: if George Eliot's fiction so thoroughly represented the ways in which commonly held prejudices and traditional practices determine the course of individual lives, how could she insist, finally, on any extensive or great power of single individuals to counteract those pressures? It is as though George Eliot's claims for Dorothea are ironically contradicted by the novel itself. As Jerome Beaty noted in his essay, the alteration of the very last word in the Finale from "nobly" in the manuscript to "tombs" in the revised proof, summarizes the difference in tone between the two versions[4] and bears witness to a victory which is, in the end, not the individual's.

It does not seem that the change can simply be explained by the wish to avoid finishing the novel with an awkward participial phrase. The effect of the change in terms of meaning is greater than that reason alone would support, and one must also consider the changes of actual words in the ending. "Having lived a hidden life faithfully", would have been as awkward as, if not more awkward than, the manuscript version, "having lived a hidden life nobly". Certainly the combined effect of replacing "nobly" with "faithfully" and finishing the novel with the word "tombs" is in keeping with the sense of version two that George Eliot was reluctant to claim too effective a power for the individual to alter social forces. Ultimately, the change shifts the focus from an evaluation of heroic character—that someone like Dorothea is "noble"—to a suggestion that the best one can say of a life such as hers is that any heroism it may have is located in a consistency of intention rather than achieved results, an idea which harks back to Dorothea's speech to Will Ladislaw about her guiding "faith" in life:

That by desiring what is perfectly good, even when we don't quite know what it is and cannot do what we would, we are part of the divine power against evil—widening the skirts of light and making the struggle with darkness narrower.

(Book IV, Chap. 39)

The final impression of the novel is that it has indicated the effective limits of that faith, while not denying the possibility of moments of success in the individual case. But they are, after all, only moments.

In summary, the most significant changes between the manuscript version and the altered proof of the Finale stress more specifically the social origins of Dorothea's "mistakes" and lead to what can only be called a more resigned and qualified belief in the efforts of individual lives to counteract the effects of those origins.

Proceeding to the alterations of 1874, one looks for explanations for the equally puzzling changes between the more explicitly feminist first edition version and the radically abridged final version, which remained the text for all editions of the novel after 1874. What had been three sentences in the first two versions is conflated to only two shortened sentences in the 1874 Finale. The move towards resignation, noted in the second version, remains, but the specific, even angry, accusations are omitted. The distinct "prosaic conditions" crucially affecting the "determining acts" of women, in particular, have been absorbed into the single, general phrase, "imperfect social state". The impression given is that the novelist had become reluctant to spell out any specific, isolated accusations which could be taken as her view on the subject.

It is important to understand whether this change is simply an example of George Eliot's almost proverbial "cold feet" in political matters getting the better of her, to determine if these changes in the final version are tantamount to the novelist being unable to face up to the implications of her own work. One has to decide if these final changes mean that the novel does not really have anything to say quite particularly about the nature of women and the forces that affect their lives, or that the novelist did not wish to make the reader feel that it does.

With regard to George Eliot's political views and her

188

reluctance to make them public, she wrote to Blackwood in 1874 that she was "no believer in Salvation by ballot",[5] and in a letter to Mrs Peter Alfred Taylor in 1868, she gave an extensive explanation of her personal position with regard to speaking on public issues:

> I thought you understood that I have grave reasons for not speaking on certain public topics. No request from the best friend in the world—even my own husband—ought to induce me to speak when I judge it my duty to be silent. If I had taken a contrary decision, I should not have remained silent till now. My function is that of the *aesthetic*, not the doctrinal teacher—the rousing of the nobler emotions, which make mankind desire the social right, not prescribing of special measures, concerning which the artistic mind, however strongly moved to social sympathy, is often not the best judge. It is one thing to feel keenly for one's fellow-beings; another to say, "this step, and this alone, will be best to take for the removal of particular calamities."[6]

Here one may safely assume that particular issue is that of the woman question.[7] But the refusal to advocate specific solutions to social questions does not render George Eliot unable to perceive the nature and implications of those questions. *Middlemarch* shows at one and the same time her ability to analyse the working of social forces and how that analysis required an artistic medium, because the novelist was engaged in a fundamental examination of the dynamic relation between the intellect and the emotions in men's and women's responses to their world. In a letter to Dr Joseph Frank Payne in January 1876 she explains the necessity she felt to work through art:

> But my writing is simply a set of experiments in life—an endeavour to see what our thoughts and emotion may be capable of—what sorts of motive, actual or hinted as possible, give promise of a better after which we may strive—what gains from past revelations and discipline we must strive to keep hold of as something more sure than shifting theory. I become more and more timid—with less daring to adopt any formula which does not get itself clothed for me in some human figure and individual experience, and perhaps that is a sign that if I help others to see at all it must be through the medium of art.[8]

This expressed position, founded on political and aesthetic conviction as well perhaps as a sensitivity to her own personal situation, and an awareness of its being particularly vulnerable to crude analyses with regard to the woman question, has its own bearing on the changes made to the *Middlemarch* Finale two years before. In a letter of 11 November 1873, John Blackwood asked George Eliot if she and Lewes had seen Alexander Main's proposed revised preface for a second edition of his *Wise, Witty and Tender Sayings* from the works of George Eliot, this edition to include extracts from *Middlemarch*. Blackwood sent her a copy of the preface with the comment,

> It seems to me that our friend puts the case rather too strong in favour of his compilation as compared with the Works. I am sure he does not intend what his words seem to convey, but will Lewes and you look at the points where I have put a query?[9]

George Eliot replied to Blackwood on 12 November:

> With regard to the preface to the "Sayings," of which I had seen nothing till you sent it, I more than agree with what you say: I totally object to the 1st clause which you have marked with a note of interrogation and to the "if at all" of the 2nd. Mr Main himself, I have no doubt, is free from the misunderstanding which the clauses are likely to convey to others.
>
> If it were true, I should be quite stultified as an artist. Unless my readers are more moved towards the ends I seek by my works as wholes than by an assemblage of extracts, my writings are a mistake. I have always exercised a severe watch against anything that could be called preaching, and if I have ever allowed myself in dissertation or in dialogue [anything] which is not part of the *structure* of my books, I have there sinned against my own laws.[10]

From about the time the above letters were written and throughout the spring of 1874, George Eliot was engaged in correcting proofs for the seven-and-sixpenny edition of *Middlemarch,* the one which would contain the third and final version of the Finale. It seems possible that the issues raised concerning Main's second preface to the *Sayings,* may have had their effect, consciously or not, on changes George Eliot chose to make to the Finale in 1874. They may have renewed her awareness of the dangers of "preaching" in her novels, and of the possibilities of extracts being taken from her work as

190

"messages" from the author. Her letter to Blackwood of 12 November makes clear that she is fully conscious of the danger that the subtle interrelation between the moral and narrative levels of her work could be missed by her readers. She goes on to say in that letter,

> Unless I am condemned by my own principles, my books are not properly separable into "direct and "indirect" teachings. My chief doubt as to the desirability of the "sayings" has always turned on the possibility that the volume might encourage such a view of my writing.[11]

One may not dismiss entirely W. J. Harvey's suggestion that George Eliot's major deletions in section two of the Finale between the first and later editions were "in response to the verdict of her reviewers"[12] who, says Harvey, "really pounced on this passage". As an example he quotes from the *British Quarterly Review*, which he says was "moderate" in its opinion that the Finale

> really had no foundation at all in the tale itself . . . We find in this passage a trace that George Eliot is, on reviewing her own work, a little dissatisfied with her own picture of the "prosaic conditions" to which she ascribes Dorothea's misadventures; and that she tries to persuade herself that they were actually more oppressive and paralysing than they really were.[13]

Harvey's summary of the *Fortnightly Review*'s position, on the other hand, seems to show a more accurate appreciation of the intricate ways the novel concerns itself with woman and society:

> While the reviewer "agrees that Dorothea does not yield to social pressures in marrying Casaubon, but is simply deluded about him, it argues that George Eliot shows that it is society which so nurtured women that their ideals cannot but be ideals of delusion."[14]

The *Fortnightly*'s analysis is more consistent with the evidence from George Eliot's letters, that she had renewed concern about the problem of "preaching" in her novels. And it would seem that the deletions and changes in the 1874 version are more probably in consequence of that concern to make the novel *as a whole* embody her vision—her teaching—than they are "proof" that she had retreated from the complex perceptions of women in the world which are fundamental to the novel's design and meaning.

But there are still more interesting aspects which relate to those changes made to the Finale in October 1872 and then in 1874 and their relation to George Eliot's treatment of the woman question in her novels. Some letters which she wrote while occupied with writing and revising the Finale in Homburg throw an interesting light on the effect actual events may have had on the alterations we have been considering. On 25 September, the third day of their stay in Homburg, George Eliot wrote to Mrs William Cross:

> The air, the waters, the plantations are all perfect—"only man is vile". I am not fond of denouncing my fellow sinners, but gambling being a vice I have no mind to, it stirs my disgust even more than my pity. The sight of dull faces bending round the gaming tables, the raking-up of the money, and the flinging of the coins towards the winners by the hard-faced croupiers, the hateful, hideous women staring at the board like stupid mon-maniacs—all this seems to me the most abject presentation of mortals grasping after something called a good than can be seen on the face of this little earth.[15]

In Lewes's diary of the 26 September there is the following entry: "Miss Leigh [Byron's granddaughter] having lost 500£, looking feverish and excited. Painful sight!"[16] Then in a letter to John Blackwood, written two days after she sent him the completed manuscript Finale to *Middlemarch*, and more than a week after the above incident took place, George Eliot returns to the topic of the gambling hall and describes Miss Leigh:

> The Kursaal is to me a Hell not only for the gambling, but for the light and heat of the gas, and we have seen enough of its monotonous hideousness. There is very little dramatic "Stoff" to be picked up by watching or listening. The saddest thing to be witnessed is the play of Miss Leigh, Byron's grand niece, who is only 26 years old, and is completely in the grasp of this mean, money-raking demon. It made me cry to see her fresh young face among the hags and brutally stupid men around her.[17]

As many people have noted, the gambling episode in the Kursaal, which captured the novelist's attention when she was writing and re-writing the first two versions of the Finale, is recognizable as the germ of the portrait of Gwendolen Harleth which opens *Daniel Deronda*.[18] In the letters, the angry disgust present in words like "hateful", "hideous", "hags", and "brutally stupid", which describe the environment of the hall, contrasts markedly with the sadness expressed at the sight of the young "fresh-faced" woman caught in the gambling world. The gambling itself and the very heat and light of the room combine to create the hellishness of the scene. One is reminded of the specific alteration George Eliot made in section four of the Finale, where she changed the moderate phrase "tone of opinion", for "social air", stressing the way that the whole of a young person's development depends on the quality of the social atmosphere, in all its senses. It comes as no surprise, moreover, that the air of Leubronn in *Daniel Deronda* is repeatedly characterised as "poisonous", and "monotonous hideousness" would indeed be a fitting phrase to describe the life Gwendolen Harleth wins when she gambles on marriage to Grandcourt.

Connections such as these between George Eliot's experiences in Homburg, her work on the Finale to *Middlemarch*, and, ultimately, the construction of *Daniel Deronda*, ironically belie the novelist's comment to Blackwood that there was "very little dramatic 'Stoff' to be picked up by watching or listening" in the Kursaal. On the contrary, it seems that George Eliot's observations there gave her a renewed, living reminder of the particular vulnerability of young women such as Rosamond Vincy in *Middlemarch*, and of the limitations of women like Dorothea to "widen the skirts of light" beyond the confines of a small domestic circle. And this recognition found its expression in the tone and accusations which make the profound difference between the manuscript and the revised proof of the *Middlemarch* Finale. But what is more, when George Eliot deleted those very accusations in 1874, in favour of the more general reference to the "imperfect social state", she was already planning *Daniel Deronda,* in which the opening paragraph presents the noisome social world whose determining influence the first edition of *Middlemarch* seemed implicitly aware of in its Finale. Although *Daniel Deronda* and *Middlemarch* are separated by some four years in actual publication, this evidence suggests strong connecting links between them. Keeping in mind this overlap between *Daniel Deronda* and *Middlemarch*, in terms of actual time and the working of artistic ideas, another sentence at the very centre of the Finale which remained unchanged in all three versions, takes on a new importance:

> But we insignificant people with our daily words and acts are preparing the lives of many *Dorotheas, some of which may present a far sadder sacrifice* than that of the Dorothea whose story we know.

It is perhaps the case that the "fresh young face" which touched George Eliot's imagination in Homburg in 1872, and which took shape in *Daniel Deronda* as Gwendolen Harleth, was felt as one of the "sadder sacrifices" included in the Finale of *Middlemarch*. If so, then the specific accusations in the first edition, which were revoked in 1874, were the more readily dispensable, not only because they smacked of "preaching", and still less because George Eliot felt they were untrue or unfaithful to her text, but because they were already acquiring fictional form, being "clothed in human figures", in the novel to come.

NOTES

1 Gordon S. Haight, ed. *The George Eliot Letters*, Vol. V, p.309.
2 *Ibid.*, p. 313.
3 *Ibid.*, p. 315.
4 Jerome Beaty, "The Text of the Novel: A Study of the Proof", in *"Middlemarch": Critical Approaches to the Novel*, ed. Barbara Hardy (1967), pp. 359-62.
5 Haight, *Letters*, Vol. VI, pp. 21-2.
6 *Ibid.*, Vol. VII, p. 44.
7 Gordon S. Haight, *George Eliot: A Biography* (London, 1968). Haight notes here that Mrs P.A. Taylor was interested in "women's rights", and that she had "urged Marian to lend her influence in support of the cause" of John Stuart Mill's bill to enfranchise women. See pp. 99 and 396.
8 Haight, *Letters*, Vol. VI, pp. 216-17.
9 *Ibid.*, Vol. V, p. 456. In a letter to Main, dated two days later, Blackwood wrote, "I am sure nothing could be farther from your thoughts than to say that the teaching of her, the most condensed and unsermonising of Writers, could be best and most easily approached from a Volume of Extracts such as yours, but that is how these passages may most naturally be interpreted. There was a preface to the first edition and my advice is

merely to add to it the fact that the second edition is further enriched by extracts from *Middlemarch* with the Author's consent." (*Letters*, Vol. V, p. 460.)

10   *Ibid.*, Vol. V, pp. 458-59.
11   *Ibid.*, p.459.
12   W.J. Harvey, "Criticism of the Novel: Contemporary Reception", in *"Middlemarch": Critical Approaches to the Novel*, p.133.
13   *Ibid.*
14   *Ibid.*, p.134.
15   Haight, *Letters*, Vol. V, pp.21-2.
16   *Ibid.*, p.314.
17   *Ibid.*
18   In his footnote referring to the episode in George Eliot's letter to Blackwood, Haight includes the following item: "In his review of Cross in the *Nineteenth Century*, 17 (March 1885), p. 483, Lord Acton says, 'a young lady over whom George Eliot wept in the gambling rooms at Homburg, and who remembers the meeting, served as the model of Gwendolen Harleth.'" (*Letters*, Vol. VI, p.314.) In his biography of George Eliot Haight connects the Kursaal episode of 1872 with the later portrait of Gwendolen Harleth, but gives no indication of its possible significance to the work the novelist was doing on *Middlemarch* at the time.

10

Gwendolen Harleth and "The Girl of the Period"

by BONNIE ZIMMERMAN

There is little disagreement that Gwendolen Harleth is among the supreme achievements of characterisation in George Eliot's works and, indeed, in the history of the novel. Like Daniel Deronda himself, critics and readers have been "arrested" upon first acquaintance with this "problematic sylph" (38).[1] We would certainly agree with John Blackwood, Eliot's publisher, that Gwendolen is a "splendid" creature.[2] Gwendolen is so fine a creation that one is rather cautious in suggesting, nonetheless, that Eliot may have had ideological as well as aesthetic impulses at work. After all, the "Jewish" half of the novel has long been criticized for being uncomfortably close to propaganda. Morals not being in fashion today, one does not like to think of George Eliot as a moral or ideological writer. But so she was considered by her contemporaries and so she considered herself, although at her best she always thoroughly transmuted her message to art.[3] Such, in particular, is the case with Gwendolen in whom Eliot joined art and ideology in nearly seamless unity.

The characterization of Gwendolen Harleth is the product of George Eliot's twenty years of literary investigation into the role of women. Eliot's novels all investigate the issues of female expectation and oppression; a principal theme in each concerns the transformation of woman's desire for power and transcendence into submission, renunciation, and the acceptance of her destiny as an agent of human sympathy. Gwendolen, like Romola, Esther, and Dorothea, exchanges egoistic rebellion for an "appropriately" feminine submission. But Gwendolen is also unique. While *The Mill on the Floss, Felix Holt,* and *Middlemarch* take place a comfortable generation in the past (and *Romola* several centuries earlier), *Daniel Deronda* is "a story of English Life, but of *our own* day" (*GEL* VI, 193). Gwendolen, unlike Dorothea, is not buried in some unvisited tomb, but was to be seen everywhere—in German gambling casinos, in London parks, in fashionable drawing rooms. Thus, the portrait of a lady in *Daniel Deronda* is very much influenced by the controversy over the "new woman" in the 1860s and '70s. George Eliot had always spoken to the women of her day, suggesting to them which "experiments in life" were most likely to bear healthy fruit. By 1876, I would suggest, Eliot feared that too many women were making poor choices and needed a clear example of where the unbridled desire for transcendence might lead. She thus created her most rebellious and egoistic heroine, her most dreadful punishment, and her most rigorous renunciation to illustrate how serious had become the problem of women's needs and duties.

George Eliot's ambivalence over the situation of women persisted throughout her life. Despite her close attachments to many notable women, particularly to feminists, one senses that she had difficulty identifying her situation with those of other women. Her commitment to women equally disposed her to serious criticism of their choices and behaviours and to empathy with their suppressed social condition. In 1861, she wrote that "women's unsatisfied diseased longings" led them into foolish preoccupation with fashion, and by 1874 she was distressed by "more and more eager scrambling after wealth and show" (*GEL* III, 402-3; VI, 17). At the same time that masses of idle, frustrated women were indulging themselves with costly dress and fashionable novels, feminists were challenging the social conditions that allowed no other options for its middle-class women. Eliot did not fear these individual conscientious feminists and social reformers, many of whom— Barbara Bodichon, Bessie Parkes, Octavia Hill, Emily Davies— were her friends and acquaintances. She thoroughly believed in careful reform and useful work for women. But in her own heart and the hearts of myriad other women, she noted an "abyss" of anger, resentment, and frustration that might so deepen that no bridges would be adequate to keep men and women together.[4] Consequently, her letters repeatedly warn against the dangers of women rejecting too quickly and extremely the role of bridge-builder, sympathizer, and nurturer. Whether tempted away by fashion or by feminism, women seemed to George Eliot to be tampering with the very moral evolution of the race. Like many other Victorian writers, she felt that domestic affection, based on the division of labour between the sexes, provided the possibility of moral advancement. Her letters and novels express this philosophy repeatedly; as she wrote to Sara Hennell, "nothing can outweigh to my mind the heavy desecration of family ties . . . One trembles to think how easily that moral wealth may be lost which it has been the work of ages to produce, in the refinement and differencing of the affectionate relations" (*GEL* V, 56).

Eliot demanded an equal but dissimilar responsibility from men and women in maintaining these affectionate relations which are essential to the moral balance of society. Woman's place in this system was spelled out by her in an 1868 letter to Emily Davies, feminist and founder of Girton College. In this letter, Eliot also refers to the social unrest that was perceived to be changing the nature of woman's role in the 1860s:

> In the face of all wrongs, mistakes, and failures, history has demonstrated that gain [of woman's special moral influence]. And here lies just that kernel of truth in the vulgar alarm of men lest women should be "unsexed." We can no more afford to part with that exquisite type of gentleness, tenderness, possible maternity suffusing a woman's being with affectionateness, which makes what we mean by the feminine character, than we can afford to part with the human love, the mutual subjection of soul between a man and a woman—which is also a growth and revelation beginning before all history. (*GEL* IV, 467-68).

The ideology that Eliot adopted to justify her heartfelt belief that woman's place was in the home was referred to at the time as "Female Influence" or "Woman's Mission".[5] Writers as varied as Mrs Sarah Ellis and Auguste Comte argued that women could be as powerful and influential within their domestic sphere as men were within their larger sociopolitical sphere. Although "Woman's Mission" is an essentially conservative ideology, it was used even by suffragists and feminists to prove woman's moral fitness and need for an expanded social role. For Eliot, this ideology offered a reconciliation of her sympathies with woman's transcendent aspirations and her own belief in social stability and fear of change. Although woman's sphere of activity and influence might be restricted to the home—the source of so much oppression in many of Eliot's novels—through love and submission to duty, woman's *place* might become the source of her greatest *power*.

She seems to have needed to affirm these ideas strongly in *Daniel Deronda*. Eliot seldom resorts to polemical outbursts in scenes primarily involving Gwendolen and her world, but at one point the narrator breaks forth with an overt statement of "Woman's Mission" that reminds us of Eliot's letter to Davies:

> Could there be a slenderer, more insignificant thread in human history than this consciousness of a girl, busy with her small inferences of the way in which she could make her life pleasant?— in a time, too, when ideas were with fresh vigour making armies of themselves, and the universal kinship was declaring itself fiercely . . .
> What in the midst of that mighty drama [the American Civil War] are girls and their blind visions? They are the Yea or Nay of that good for which men are enduring and fighting. In these delicate vessels is borne onward through the ages the treasure of human affection. (159-60)

This outburst reminds us that George Eliot took women very seriously, that they were crucial to her analysis of social order. When, in *Middlemarch*, she takes "a woman's lot" as a starting point for her story of provincial life, she is not merely expounding an interesting bit of narrative theory. Nor, when she explains that "Gwendolen and her equivocal fate moved as busy images of what was amiss in the world" (685), are we to interpret this only as an association in Daniel's mind. Woman's lot *was* a starting point for Eliot's social analysis; women and their equivocal fates *do* reflect or influence the ills of the world.[6]

Thus, while anatomy may be destiny, the maternal role has been spiritualized and universalized.[7] *Women* bear human affection through the ages, and for Eliot love was virtually a panacea for human malaise. That she felt womanly affection under attack during the period in which she wrote *Daniel Deronda* is also borne out by the numerous letters of that period emphasizing the theme of womanliness and of loving domestic relations. Eliot commended, almost obsessively, "the high type of womanly grace", "the most charming [type] of womanliness, and . . . a woman's best blessings", "the grander feminine type", and "the excellent wheaten bread of a loving woman's [heart] nature" (*GEL* VI, 25, 57, 117, 360). As she wrote to Emily Cross, "That is really the highest good of a wife—to be quite [certain] sure in the midst of the dimness and doubt which this difficult world surrounds us with, that there is one close to her whose life is everyday the better for her . . . " [*GEL* VI, 116-17].

George Eliot was not alone in worrying about the future of her generation of women. Although every generation searches the past for its lost ideals, the decade of the 1860s seemed particularly preoccupied with the deterioration of the English ideal of womanhood. Journalists crowded the pages of quarterlies and periodicals with denunciations of the sensation novel heroine and of the romp (popularized in novels by Rhoda Broughton and Ouida). The high (or low) point of this popular dismay occurred in 1868 when *The Saturday Review* published "The Girl of the Period", first of a phenomenally influential series of articles. The author, Eliza Lynn Linton, a third-rate novelist and hack journalist, was an acquaintance and, in her mind, rival of Eliot. The latter could hardly have been unaware of this phenomenon. There is some circumstantial evidence to suggest that Eliot read "The Girl of the Period" articles— Linton called at The Priory during the late sixties, the "Woman Question" was often discussed there during this period, and Edith Simcox, a regular visitor, wrote an angry rebuttal to the series—although one would like proof that friends brought copies of *The Saturday Review* when they came to call.[8] But although the connection must remain conjectural, a comparison between Linton's articles and *Daniel Deronda* reveals some interesting links between the two.

In "The Girl of the Period", Linton mourned the loss of the "fair young English girl . . . a creature generous, capable, modest", who was distinguished by the "innate purity and dignity of her nature . . . and [who] was neither bold in bearing nor masculine in mind."[9] This mythical creature—the "Daughter of England" or "Angel in the House"—had once expressed the supreme values of Victorian womanhood.[10] The mercenary air of the high Victorian age, however, had led to her presumed demise and replacement by a new mythic heroine, "a creature whose sole idea of life is fun; whose sole aim is unbounded luxury." The Girl of the Period, in Linton's words, was addicted to "slang, bold talk and general fastness; to the love of pleasure before either love or happiness; to uselessness at home, dissatisfaction with the monotony of ordinary life, horror of all useful work; in a word, to the worst forms of luxury and selfishness—to the most fatal effects arising from want of high principle and absence of tender feeling." Linton's was the principal voice of this criticism—her articles appeared regularly and eventually filled three volumes—but she was not alone in her jeremiad. *The Christian Remembrancer* antedated her argument by unfavourably contrasting "the popular ideal of charming womanhood in the times we remember" with "what seems to constitute the modern ideal of the same thing".[11] Book reviewers gleefully exposed the sinister implications of the sensation heroine, who was called "no longer the Angel, but the Devil in the House", and a "Lady Macbeth, who is half unsexed."[12] Like Linton, Geraldine Jewsbury feared that modern maidens were too fascinated with the demi-monde: "If I were a *man* reading this MS I should enquire 'are the young women of England trying to qualify themselves for Courtesans?'—the breaking down of all sense of shame and modesty, opens the way to that bottomless pit."[13]

To Linton and many of her contemporaries, the Girl of the Period manifested shocking and dangerous new characteristics. Instead of being selfless, she was selfish. Instead of professing Christian morality, she worshipped Mammon. She was disturbingly independent, unsentimental, and sexually free (in word if not in deed). Most horrifying of all, the Girl of the Period was no longer a truly feminine woman; she had discarded the traditional female virtues of submission, dependency, and maternal love in favour of self-assertion and power. In this way, Linton and others connected—with varying degrees of insight—this new phenomenon of role rejection with the emergence of a feminist movement.

Linton, for example, defended many modern women who rejected the ideology of the Angel in the House. Herself a victim of an unhappy marriage, she accepted the inevitability of women breaking out of the "claustral home".[14] Nonetheless, she pointed out that "the whole question is a tangled web from first to last, and no one can see his way quite clearly through its mazes. Of course *it is utterly revolutionary and subversive of the whole existing order of things;* but that is no argument against a fair trial of its merits . . . " (emphasis mine).[15] Margaret Oliphant also felt that the new woman, addicted to sensation novels and fast living, was paying too much attention to the discussion of "women's rights and women's duties".[16] She too longed for a return to the days of pure and innocent young girls. An anonymous reviewer in *Temple Bar* made a similar comparison between "the fast school" of novels and women's rights, in the "shallow jargon of the period".[17] These critics support Vineta Colby's observation that the mid-century woman was "blossoming out in rebellion against the codes and crinolines of mid-Victorianism and flowering (or degenerating, according to one's feminist views) into the belligerent crusading suffragette of the 90s and later."[18]

It is difficult to determine whether or not English women had changed their behaviour and expectations as drastically as Linton maintained (although the *perception* of change can be as crucial to the creation of a social myth as the material change itself). But today we can note that changes in the nature of woman's work, the increasing wealth of the middle class, and liberal ideology all contributed to a continuous evolution in woman's role throughout the nineteenth century.[19] By mid-century, genteel women no longer performed concrete work in the home; cheap labour and industrialization devalued a woman's household skills. Gwendolen, for example, need not know who does the work of her home as long as she can employ a housekeeper; her needlework is useful only to entice a lover, not to keep her white silk gowns in repair. In an era of increasing wealth, the lady's primary occupation was to enhance her father's or husband's material status. Gwendolen's looks and bearing are "really worth some expense" (66); her assets ought to bring at least a few thousand a year on the open market. But while woman's practical value declined, the ideology of individualism sparked by the Enlightenment and French Revolution led women to demand that their power and influence be acknowledged. Woman, it was cried, was no longer a household drudge; what then was she? From this conflict between declining material power and rising ideological expectations comes the emphasis on Female Influence, the groping for greater freedom, and the rise of feminism. The Girl of the Period is, in this way, the less socially-conscious, more ornamental sister of the feminist.

It is not surprising that Eliot, always interested in the proper duties and powers of womankind, should have responded to the "vulgar alarms" (as she put it in her letter to Davies) of the journalists. Gwendolen Harleth is her response: a portrait of the female egoist placed in its historical setting by the language and mythology adopted from the Girl of the Period controversy. Rather than merely nodding at an amusing quirk of popular culture, Eliot uses this phenomenon to create a scenario her contemporaries would recognize. Gwendolen, like the Girl of the Period, is criticized for her "ambitious vanity and desire for luxury", for her "strong determination to have what was pleasant", and for her "practical ignorance" (401, 71, 276). Her girlish ideal is "to be daring in speech and reckless in braving dangers, both moral and physical" (94). She is selfish and a "princess in exile"; she is useless (she "really did not know who did the work of the house"); and she is "always bored" (53, 339, 42). She has "no permanent consciousness of . . . spiritual restraints" or of "the sweetness of labour and fulfilled claims" (94, 317). She has little affection or regard for others; she is thoroughly indifferent to duty. Her uncle's wish, which she avidly seconds, for "parks, carriages, a title—everything that would make this world a pleasant abode", (179-80) is strikingly parallel to Linton's criticism of mercenary marriages: "She has married his house, his carriage, his balance at the banker's, his title . . ." (*GOP*, 339). Finally, just as Linton traces the moral degradation of the Girl of the Period to her slavish imitation of the demi-monde, Gwendolen, led by her taste for luxury to marry a man already bound to another woman, becomes, in terms of her moral position, a courtesan herself.

In short, *Daniel Deronda* recreates the upper-class society of England in the 1860s whose flower, or blight, was the dazzling Girl of the Period. Eliot uses historical research as precisely as she did to create Quattrocento Florence or Reform-era England.

(She is so scrupulously attentive to detail that one feels she used Linton's articles as primary source material.) For example, both authors adopt similar clichés for their titles: "The Spoiled Child" and "Maidens Choosing" allude to "Spoilt Women" and "Modern Maidens"; furthermore, Gwendolen's is certainly a "Fashionable World" of "Foolish Virgins", "Nymphs", "Aesthetic Women", and "Fine Ladies". Lady Mallinger's reddish blonde hair is, of course, "the hair of the period"—Eliot could not resist a direct slap at the cliché (368). She is precise about her fashions: archery was a recently-revived and vogueish sport and we are told exactly what style of dress was modish at competitions and dances.[20] (In *Middlemarch*, by contrast, dress symbolizes moral qualities.) Gwendolen's "superfluous stepsisters" evoke W. R. Greg's "redundant women", mercenary marriages provided a staple topic for novelists and moralists, and in one swift epigram—"I would rather emigrate than be a governess" (276)—Gwendolen raises two of the foremost concerns of Victorian feminists.[21] With additional references to *tableaux vivants*, romps and tomboys, croquet, Wagner, natural selection, boarding-school education, and the *femme sole*, George Eliot roots her study of female egoism in the firm ground of historical reality.[22]

Further observations are made by both Eliot and Linton. The fast and frivolous Girl of the Period does not marry easily because men are afraid of her, insists Linton; Gwendolen, with her dangerous Lamia beauty and sharp tongue, is admired by the local gentry but receives few offers of marriage. The Girl of the Period, unlike the tender-hearted English maiden, is no longer seduced into an unwise marriage by the dream of "love in a cottage" (*GOP*, 340); Gwendolen, petrified by her wealthy husband, is compared to a poor cottage-woman waiting for the music of her mate's returning footsteps (734). Like Eliot, Linton criticizes her "Foolish Virgin" for not observing that "there is a great portion of a universe outside her own circle and her own mind."[23] Corrupted by luxury and avarice, the Girl of the Period is soon overgrown "with flaunting poison plants";[24] Gwendolen uses the same language to explain the effects of boredom on women (171). The most serious charge that Linton raises against the Girl of the Period is that she married not for love "but as a means of securing independence" and once married declines to be a mother.[25] As we shall see, this is essentially Eliot's criticism of Gwendolen. In short, then, the characterization of Gwendolen Harleth is in line with the popular stereotype of the Girl of the Period. As the Leubronn dowager acidly observes, "It is wonderful what unpleasant girls get into vogue" (41).

Gwendolen, however, is more than unpleasant—she is dangerous. George Eliot pursues the implications that Linton had called a "tangled web" by demonstrating that the Girl of the Period was one manifestation of a general unrest leading to a possible feminist uprising. In this novel, as in many of her letters, Eliot explored the social conditions that led women to reject their role, whether for an expanded social and political sphere of activity, or for a more narcissistic pursuit of pleasure. As I have suggested, the Girl of the Period and the new feminists were sisters of a sort; *Daniel Deronda* is one of the most sophisticated explorations of this sisterhood. Eliot, who sensed a revolution in the making, hoped to influence this nascent feminism away from the clamorous call for equality and toward her own vision of moral evolution.

The opening scene of *Daniel Deronda* illustrates this preoccupation with "equality". Chronologically, Gwendolen's story begins and ends at Offendene, the locus and symbol of family, domesticity, and affective virtues. But, narratively, the novel begins in the Leubronn gambling casino, allowing Eliot to quickly contrast the quiet English countryside that potentially nourishes human affection with the casino that starves it. The casino provides "a striking admission of human equality" where countess sits next to tradesman: class is levelled here and so is sex (36). Gwendolen, seduced by this perverse atmosphere of equality, is lost in visions of herself as a goddess of luck: "Such things had been known of male gamblers; why should not a woman have a like supremacy?" (39). Vanity's family, we are told, is both male and female. When Gwendolen, a favourite daughter, enters the casino dressed in green and silver, one gentleman quips, "woman was tempted by a serpent: why not a man?" (41). This observation of sexual equality in egoism echoes throughout Philistia. Eliot settles her earlier quarrel with lady novelists and their silly novels by noting that "the production of feeble literature . . . [is] compatible with the most

diverse forms of *physique,* masculine as well as feminine" (74).
The Motto to chapter ten suggests that not only is "men's taste
. . . woman's test", but that this bit of social wisdom could be
effectively turned around (132). The deterioration of polite
society is satirized by the sexually segregated archery banquets;
such a drastic action has been called for because of the
"epicurism of the ladies, who had somehow been reported to
show a revoltingly masculine judgement in venison, even asking
for the fat—a proof of the frightful rate at which corruption
might go on in women, but for severe social restraint" (150).
Even Lydia Glasher's fateful letter provokes the narrator to a
jarring mock lamentation over the loss of sexual distinctions in
handwriting (186).

Through such occasionally heavy-handed mockery of the
battle of the sexes, Eliot sets the stage for Gwendolen's assertion
of a claim to equality. Her drive for dominance culminates in
her fateful and ultimately futile struggle for mastery with
Grandcourt. "Ah, piteous equality in the need to dominate!"
cries the narrator, but Gwendolen has been outmanoeuvred
from the start (346). Before she falls under the spell of
Grandcourt's superior egoism, however, Gwendolen demands
not merely equal but superior claims for her sex. Whether as
gamblers or criminals, she gives women the edge: "Oh mamma,
you are so dreadfully prosaic! As if all the great poetic criminals
were not women! I think the men are poor cautious creatures"
(85). When her family's bankruptcy propels her down the path
to real, not poetic, criminality, her troubles elicit a response
equal in egoism to that of a man: "Her griefs were feminine; but
to her as a woman they were not the less hard to bear, and she
felt an equal right to the Promethean tone" (321).

Despite the ironic tone of this last passage, we ought not to
overlook that the "equal rights of women" was an inflammatory
phrase in an era of feminist agitation and counter-agitation.
Eliot does not use her words lightly. To emphasize her
perception that traditional feminine subordination was
deteriorating, she puts many superficially feminist complaints
and quips in Gwendolen's mouth. To Rex Gascoigne,
Gwendolen complains, "Girls' lives are so stupid: they never do
what they like" (101). In her more fateful sparring with
Grandcourt she repeats this complaint: "We women can't go in

search of adventures . . . We must stay where we grow, or where the gardeners like to transplant us" (171). Both men, however, correct her complaints by observing that men's lives are often hampered by similar circumstances. She never adopts this bantering tone with Deronda, yet her first query to him has just such a feminist implication: "I want to know why you thought it wrong for me to gamble. Is is because I am a woman?" (382). Deronda also leads her away from what Eliot perceived as a one-sided conclusion, to a serious discussion of the need for each sex to serve the other as a moral guide.

For all her clever and lively speech, however, Gwendolen is no real feminist: ". . . this delicate-limbed sylph of twenty meant to lead. For such passions dwell in feminine breasts also. In Gwendolen's however, they dwelt among strictly feminine furniture, and had no disturbing reference to the advancement of learning or the balance of the constitution; her knowledge being such as with no sort of standing-room or length of lever could have been expected to move the world" (69).

Gwendolen's energy and ambition thus dissipates in unfocused idle dreams of gathering the chariot reins into her own hands.[26] Since women of fashion must conform to the feminine role if they are to wield any command at all, Gwendolen carefully observes the proper limitations: "Gwendolen was as inwardly rebellious against the restraints of family conditions, and as ready to look through obligations into her own fundamental want of feeling for them, as if she had been sustained by the boldest speculations; but she really had no such speculations, and would at once have marked herself off from any sort of theoretical or practically reforming women by satirizing them" (83). Gwendolen, this passage suggests, does have a distant connection to such "theoretical or practically reforming women" as Edith Simcox, Bessie Parkes, Emily Davies, or even Barbara Bodichon—shocking as that comparison may seem. Gwendolen on the one hand and the feminists on the other were rebelling against "the restraints of family conditions", against patriarchal assumptions. Like Linton, Oliphant, and other critics of the age, Eliot surmised that the Girl of the Period, Gwendolen Harleth in this case, represented a mass of uninformed, bored, easily-swayed women who—in Eliot's terms—could turn the feminist cause away from the

207

cautious amelioration of the human condition toward an explosive exercise in ego and self-indulgence.

Like Linton, Eliot was concerned that the great loss in this drive for equality would be those qualities of womanly affection, commiseration, and sympathy that she treasured as a linkage between separate souls. She illustrates this concern in Gwendolen, who is only superficially feminine and not a "real woman" at all. Gwendolen dons the *livery* of womanhood much as she dons her Greek dress in the *tableaux vivants*. In this way, acting imagery is used to suggest that Gwendolen (unlike Mirah, who finds the stage "no better than a fiery furnace" [258]) only mimics a brittle, artificial femininity.[27] Her true nature is instead revealed through that cluster of images—sylph, witch, Lamia—that describe her as an inhuman creature.

One incident from Gwendolen's girlhood highlights this contrast between real and artificial femininity. The canary that the young Gwendolen strangled in a fit of pique has been often noted as a symbol of her violence and easy remorse and a foreshadowing of her murderous impulses toward Grandcourt. But Eliot is so sparing of childhood incidents in this novel that yet another meaning might be discerned. The "bird in the gilded cage" is a familiar cliché, used effectively by Mary Wollstonecraft and Charlotte Brontë, among others, to symbolize the oppressed condition of women. In *Daniel Deronda*, Eliot makes admirable use of the comparison between women and caged birds. When Gwendolen strangled that canary, she was, in effect, strangling the woman inside herself; it was one minor, unfeminine act leading her inexorably down the path of ego to her mercenary marriage. It is appropriate that, just as she had killed the canary because its singing blended inharmoniously with her own, her own singing is strangled by Grandcourt's command. Thus, the splendid Mrs Grandcourt is only "an imprisoned dumb creature, not recognising herself in the glass panels, not noting any object around her in the painted gilded prison" (651). Glass panels no longer restore the ascendency of Vanity's daughter; Gwendolen is to pay a higher price in remorse than the white mouse with which she had replaced her sister's strangled bird.

This incident, along with others, is used by Eliot to convey the message that Gwendolen has become "unsexed" by her pursuit of mastery. All of the novel's superfluous sisters are measured by a "distorting male standard", but Gwendolen is the sole standard in her family of girls (717). She thus abrogates the rights of a son in patriarchy. She is further characterized by gambling and hunting, activities that excite her even as they unsex and almost declass her. Anna may ride a feminine pony, but Gwendolen needs a more spirited mount; she is twice compared to a high-mettled racer. She considers herself an exception to the routine lot of womankind; her "favourite formula" is that she is "not going to do as other women did" (168). Consequently, women do not like her and to Gwendolen they are little better than "empty benches" (150); this rejection of and by other women is further evidence that Gwendolen rejects the woman in herself. Little wonder, then, that her tears affect Mrs Davilow like "the sight of overpowering sorrow in a strong man" (414).

These details of characterization might, in themselves, only portray a spirited, somewhat reckless girl. But in Gwendolen's attitude toward marriage, motherhood and men, Eliot provides her serious criticism of these unsexed Girls of the Period. The sacramental nature of marriage and motherhood is acclaimed by the narrator, who says that marriage symbolizes "all the wondrous combinations of the universe", and by Mrs Meyrick, one of Eliot's most highly approved characters, who explains that a mother's love is the deepest and longest-lasting of all loves (812, 424). But to Gwendolen, obsessed by mastery and personal power, marriage is only a state of servitude: "her thoughts never dwelt on marriage as the fulfilment of her ambition . . . Her observation of matrimony had inclined her to think it rather a dreary state, in which a woman could not do what she liked, had more children than were desirable, was consequently dull, and became irrevocably immersed in humdrum" (68). Since marriage is, at best, a social promotion, Gwendolen questions whether she can have more freedom as a wife or as an unmarried woman. When she is brought to the choice between serving as the Momperts' governess or as Grandcourt's wife, the question becomes moot, but at no point does she appreciate the "mutual influences, demands, duties of man and woman in the state of matrimony" (342). In the naïve cruelty of youth, Gwendolen had stripped away her mother's pretense of matrimonial felicity: "Why did you marry again, mamma? It would have been nicer if you had not." Mrs Davilow's reply, "You have no feeling, child", is prophetic, for Gwendolen's heart—the emblem of her womanliness—"has never been in the least touched" (52, 110). Eliot allows us a rare moment of empathy with Gwendolen in her searing confession, "I shall never love anybody. I can't love people. I hate them" (115). Such misanthropy voiced by a "delicate vessel" of human affection is a cry of emotional suicide. Gwendolen, who also lives in a dread lest her own unborn child disinherit Grandcourt's illegitimate son, is thus as barren spiritually as she is physically.

Not only is Gwendolen's rejection of marriage seen as an inability to love, Eliot suggests that it also results from a rejection of men and sexuality. All men except Deronda inspire Gwendolen with a mixture of fear, revulsion, and loathing. Sex threatens the loss of self-control and the possibility of control by men; thus, Gwendolen recoils like a sea-anemone from the sexual approach of a man, curling protectively around her centre to prevent any penetration of her self (113). Linton also found the Girl of the Period sexually cold, but Eliot analyzes the reasons behind this observation. Just as Gwendolen rejects sex, her experiences lead her to reject men themselves. When she discovers the existence of Grandcourt's mistress and illegitimate children, as well as the presumed illegitimacy of Deronda, she declares forthrightly that "all men are bad, and I hate them" (192). If this is the consequence of male sexuality, Gwendolen will cling to her "fierceness of maidenhood" (102).

In fact, the refusal to acknowledge male authority lies at the core of Gwendolen's being. With only her uncle as a representative of patriarchy—and uncles are a comfortable degree further in authority than fathers—Gwendolen is used to being the master. Deronda traumatizes her because he assumes superior judgement over her actions. His "evil eye" freezes her at the gambling table and turns her luck for her. But by redeeming her turquoise chain from the pawnbroker, he also turns her luck in a different direction. Pawning this single momento of her dead father is a metaphor for Gwendolen's rejection of the entire patriarchal structure; Deronda thus slowly restores her faith and trust in the male order. She rebels later against

Klesmer's superior authority, which stems as much from his masculinity as from his musicianship (Catherine Arrowpoint, also a superior musician, is too much a lady to criticize Gwendolen) and futilely rages against the ecomomic structure that allows men to run off with her mother's fortune. Finally, Gwendolen marries Grandcourt precisely because she believes him to be a man easily commandable.

Gwendolen is thus a complex portrait of a female egoist whose desire for power throws her into direct conflict with the patriarchal system. She rejects her own place as a woman in this system and clashes repeatedly with representatives of its values. Her education into submission—which all Eliot's heroines must undergo—forces her to acquiesce to the male authority she tried to defy. Her repeated assertion of, "I will not submit", is a cry no woman in Eliot's world can dare utter. Once she has learned the limits of her freedom, both as a woman and as a moral being, Gwendolen dimly perceives a positive image of womanhood that inspires her to become "the best of women". But Eliot is not offering a pious version of Mrs Ellis's strictures. Grandcourt's sadism makes the text, "wives, submit unto your husbands", a grim joke. Eliot must first teach Gwendolen the true meaning of submission and the proper sphere for rebellion and power. Gwendolen must learn to discriminate between what Eliot establishes as legitimate male authority — represented by Deronda and Klesmer and later by Mallinger and Gascoigne—and Grandcourt's abusive authority. Since she has sold herself into a mercenary marriage, she can at first only submit to shame and degradation. The inevitable result of such submission for a powerful personality like Gwendolen is madness or murder, both of which tempt her perilously. Gwendolen must submit instead to Deronda's values, which are the values of an integrated, balanced, benevolently patriarchal society. Yet everywhere she turns, the abusive power of male dominance threatens her redemption. Eliot is unequivocally clear about the social forces that prevent Gwendolen's "constructive rebellion" against the deadly values of Philistine society (607):

> How could she run away to her own family—carry distress
> among them, and render herself an object of scandal in the

211

> society she had left behind her? . . . What could she say to justify
> her flight? Her uncle would tell her to go back. Her mother would
> cry. Her aunt and Anna would look at her with wondering alarm.
> Her husband would have power to compel her. She had
> absolutely nothing that she could allege against him in judicious
> or judicial ears. And to "insist on separation!" That was an
> uneasy combination of words; but considered as an action to be
> executed against Grandcourt, it would be about as practicable as
> to give him a pliant disposition and a dread of other people's
> unwillingness. (655)

If these unsexed Girls of the Period are to make the correct
choice and dedicate themselves to womanly virtues, familial
duties, and useful work, Eliot suggests, then many of the
structures of the old society that inspired them to rebel must be
changed. Mercenary marriages, spoiled children, false
equality, abusive husbands, crippling domestic laws—all are
part of an unhealthy contemporary society that must be
changed if its children are to be saved, as Eliot insisted
Gwendolen was to be. Yet here is where the problems and
ambivalences of Eliot's moral position become most evident.
The agent of change is Daniel Deronda, and we must seriously
question the adequacy of his advice. Given the narrow distance
between Deronda and his creator, we must also question Eliot's
message to women of her time.

Gwendolen turns to Deronda because his new standards of
judgement inspire her to startlingly new questions. As I have
pointed out, she first questions him about her behaviour as a
woman: "do you object to my hunting?" (377) and "I want to
know why you thought it wrong for me to gamble. Is it because I
am a woman?" (382). The model for all her questions is, "is that
the best I can do?" But in the chiselled syntax of his replies,
Deronda switches the verb "to be" for "to do". He assures her
that, "You can, you will, be among the best of women, such as
make others glad that they were born" (840). Yet Eliot was fond
of quoting Comte's prescription of *"resignation* et *d'activité"*
(*GEL* I, 359; II, 127, 134). What does Deronda offer
Gwendolen of the "more independent life" that women need as
a "sort of defense against passionate afflication" (*GEL* V, 107)?
He can, in fact, do little better than advise her to resume her
music lessons, and Grandcourt, the representation of abusive

male power, immediately countermands his advice with his quiet drawl that "one doesn't want to hear squalling in private" (648). Deronda's abstract faith that Gwendolen might be among the best of women gives little hint of the value Eliot actually found in steady, productive labour.

It is difficult to accept that Deronda can give Gwendolen the seeds for her salvation or that the author herself had a clear idea of what those seeds might be. Deronda assures Gwendolen that kindness to her family is the best she can do with her life:

> Other duties will spring from it. Looking at your life as a debt may seem the dreariest view of things at a distance; but it cannot really be so. What makes life dreary is the want of motive; but once beginning to act with that penitential, loving purpose you have in your mind, there will be unexpected satisfactions—there will be newly-opening needs—continually coming to carry you on from day to day. You will find your life growing like a plant.
>
> (839)

This emphasis on debt, dreariness, and penitence suggests that Gwendolen has not been released from prison but, rather, sentenced to a life term. Deronda's stiff assurance that she will grow "like a plant" recalls her own frivolous repartee with Grandcourt: "We are brought up like the flowers, to look as pretty as we can, and be dull without complaining. That is my notion about the plants: they are often bored, and that is the reason why some of them have got poisonous" (171). Has Gwendolen grown past her poisonous boredom only to be returned to it full circle?

In *Daniel Deronda*, I would suggest, Eliot was more acutely aware of the conflicts and contradictions raised by woman's heightened consciousness in the 1860s and 70s than she was of possible political or social alternatives. Like other contemporary moralists, she deplored the Girl of the Period and mistrusted the "emancipated woman". Yet, much as she believed in the ideology of "Women's Mission", alluding to it directly in *Daniel Deronda*, she did not neatly wind up Gwendolen's tale of remorse with marriage and motherhood. Gwendolen smiles ironically at Gascoigne's homily that "a wife has great influence with her husband" (611) and, in the end, Deronda alone has a "mission" to the East. Gwendolen's end is open and uncertain, as I believe Eliot saw the future to be. In this way, *Daniel Deronda* is a more ambivalent novel than any of its predecessors.

Daniel Deronda suggests, through subversive details, an emerging female role superior to that of the Women of England or the Girls of the Period. Every female character is in revolt, either openly or tacitly, against patriarchal society. Gwendolen and the Alcharisi are self-conscious rebels, but even passive Anna Gascoigne longs to reject the irksome restraints of "coming out". Catherine Arrowpoint rebels against her parents' matrimonial plans, the Meyrick sisters support themselves and quietly satirize the male bias of society, and shadowy Mirah is herself a talented, self-supporting artist who runs away from her father. Eliot further demands that Gwendolen herself wake to the historical and political reality of her world in a way that no other heroine—not even Dorothea—is expected to do. Although Gwendolen had no more thought of the Jews "as likely to make a difference in her destiny, than of the fermenting political and social leaven which was making a difference in the history of the world", the shock of discovering the details of Deronda's birth gives her "a sense that her horizon was but a dipping onward of an existence with which her own was revolving" (843, 876). Eliot thus insists that the lives of idle, fashionable women expand beyond the limits of decorated drawing rooms.

Nevertheless, given Eliot's fundamental ambivalence, this female revolt and expansion must be contained and controlled. While abandoning her selfishness and misguided quest for power, Gwendolen also is stripped of her energy, spirit, wit, and ambition. Her final acceptance of her mother and stepsisters represents her acceptance of the woman within herself, an acceptance that has both positive and negative implications. Although her domestic end suggests the creation of the female culture so critical to all social and feminist reform in the nineteenth century, it seems also like a retreat to the womb.[28] Gwendolen's end seems even more equivocal than Dorothea's, for the latter exchanges provincial England for an active life in London. Gwendolen, however, returns to the great good place, and a retired life of county visits, balls at Diplow, and a possible marriage to Rex Gascoigne. Eliot herself criticizes Gwendolen for a spiritual and social isolation comparable to that of "a man in a lighthouse". Is her solitude more laudable because it is lighted by the "little lot of stars belonging to [her own] homestead" (50)?

Ultimately, the greatest value of George Eliot as a theorist about women is her final ambivalence. On the one hand, we find Gwendolen so egoless and passive that "when he [Deronda] was quite gone, her mother came in and found her sitting quite motionless" (879). Might this paralysis be taken as a symbol of Eliot's chosen position as one of the "epicurean gods" whose cautious balancing act denies the efficacy of action in an increasingly complex world (*GEL* II, 396)? This was Eliot's own way of handling the disturbing ambiguities of the "Woman Question". But, on the other hand, there is a wrenching combination of love, hope, and despair in Gwendolen's final words: ". . . she looked fixedly at her mother and said tenderly, 'Ah, poor mamma! You have been sitting up with me. Don't be unhappy. I shall live. I shall be better!'" (879). Gwendolen's reassurance to her mother is, in the final analysis, an overt message of resignation nurturing a personal, subtextual message of determination: exactly the attitude Eliot was always to maintain toward her "spiritual daughters". Gwendolen Harleth, a profound example of the unsexed Girl of the Period, and her open future thus symbolise a turning point in history: the transformation of the long tradition of Female Influence and Women's Mission into the feminism that would soon shatter the calm surface of domestic England.

NOTES

1 *Daniel Deronda*, p. 38. Penguin English Library edition, edited with an introduction by Barbara Hardy. All subsequent references will appear in the text.

2 *The George Eliot Letters*, ed. Gordon S. Haight (New Haven, 1954), VI, 183. Subsequent references will appear in the text as *GEL*.

3 A reviewer in *The Examiner* (2 September 1876) commented that George Eliot might have more effectively taught "the girls of the period" a lesson of womanly duties and destinies by increasing Gwendolen's punishment. Quoted in *George Eliot and Her Readers*, ed. John Holstrom and Laurence Lerner (London, 1966), p. 137. The editors reject this as "wrong-headed" and ask, "did George Eliot have so moralizing a purpose?"

(162). I would answer yes. We might remember that in Eliot's famous self-description as an "aesthetic teacher", the emphasis is equally on the teacher as on the aesthete.

4   *GEL* V, 58. This letter contains one of Eliot's most troubled comments on feminism: "There is no subject on which I am more inclined to hold my peace and learn, than on the 'women question'. It seems to me to overhang abysses, of which even prostitution is not the worst. Conclusions seem easy so long as we keep large blinkers on and look in the direction of our own private path."

5   See my paper, *"Felix Holt* and the True Power of Womanhood", to appear in *English Literary History*. Major discussions of domestic feminism include Ann Douglas, *The Feminization of American Culture* (New York, 1977); Kathryn Kish Sklar, *Catharine Beecher: A Study in American Domesticity* (New Haven, 1973); and Daniel Scott Smith, "Family Limitation, Sexual Control, and Domestic Feminism in Victorian America", in *Clio's Consciousness Raised,* ed. Mary Hartman and Lois W. Banner (New York, 1974).

6   Also noted by U. S. Knoepflmacher in *Religious Humanism and the Victorian Novel* (Princeton, 1965), p. 121.

7   For more on Eliot's position on motherhood, see my essay, "The Mother's History in George Eliot's Life, Literature, and Political Ideology", to appear in *The Lost Tradition: Mothers and Daughters in Literature,* ed. C. N. Davidson and E. M. Broner (New York, 1980).

8   On Linton's visits see Gordon S. Haight, *George Eliot: A Biography* (New York, 1968), pp. 407, 411. On discussions of the "Women Question" see *GEL* IV, 364 and VI, 394; *Biography,* p. 391; and Cross's *Life of George Eliot,* III, 95. For the Simcox article, see [H. Lawrenny] "Custom and Sex", *The Fortnightly Review,* XI (1872), 310-23.

9   "The Girl of the Period", *The Saturday Review,* 25 (14 March 1868), 339 (hereafter *GOP*).

10   The "Daughters of England" comes from the title of one of Mrs Sarah Stickney Ellis's series of behaviour guides for women; "The Angel in the House" is the title of Coventry Patmore's famous praise of marriage and femininity.

11   "Four Female Sensation Novelists", *The Christian Remembrancer,* 46 (July, 1863), 209.

12   "Belles Letters", *Westminster Review,* 84 (October, 1865), 568; "Sensation Novelists: Miss Braddon", *North British Review,* 43 (September, 1865), 186.

13   Quoted in Jeanne Rosenmayer Fahnstock, "Geraldine Jewsbury: The Power of the Publisher's Reader", *Nineteenth Century Fiction,* 28 (December, 1973), 262. Note the similarity between Jewsbury's image of the "bottomless pit" and Eliot's "abysses".

14   "Womanly Dependence", reprinted in *Ourselves: Essays on Women* (London, 1893), p. 235.

15   "Womanly Dependence", p. 237.

16   "Novels", *Blackwood's Edinburgh Magazine,* 102 (September, 1867), 259.
17   "Our Novels: The Fast School", *Temple Bar,* 29 (May, 1870), 190.
18   Vineta Colby, *The Singular Anomaly* (London, 1970), p. 17.
19   For sources on the historical development of woman's role and social expectations, see Barbara Sicherman, "Review Essay: American History", *Signs,* 1, 2, (Winter, 1975), 461-85; and Carolyn C. Lougee, "Review Essay: Modern European History", *Signs,* 2, 3, (Spring, 1977), 628-50.
20   See William Veeder, *Henry James: The Lessons of the Master* (Chicago, 1975), p. 166.
21   W. R. Greg, "Why are Women Redundant?" in *Literary and Social Judgements* (London, 1877 [1862]). For a contemporary investigation of the issue of mercenary marrriages, see Sondra R. Herman, "Loving Courtship or the Marriage Market? The Ideal and its Critics 1871-1911", *American Quarterly,* 25 (May, 1973), 235-42. On governesses, see M. Jeanne Peterson, "The Victorian Governess: Status Incongruence in Family and Society", in *Suffer and Be Still,* ed. Martha Vicinus (Bloomington, 1972). On emigration, see A. James Hammerton, "Feminism and Female Emigration, 1861-1886", in *A Widening Sphere,* ed. Vicinus (Bloomington, 1977).
22   *Fraser's Magazine* ("Women's Education", May, 1869) derides the *tableaux vivants,* p. 539; boarding-schools were rather more a topic of the 1830s and 40s; Eliot wrote of the *femme sole* to Sara Hennell, *GEL* V, 67.
23   "Foolish Virgins", *The Saturday Review* (August 17, 1867), p. 212.
24   "Foolish Virgins", p. 211.
25   "Woman and the World", *The Saturday Review* (11 April 1868), p. 479.
26   Imagery of whips, reins and chariots are used in *Daniel Deronda* to symbolise the power struggle between Gwendolen and Grandcourt (for example, pp. 173, 343, 482). Linton also, in "Womanly Dependence" asks the question, does man flourish the whip or woman hold the reins? It might also be noted how effectively Eliot uses horses, a traditional symbol of male potency, in this novel. Not only are they a symbol of command for Gwendolen, and later of her own position as one of Grandcourt's possessions, but many of her most momentous sexual manoeuvrings, with Rex and Deronda as well as with Grandcourt, take place on horseback.
27   Eliot's use of demonic imagery to question true femininity is analyzed by Nina Auerbach in "The Power of Hunger: Demonism and Maggie Tulliver", *Nineteenth Century Fiction,* 30, 2 (September, 1975), 150-71.
28   See Carroll Smith-Rosenberg, "The Female World of Love and Ritual: Relations between Women in Nineteenth-Century America", *Signs* 1, 1 (Autumn, 1975), 1-29; and Blanche Wiesen Cook, "Female Support Networks and Political Activism", *Chrysalis,* No. 3 (1977), 43-61.

Index